A COSMOPOLITAN LEGAL ORDER

A Cosmopolitan Legal Order

Kant, Constitutional Justice, and the European Convention on Human Rights

ALEC STONE SWEET
and
CLARE RYAN

OXFORD
UNIVERSITY PRESS

OXFORD
UNIVERSITY PRESS

Great Clarendon Street, Oxford, OX2 6DP,
United Kingdom

Oxford University Press is a department of the University of Oxford.
It furthers the University's objective of excellence in research, scholarship,
and education by publishing worldwide. Oxford is a registered trade mark of
Oxford University Press in the UK and in certain other countries

First Edition published in 2018

Impression: 1

Published in the United States of America by Oxford University Press
198 Madison Avenue, New York, NY 10016, United States of America

British Library Cataloguing in Publication Data
Data available

Library of Congress Control Number: 2018930532

ISBN 978–0–19–882534–0

Printed and bound by
CPI Group (UK) Ltd, Croydon, CR0 4YY

To the Camargo Foundation, a refuge for cosmopolitans.
Alec Stone Sweet

To my grandparents, whose stories set me down this path.
Clare Ryan

Acknowledgments

For their painstaking analysis of judgments of the European Court of Human Rights, I am indebted to Eliška Holubová (LLM, Yale Law School, 2015), Dominik Rennert (LLM, Yale Law School, 2015), and Jolin Chen (LLB, Faculty of Law, the National University of Singapore, 2017), and to Professor Christine Landfried for her help in organizing the data collection. Eric Palmer (JD, Yale Law School, 2017) co-authored chapter 2, parts of which appeared as a "Kantian System of Constitutional Justice: Rights, Trusteeship, Balancing" in the *Journal of Global Constitutionalism* (2017). We benefitted enormously from discussions of early versions of chapters presented in the Seminar Series, Centre for Legal Theory, Faculty of Law, National University of Singapore (April 2016); the Workshop on Courts and Public Reason in Global Public Law, WZB Berlin Social Science Centre (July 2016); and the Seminar Series, Edinburgh Centre for Legal Theory (November 2016). PluriCourts, the University of Oslo, organized a workshop on a first draft of the manuscript in May 2017; we are particularly grateful to its co-director, Andreas Føllesdal, for both the idea and its execution. We also thank the participants of the PluriCourts Workshop—including Damiano Canale, Giacinto della Cananea, Claudio Corradetti, Eirik Bjorge, Andreas Føllesdal, Reidar Maliks, Neil Walker, Jacob Weinrib, and Ariel Zylberman—for detailed comments that greatly improved the book. Garrett Wallace Brown also read the draft and provided invaluable insight on matters Kantian. Alex Flach and John Louth at Oxford University Press had the good idea to propose the book and to shelter it from dogmatic scholasticism. I again thank Julie Chenot, Director of the Camargo Foundation, for the opportunity to complete another book in Cassis.

Finally, Martha Lewis, an artist drawn to the consideration of complex pluralist systems, made the painting that graces the cover.

Alec Stone Sweet

I am grateful to my friends and colleagues in Strasbourg for teaching me so much about the Convention system. The transformative year I spent at the Strasbourg Court (2014–15) was made possible by Yale Law School's Robina Foundation Human Rights Fellowship. I am also indebted to the participants at the PluriCourts Workshop in Oslo whose advice proved invaluable in writing this book. My thanks as well to Yale Law School and the PhD in Law program, which afforded me the time and resources to undertake this project. Finally, my deepest thanks to Alec Stone Sweet, who first introduced me to the European Court of Human Rights and, later, to Kantian cosmopolitanism.

Clare Ryan

Contents

List of Abbreviations

ACHR	American Convention on Human Rights
CIA	Central Intelligence Agency
CJEU	Court of Justice of the European Union
CLO	cosmopolitan legal order
ECHR	European Convention on Human Rights
ECOWAS	Economic Community of West African States
EU	European Union
FYROM	Former Yugoslav Republic of Macedonia
GCEU	General Court of the EU
GFCC	German Federal Constitutional Court
IACHR	Inter-American Convention on Human Rights
ICC	Italian Constitutional Court
NATO	North Atlantic Treaty Organization
PA	proportionality analysis
UPR	Universal Principle of Right

Introduction and Overview

A *cosmopolitan legal order* is a multi-level, transnational legal system in which (i) justiciable rights are held by individuals; (ii) all public officials bear the obligation to fulfill the fundamental rights of every person within their jurisdiction, without respect to nationality or citizenship; and (iii) both domestic and transnational judges supervise how officials do so. In Europe, such an order emerged as a product of the combined effects of Protocol no. 11 (1998) of the European Convention on Human Rights (ECHR), and the incorporation of the Convention into national law. Protocol no. 11 established the right of individual petition, directly to the European Convention on Human Rights, upon the exhaustion of domestic remedies. Incorporation made Convention rights directly enforceable by national judges, as a matter of domestic law. The resulting system is governed by a "decentralized sovereign": a community of courts whose activities are coordinated through the rulings of the European Court, based in Strasbourg. Although imperfect and still maturing, the regime meets significant criteria of effectiveness. It routinely succeeds in raising standards of rights protection. It has anchored transitions to constitutional democracy in post-authoritarian states. And it has steadily developed the capacity to render justice to all people that come under its jurisdiction, even non-citizens who live—and whose rights are violated—beyond Europe. Today, the Convention comprises an important component

A Cosmopolitan Legal Order: Kant, Constitutional Justice, and the European Convention on Human Rights. Alec Stone Sweet and Clare Ryan. Published 2018 by Oxford University Press.

of a cosmopolitan constitution, and the Strasbourg Court is the single most active and important rights-protecting body in the world.[1]

This book explicates and defends these claims in light of Kantian constitutional theory. Its ambition is to provide a Kantian-congruent account of the ECHR, understood as an instantiation of a legal system capable of optimizing progress toward what Immanuel Kant called a "Rightful" constitutional condition. Moral and political philosophy have experienced a powerful revival of interest in Kantian theory, including a sustained effort to extend and modernize his ideas,[2] and to build a rights-based cosmopolitanism.[3] We share these orientations. For their part, political scientists have subjected Kant's blueprint for "perpetual peace" among liberal states to rigorous testing, with impressive results.[4] We build on this agenda, though our aim is to explain the emergence of a cosmopolitan legal order (CLO), not the absence of war.

The project also engages scholarship on matters beyond Kantian theory and European law. In particular, we respond to a tenacious controversy concerning the nature and scope of human rights.[5] Simplifying, the debate has focused on the tension between (i) the universalistic claims of rights, and (ii) the diversity of culture and moral views in the world. This tension is typically resolved in one of two ways. Either the analyst identifies the content of rights from those elements that are common to moral systems, or conceptions of justice, across state boundaries and cultural divides. Or she takes a universalistic stance, deriving rights from normative arguments that every person would be required to accept regardless of differences in cultural standpoints.[6] While the approaches are incommensurate, they produce a convergent outcome: the view that rights can (and should) only have minimal content.[7] Minimalism has its detractors,[8]

[1] Stone Sweet (2012b).

[2] Brown and Held, eds. (2010); Held (2010); Flikschuh (2000); Pogge (1988); Ripstein (2009); Føllesdal and Maliks, eds. (2015).

[3] Anderson-Gold (2001); Benhabib (2004, 2009); Brown (2009); Habermas (1997); Kleingeld (2011).

[4] O'Neal and Russett (1999). For a general critique of the literature on the "liberal peace," see Brown, Lynn-Jones, and Miller, eds. (1996).

[5] Beitz (2001); Sajo, ed. (2004).

[6] Finnis (1980); Nickel (2006).

[7] Ferrara (2003); Ignatieff (2001); Rawls (1999); Walzer (1994).

[8] Benhabib (2009); Pogge (2000).

who worry that it drains rights of their intrinsic moral and legal force. The minimal view also conflicts with the expansive trajectory of rights discourse, politics, and adjudication since the end of the Second World War.[9] Cohen, a reluctant proponent of minimalism, puts it this way:

> We can be tolerant of fundamentally different outlooks on life, or we can be ambitious in our understanding of what human rights demand, but we cannot—contrary to the aims of . . . activists—be both tolerant and ambitious.[10]

One strong empirical claim of this book is that the European CLO has transcended rights minimalism, while maintaining a meaningful commitment to principles of democracy, national diversity, and regime subsidiarity.

The book follows in a line of research on how new forms of judicial authority emerge and evolve, with what consequences for politics, society, and the economy.[11] Courts famously govern not through the sword or the purse, but through reason-based justification and the propagation of argumentation frameworks—what lawyers call "doctrine." Judges will be effective only to the extent that they draw citizens and non-judicial officials into dynamic, "jurisgenerative" and "judicialized," fields of action.[12] The ECHR is both a source and product of such processes, and an expansive politics of rights protection has been the result.[13] The CLO is also a novel, transnational legal system, constituted on the basis of a structural characteristic: "constitutional pluralism."[14] Research on law and courts "beyond the state"[15] can no longer avoid the question of how to understand both the "constitutional" and "pluralist" features of global governance

[9] Epp (1998); Stone Sweet (2017).
[10] Cohen (2004: 192).
[11] Stone Sweet (1999, 2000, 2004).
[12] Benhabib (2009); Shapiro and Stone Sweet (2002).
[13] Keller and Stone Sweet (2008: ch. 11).
[14] Following Walker (2002). See Kumm (2009); Maduro (2009); Stone Sweet (2013).
[15] Krisch (2010); Walker (2008a).

arrangements.[16] Today, Europe possesses an overarching "constitutional" structure, comprised of fundamental rights and the shared authority of judges to adjudicate individual claims. Yet the system is pluralist: no single organ possesses the "final word" when it comes to a conflict between incompatible interpretations of the content and scope of rights. Instead, activated by a steady stream of cases, the system evolves in large part through inter-court dialogues, both co-operative and competitive.

Since we engage the scholarship on European rights protection throughout the book, we do not survey that literature here, beyond stressing the following preliminary points. In the vast bulk of research on the ECHR,[17] scholars either prioritize the perspective of the Convention (the Strasbourg Court and its judgments), or that of a single domestic regime (national law, courts, and politics), as it relates to, is influenced by, or resists the ECHR. Our goal is not to refute or debunk other approaches to rights adjudication. Indeed, we expressly build on existing research on the Court, and on the impact of the Court's evolving case law on domestic officials. The very idea of a CLO, as defined above, stipulates our primary unit of analysis: a multi-level, transnational, composite system of rights protection. While we recognize that domestic systems comprise meaningfully autonomous legal orders, every state party to the ECHR has incorporated the Convention in ways that mitigate this autonomy, as scholars are beginning to document and assess.[18] In Europe, diverse arenas of rights protection, operating at different levels of governance, have become deeply embedded in one another, through the effects of overlapping sources of rights, procedures, and jurisdiction.

[16] Dunoff and Trachtman, eds. (2009); Klabbers, Peters, and Ulfstein (2009); Stone Sweet (2009a).

[17] Important exceptions include the scholarship cited in chapters 4 and 5.

[18] Keller and Stone Sweet, eds. (2008); Brems and Gerards, eds. (2014); Anagnostou, ed. (2013); Bjorge (2015).

OVERVIEW OF THE BOOK

This book develops a Kantian-congruent account of constitutional justice, both within and beyond the state, which is then applied, as a theoretical framework, to explain the construction of the European CLO, and to assess how it functions. We have sought to provide a short and relatively non-technical introduction to (i) Kantian constitutional theory and (ii) the law and politics of European rights protection, in light of their deep connections with one another. Every effort has been made to engage readers who are neither versed in Kant or philosophical method, nor specialists in human rights and European law. Nonetheless, we are aware that many of the book's most important topics are, in fact, technically complex and normatively fraught. The project's wide scope, coupled with our commitment to brevity, has obvious costs. We expect that the summary nature of some of the arguments, including the normative stances taken, will give some readers reasons for skepticism. We address these potential shortcomings at relevant points in each chapter.[19]

The book proceeds as follows. Part I is devoted to Kantian constitutional theory and its application to modern systems of constitutional justice. In chapter 1, we discuss Kant's blueprint for achieving perpetual peace and a condition of Public Right, and argue that the conditions necessary for a CLO to materialize were gradually fulfilled in Europe after the Second World War. Chapter 2 presents a model of a *domestic* system of constitutional justice rooted in the precepts of Kantian constitutional theory. It is a blunt fact that Kant had little to say about rights, courts, and judicial review in the modern sense. We fill this gap, providing a response to the crucial institutional question: what structural properties must a legal system exhibit for

[19] It is also important to state up-front what this book is not about. We do not directly engage the burgeoning neo-Kantian scholarship on global justice undertaken under the "cosmopolitan" banner. We briefly address some of these issues in the conclusion, in light of this book's priorities.

it to render justice in a Kantian sense? Chapter 3 extends and adapts these ideas to a transnational system of rights protection, considers key structural features of a cosmopolitan legal order, and tracks the consolidation of a foundational component of the European CLO: constitutional pluralism. The book thus extends Kant's constitutional ideas into realms in which he had hardly considered.

It is also important to highlight what Part I does not do, which may strike some as an important limitation of the book. We develop a Kantian-congruent account of the structural foundations of a domestic and transnational system of justice. We do not develop a theory purporting to accurately "predict" how a constitutional court would resolve a hard case coming before it, as a matter of substantive law. The usefulness of Kantian theory to help explain a cosmopolitan system of rights protection does not depend on its ability to determine the niceties of the case law it produces. The philosopher himself strongly rejected the view that correct "decisions in concrete situations" could "be deduced from abstract concepts,"[20] and he declined to engage in casuistry in the *Doctrine of Right*, which is at the core of his constitutional theory. Nonetheless, Part II gives pride of place to the Strasbourg Court's jurisprudence, the most important strains of which, we argue, display a clear Kantian gloss. The Court has aggressively sought to remedy situations in which individuals and groups (homosexuals and the Roma community, for example) have been denied full juridical status by national law and practices. It has been uncompromising in its approach to the so-called "absolute rights" (including the prohibition of torture and inhuman treatment), adopting strong cosmopolitan positions that it has worked diligently to impose upon the member states. And it has adjudicated the qualified rights in ways that are broadly congruent with the major features of the approach we develop in chapters 2 and 3, in particular through the enforcement of the proportionality principle.

[20] Von Bogdandy and Venzka (2012), citing to Kant, *Critique of Pure Reason*.

Part II focuses on the evolution of the post-1998 European regime. In chapter 4, we track the constitutionalization of the ECHR, as registered in the accretion of the European Court's powers, and its capacity to enhance the effectiveness of the Convention in the face of chronic failures of rights protection at the national level. Chapter 5 focuses on the adjudication of the Convention's "qualified" rights, which cover privacy and family life, speech, assembly, and the press, and conscience and religion. These provisions contain a limitation clause permitting a state to legally restrict rights, but only to the extent that such limitations are "necessary" to achieve important public policy purposes. We examine how the Court has adjudicated limitation clauses, and the extent to which the regime has overcome rights minimalism. Chapter 6 attends to the Court's enforcement of the "absolute" rights: the right to life; and the prohibition of torture and inhuman treatment. The Court has also treated access to justice, and the right to an effective judicial remedy, as quasi-absolute. It is through these provisions that the Court has asserted, sometimes aggressively so, its own cosmopolitan *bona fides*, demonstrating that it can protect rights beyond the confines of citizenship and territory. A nascent pluralist and Kantian-constitutional structure to the international level is now discernible. For each of these chapters, we present aggregate data analysis of Grand Chamber rulings and case studies of interactions between the European Court and national officials. In the conclusion, we briefly consider the emergence of cosmopolitan legal systems beyond Europe.

Part I

Kantian Imperatives

1

Perpetual Peace and the Cosmopolitan Constitution

INTRODUCTION

This chapter connects the social science on the "Kantian peace"—which purports to explain the absence of war among "liberal" states—to the account of the cosmopolitan legal order (CLO) we develop in this book. In *Toward Perpetual Peace among States* (1795),[1] Kant claimed that perpetual peace could be achieved only once a group of "republican" states joined together in a "league" that would recognize and secure the effectiveness of "the universal principle of hospitality," and of the equal freedom and juridical status of all human beings. Over the past three decades, political scientists, treating these and other factors as causal variables and finding strong support for some of the basics of Kant's theory, have transformed the field of international relations. Yet, international relations scholars have hardly addressed Kant's own priority, as announced in his essay: the achievement in law of a Rightful condition beyond the state. We do so here.

[1] Hereinafter PP.

A Cosmopolitan Legal Order: Kant, Constitutional Justice, and the European Convention on Human Rights. Alec Stone Sweet and Clare Ryan. Published 2018 by Oxford University Press.

KANTIAN ANALOGS

In *Perpetual Peace*, Kant held that in a "state of nature," nations would find themselves recurrently beset by conflict and war, and thus incapable of establishing freedom through law—what he called "Right"—to govern their relations with one another. States, he insisted, could achieve a Rightful condition only by subjecting themselves to "universally valid public laws," which he associated with a "constitution."[2] Constructions of sovereignty and international law that dominated in Kant's day, by contrast, supported the very evils he sought to eradicate.[3] As every student of international relations knows, political scientists too had long presumed that, in the international system, the absence of an authoritative, hierarchical government made the threat of violence and war omnipresent. This premise could only be dispelled by compelling reasons and evidence to the contrary.[4]

Kant outlined a blueprint for achieving peace and Right on the basis of six preliminary and three definitive articles, which are stated in the form of a treaty or constitution. The preliminary articles prohibit colonial subjugation and the accumulation of foreign debt, ban treacherous dealings among states (including preparation for war), and proclaim a rule of non-interference in the internal affairs of any other state. In subscribing to these laws, states would create a first pillar of what today is known as a "security community,"[5] whose purpose is to reduce the threat of armed conflict among its members to nil.

[2] PP, 8: 348–60.

[3] Kant took pains to dismiss the then-dominant theorists of international law (singling out Grotius, Vattel, and Pufendorf), as "tiresome comforters," who devoted enormous efforts to "justify offensive war"; PP, 8: 355.

[4] For an overview of the literature on the structural determinants of war and peaceful cooperation, from an explicitly constitutional perspective, see Stone (Sweet) (1994). The most influential proponent of the presumption that war, and preparation for war, is the normal state of affairs in an "anarchic" international system is Waltz (1979). Those who argue the contrary, at least under certain specified conditions, include Doyle (1986) and other adherents to Kantian approaches to peace and war, as well as other "liberal" theorists, including Moravcsik (1997), and Rosecrance (1986).

[5] Deutsch et al. (1957).

The definitive articles establish the laws that Kant deemed necessary for sustaining peace, which he distinguished from "a mere cease-fire" or "postponement of hostilities."[6] Since Doyle's path-breaking papers of the 1980s,[7] political scientists have treated the definitive articles as causal variables, Kant's explications of the "laws" as mechanisms, and his overall arguments, once teased out and updated, as testable hypotheses.

Box 1 lists the preliminary and definitive articles, accompanied by selected commentary by Kant. While there is no substitute for a close reading of Kant's essay, we provide a summary exposition of the definitive articles here, in light of how social scientists have operationalized them over the past three decades.

Box 1 Toward Perpetual Peace: the Preliminary and Definitive Articles

In *Toward Perpetual Peace* [8: 343–60] Kant elaborates six "preliminary" and three "definitive" articles that states must honor and respect if they are to achieve the Perpetual Peace. [Emphases in original.]

The Six Preliminary Articles:

1. No peace settlement which secretly reserves issues for a future war shall be considered valid.[PP, 8: 343]

For such a treaty would resemble a mere cease-fire, a postponement of hostilities, and not peace.[PP, 8: 343]

2. No independently existing state (irrespective of whether it is large or small) shall be able to be acquired by another state . . . [PP, 8: 344]

To annex a state, which, like a tree trunk, has its own roots, and thus to treat it like a graft onto another state, is to annul its existence as a moral person and to treat this moral person as a mere thing.[PP, 8: 344]

3. Standing armies shall gradually be abolished entirely.[PP, 8: 345]

For they continually threaten other states with war . . . and prompt other states to outclass each other the number of those armed in battle.[PP, 8: 345]

4. The state shall not contract debts in connection with its foreign affairs.[PP, 8: 345]

[6] PP, 8: 343. [7] Doyle (1983a, 1983b, 1986).

This credit system can be used as a war chest that surpasses in size the wealth of all other states combined . . . [PP, 8: 345]

5. No state shall forcibly interfere in the constitution and government of another state. [PP, 8: 346]

For what can justify it doing so? [PP, 8: 346]

6. No state shall allow itself such hostilities in wartime as would make mutual trust in a future period of peace impossible. Such acts would include the employment of assassins, poisoners, breach of surrender, incitement of treason within the enemy state, etc. [PP, 8: 346]

These are dishonorable stratagems. For there must remain, even in the middle of war, some degree of trust in the enemy's manner of thinking, since otherwise no peace could possibly be reached, and hostilities would degenerate into a war . . . For war is only the regrettable expedient in the state of nature (where there exists no court that could adjudicate the matter with legal authority) to assert one's rights by means of violence. [PP, 8: 346]

The Three Definitive Articles:

The state of nature *(status naturalis)* is not a state of peace among human beings who live next to one another but a state of war, that is, if not always an outbreak of hostilities, then at least the constant threat of such hostilities. Hence the state of peace must be *established.*[PP, 8: 348–9]

1. The Civil Constitution of every state shall be republican.[PP, 8: 349]

The republican constitution is a constitution that is established, first, according to principles of the *freedom* of the members of society (as human beings), second, according to the *dependence* of all on a single, common legislation (as subjects), and third, according to the law of the *equality* of the latter (as *citizens of the state*).[PP, 8: 349–50]

The state . . . is either republican or despotic. Republicanism is the principle by which the executive power . . . is separated from the legislative power . . . Under despotism, the public will is . . . treated by the monarch as his individual will. . . . If it is to be in accordance with Right, the form of government must include a representative system, the only kind of system in which a republican form of government is possible, and without which the government will be despotic and violent . . . [PP, 8: 352–3]

2. International Right shall be based on the federalism of free states.[PP, 8: 354]

Peoples, as states, can be judged as individual human beings who, when in the state of nature (that is when they are independent of external laws), bring harm to one another already with their proximity to one another, and each of whom, for the sake of his own security, can and ought to demand of others that they enter into a constitution, similar to that of a civil one, under which each is guaranteed his rights. This would constitute a federation of peoples, which would not, however, necessarily be a state of peoples.[PP, 8: 354]

Although states can [now] pursue their rights only through war, and never by means of a trial before an external tribunal, war and its favorable conclusion—*victory*—never determines Right.[PP, 8: 355]

> [F]rom the throne of highest moral legislative authority, reason looks down on and condemns war as a means of pursuing one's rights, and makes peace an immediate duty. [A] special sort of federation must be created, which one might call a pacific federation . . . This federation aims . . . [to secure and maintain] the freedom of a state for itself and also the freedom of other confederated states without these states therefore being required . . . to subject themselves to public laws and coercion under such laws. It can be shown that the idea of federalism, which could gradually encompass all states and thereby lead to perpetual peace, is practicable (that is, has objective reality). For if fortune so determines that a powerful and enlightened people can constitute itself as a republic (which according to its nature tends necessarily toward perpetual peace), then this republic provides a focus point for other states, so that they might join this federative union and thereby secure the condition of peace among states in accordance with the idea of International Right and gradually extend this union further and further through several such associations.[PP, 8: 356]
>
> 3. Cosmopolitan Right shall be limited to the conditions of universal hospitality.[PP, 8: 357]
>
> As in the previous articles, we are concerned here with Right, not with philanthropy, and in this context *hospitality* means the right of a stranger not to be treated in a hostile manner by another on his arrival in another's territory. . . . It is not the *right of a guest* that the stranger has a claim to . . . but rather a right to visit, to which all human beings have a claim, to present oneself to society by virtue of the right to common possession of the surface of the earth. Since it is the surface of a sphere, they cannot scatter themselves on it without limit, but they must always ultimately tolerate one another as neighbors, and originally no one has a right to be at a given place on the earth than anyone else.[PP, 8: 358]

The first factor (definitive article) concerns the political organization of the state, which must be "republican." It merits emphasis that Kant's essay appeared just as the first constitutional democracies were emerging in the United States and France; and the philosopher himself never journeyed beyond a small region of autocratic Prussia. Not surprisingly, there are obvious tensions between the philosopher's characterization of "democracy," and modern constitutional forms (see also chapter 2). In *Perpetual Peace*, Kant equated democracy with mob rule, in which "everyone wishes to be ruler," and minority views (however Rightful) could be quashed.[8] By "republican," Kant meant self-government, by a

[8] PP, 8: 352. Scholars robustly debate the issue of Kant's understanding of democracy, which evolved; see Hanisch (2016). Taylor (2006) argues, compellingly, that Kant thought representative, democratic self-governance would emerge, gradually, through the decisions of benevolent monarchs.

People constituting a state, in which equality among citizens could be secured, separation of powers respected, and tyranny avoided.[9]

Kant also proposed what a social scientist would today call a "mechanism," a causal logic for *why* the republican form will tend to favor peace.

> [T]he Republican Constitution . . . offers the prospect for the desired consequence, namely, perpetual peace. The reason for this is as follows: if (as must be the case in such a constitution) the agreement of the citizens is required to decide whether or not one ought to wage war, then nothing is more natural than that they would consider very carefully whether to enter into such a terrible game, since they would have to resolve to bring the hardships of war upon themselves (which would include themselves fighting, paying the costs of the war from their own possessions, meagerly repairing the ravages that war leaves behind, and finally, on top of all such malady, assuming a burden of debt that burdens the peace . . .). By contrast, in the case of a [despotic] constitution . . . declaring war is the easiest thing in the world, because the head of the state is not a fellow citizen, but the owner of the state, and forfeits nothing . . . The head of the state can decide to wage war for insignificant reasons . . . [10]

The Republican Constitution constrains the decision to go to war, by requiring the People's consent. At the very least, representative government and separation of powers mean that significant veto points in the decision-making process must be overcome if a war is to be prosecuted.

Contemporary Kantians[11] and political scientists[12] script the variable in terms of standard conceptions of liberal democracy. This

[9] A state "is a society of human beings"; PP, 8: 344. In *The Metaphysics of Morals* (6: 315) (hereinafter MM), Kant stipulates that "it is only in conformity with the conditions of freedom and equality that [the] people can become a state and enter into a civil constitution"; see chapter 2.

[10] PP, 8: 350–1.

[11] Brown (2009: 93–9); Hanisch (2016); Kleingeld (2011: 190–3).

[12] Doyle (1986); Gaubatz (1996).

includes: (i) a polity that features an elected legislature and a competitive party system, (ii) independent courts capable of protecting rights, and (iii) basic market freedoms.

The second factor is international organization: the building of a constitutionally-grounded "federalism of free states." Kant contemplated a world in which some states, weary with war, would choose to form a league designed for the "maintenance and security" of its members. He emphasized that, at least at the outset, the federation would not extinguish state sovereignty: the league would not exercise coercive powers within any national order and every state would be free to leave it.[13] Nonetheless, states must enter into a federation if they are to escape the state of nature:

> [T]here can be no other way for [states] to emerge from the lawless condition, which contains only war, than for them to relinquish, just as do individual human beings, their wild (lawless) freedom, to accustom themselves to public binding laws, and to thereby form a state of peoples *(civitas gentium),* which, continually expanding, could ultimately comprise all of the peoples of the world.[14]

Kant also suggests a mechanism for the federation's expansion, which rests on logics of increasing returns to republican government (positive feedback that produces a bandwagon effect). Once a "powerful and enlightened people" demonstrates the advantages of abandoning despotism, other nations will follow.[15] Social scientists operationalize this variable with reference to state membership in international organizations and in the type of organizations to which states belong.

The third factor directs attention to a normative duty: the obligation of all within a state to provide "hospitality" to non-citizens. In *Perpetual Peace*, Kant gives this definitive article a narrow

[13] "This alliance must, however, involve no sovereign authority (as in a civil constitution), but only an *association* (federation); it must be an alliance that can be renounced at any time and so must be renewed from time to time." MM, 6: 345.

[14] PP, 8: 357. [15] PP, 8: 356.

scope: "Hospitality means the right of a stranger not to be treated as an enemy when he arrives in the land of another." Strangers are to be welcomed, but they do not possess an entitlement to permanent settlement or citizenship; and, in contrast to citizens, a state may expel foreigners who do not abide by its laws. Kant then immediately derives from hospitality an entitlement "to present oneself to society by virtue of the right of common possession of the surface of the earth."[16] It is important to recall that Kant wrote before international human rights, as such, had been established.

Political scientists operationalize the "hospitality" variable with reference to cross-border trade and other measures of interdependence between states. Kant stressed that hospitality would both express and facilitate "a spirit of trade, which cannot coexist with war"; and, in the section devoted to Cosmopolitan Right in the *Metaphysics of Morals* (1797), Kant asserted that each nation has a "right" to "offer to engage in commerce with any other."[17] The norms covered by hospitality are thus associated with a mechanism: the greater the level of interdependence between any two states, the more costly it will be to go to war. As Doyle insists,[18] all three variables must reinforce one another, as constraints, for the liberal peace to be secured. War will be maximally unlikely between democratic states, whose economies are tightly connected, and who cooperate with one another within international organizations.

While outsiders to the international relations field might not fully appreciate their importance, these moves directly challenged long dominant "realist" approaches to security that had staunchly rejected views to the effect that (i) the internal organization of states, (ii) treaty-based international organization, and (iii) international law, including rights, could make any appreciable difference to affairs of war and peace.[19] Over the past thirty years, political scientists have generated

[16] PP, 8: 358. [17] MM, 6: 352. [18] Doyle (1986, 2005).

[19] Realists argue that the distribution of power and the constellation of state interests at the level of the international system are the main forces driving outcomes

a massive research project designed to test Kant's theory, and to assess the robustness of the proposed mechanisms. Although scholars continue to refine methods and debate findings,[20] the Kantian peace has been shown to be remarkably robust, and the independent causal influence of the three definitive articles (the independent variables) on the outcome to be explained (the dependent variable—the absence of war between liberal states) has been impressively demonstrated.[21] Indeed, a testable theory of why liberal democracies do not go to war with one another produced what is, arguably, the single most important finding of contemporary political science.

But political scientists have largely ignored Kant's overarching purpose: to demonstrate that states must (as a moral imperative), and could (in practice) achieve a Rightful constitutional condition at both the domestic and international levels.[22]

Kant conceptualized perpetual peace in terms of freedom and justice—what he called Right—and not merely as the absence of war.[23] In commentary on hospitality, for example, he reflected on the consequences of a shrinking world, in strikingly contemporary terms:[24]

> The growing prevalence of a . . . community among the peoples of the earth has now reached a point that the violation of Right at any *one* place on the earth is felt in *all* places. For this reason, the idea of Cosmopolitan Right is no fantastic or exaggerated conception of

that matter most. Literature cited in note 4 above. While some realists continue to consider the Kantian peace a "myth" (Layne (1994)), many have engaged Kant in diverse and productive ways.

[20] Brown, Lynn-Jones, and Miller, eds. (1996).

[21] O'Neal and Russett (1999).

[22] But see short comments by Doyle (1986: 1161, 2005).

[23] Indeed, for Kant, "perpetual peace" could not be dissociated from a Rightful condition; see chapters 2 and 3.

[24] This type of analysis will be familiar to social scientists who view international regimes in functionalist terms, that is, as institutions that help states resolve dilemmas of governance which would be either impossible or too costly to resolve on their own. The seminal book is Krasner, ed. (1983).

> Right. Rather it is a necessary supplement to the unwritten code of Constitutional and International Right, for Public Human Right in general, and hence for perpetual peace. Only under this condition can one flatter oneself to be continually progressing toward perpetual peace.[25] [Emphases in the original.]

This passage suggests another mechanism for advancement: the codification of hospitality in positive law. Through the gradual acceptance of hospitality, Kant wrote, "remote parts of the world [might] establish relations peacefully with one another, relations which ultimately become regulated by public laws and [might] thus finally bring the human species ever closer to a cosmopolitan constitution."[26]

In other writings, the philosopher suggested that a wider range of human rights were implicated in the notion of hospitality and Cosmopolitan Right,[27] including the freedom "to make public use of one's reason,"[28] and "the right of citizens of the world to try to establish community with all."[29] It is difficult to see how these freedoms could be fully enjoyed without the provision of rights more generally.

A decade after Doyle's pioneering papers, Habermas' reconstruction of *Perpetual Peace* established a base from which to explore the implications of these ideas for contemporary (and normative) theories of justice, democracy, and globalization.[30] Most important for us, Habermas directed attention to the juridical foundations of Kant's cosmopolitanism, and linked the concept of hospitality to the norms and discursive politics of the international bill of rights.[31] Other theorists of cosmopolitanism, including Anderson-Gold and

[25] PP, 8: 360. [26] PP, 8: 358. [27] Brown (2006).

[28] *What is Enlightenment?* (Kant (1994) [1784]: 55). [29] MM, 6: 353.

[30] Habermas (1997).

[31] See Banham (2007: 33–4). The international bill of rights includes: the United Nations Declaration of Human Rights (1948); the International Covenant on Economic, Social, and Political Rights (1966, entry into force in 1976); and the International Covenant on Civil and Political Rights (1966, entry into force in 1976). Benhabib (2009, Appendix: 702).

Benhabib,[32] have further integrated human rights into what is now a vibrant neo-Kantian project. As Benhabib puts it, rights cosmopolitanism flows from "the recognition that human beings are moral persons equally entitled to legal protection in virtue of rights that accrue to them not as nationals, or members of an ethnic group, but as human beings as such";[33] a view that is bedrock Kantian.[34]

We embrace this more expansive view of rights, if on somewhat different, though compatible grounds. The expository sections of *Perpetual Peace* make it clear that progress toward a Rightful condition could only take place through complex, historically-contingent processes laden with obstacles; and Kant did not believe that the content of the laws could be precisely determined in advance. As Brown suggests, "the laws of hospitality," as restrictively defined in *Perpetual Peace*, "do not represent [Kant's] final vision" of the content of the cosmopolitan constitution:

> [They] only represent the minimal conditions that are necessary for peaceful interaction to occur, which may eventually, with consistent application, evolve into a more thoroughgoing condition of cosmopolitan law.

The "principle of hospitable reciprocity" functions as a start-up mechanism: a "first . . . iteration in a move to ground all future legal relations."[35]

In our view, it makes no sense to consider the development of human rights as a process exogenous to Kant's theory. Rather, the codification of rights since 1950 permeates the pertinent normative and institutional contexts covered by each of the three definitive articles. Today, (i) charters of rights and guarantees of judicial protection

[32] Anderson-Gold (1988); Benhabib (2004, 2009). [33] Benhabib (2011).

[34] Others have rejected extending hospitality in this way; for a critical assessment of the debate, see Brown (2009: ch. 2; and 198–202), who rejects narrow accounts.

[35] Brown (2009: 65).

have become core components of domestic constitutional democracy (first definitive article); (ii) international organizations have promulgated bills of rights of universal content and scope (second definitive article); and (iii) the content of such rights covers virtually every aspect of individuals' relationships to public authority (third definitive article).[36] While the horrors of two catastrophic world wars catalyzed this turn to rights, rights-based constitutionalism quickly generated its own jurisgenerative dynamics and momentum.[37] Doyle, in a recent commentary, now explicitly incorporates the "ideological commitment to fundamental human rights" into the causal theory, supplementing mechanisms rooted in "republican representation" and "transnational interdependence."[38]

RIGHT BEYOND THE STATE

Under conditions of perpetual war, Kant argued, achieving Cosmopolitan Right[39]—an "international rule of law"[40] rooted in freedom and the respect for fundamental rights of all persons—would be impossible. The philosopher defined Right as "the sum of the conditions under which the choice of one can be united with the choice of the other in accordance with a universal law of freedom."[41] These conditions are "constitutional" in that they ground the legitimacy of all political arrangements, including treaty-based organizations:

> Public Right is . . . a system of laws for a people, that is, a multitude of human beings, or for a multitude of peoples, which, because they affect one another, need a Rightful condition under . . . a

[36] Chapters 2 and 3. [37] Stone Sweet (2017). [38] Doyle (2005: 463).

[39] The "cosmopolitan constitution," as Brown (2006: 674) puts it, is a set of "normative and juridical principles of . . . cosmopolitan Right."

[40] Huntley (1996: 49). [41] MM, 6: 230.

> *constitution* . . . so that they may enjoy what is laid down as Right.[42] [Emphasis in original.]

We discuss Kant's constitutional theory in detail in chapter 2, and apply it to transnational arrangements in chapter 3. For now, it is enough to highlight two overlapping points.

First, Kant's theory of justice among a People *within the state* (Public Right) rests on many of the same concepts and ideas as his notions of justice *between* states (International and Cosmopolitan Right).[43] He insisted that states are "moral persons" subject to the moral duty to pursue both "the sweet dream of perpetual peace"[44] and a stable, Rightful condition.[45] In practice, Kant believed, progress would entail altering the mode of governance "gradually and continuously, so that it harmonizes *in its effect* with the only constitution that accords with Right."[46]

Second, because individuals (and states) must coexist in a limited space with finite resources, their choices and actions will chronically produce conflict. In *Metaphysics of Morals*, Kant contended that both persons and states must accept public laws that meet the Universal Principle of Right,[47] if they are to be truly free. Although

[42] MM, 6: 311.

[43] To take just one example, compare MM, 6: 230–3 (on the Doctrine of Right) with 6: 352–3 (Cosmopolitan Right). See also chapter 3, note 6.

[44] PP, 8: 343.

[45] The republican state and the federation of republican states are linked conceptually to one another, and then both are causally connected to prospects for peace. Kant implies that the people too declare the peace when they select a republican form of state: "There shall be no war among us, for we desire to form ourselves into a state, that is, to establish a supreme legislative, executive, and judicial authority over ourselves that will settle our disputes in a peaceful manner." He then treats the federation as a "surrogate"—a functional equivalent—of the "compact of civil society," in "which reason must necessarily connect with the scope of International Right, if the latter is to mean anything at all." PP, 8: 356.

[46] MM, 6: 340–1. In this passage, Kant addresses domestic arrangements, but the basic notion of a gradual but continuous perfecting of Right applies to the cosmopolitan version as well; see the conclusion to the Doctrine of Right (quoted below, note 68), at 6: 354–5.

[47] MM, 6: 229–33.

conflict can be debilitating, its very inevitability requires the provision of law to protect everyone in their "external freedom,"[48] that is, when they interact with one another. Kant conceived of the domain of justice—and of the Rightful exercise of public coercive authority, more generally[49]—as those constitutional arrangements capable of authoritatively establishing the legitimate reasons for hindering an individual's freedom when necessary to guarantee the freedom of all. It follows that, with few exceptions (e.g., the prohibition of slavery), rights will not be "absolute." Rather, most rights will be "qualified," that is, subject to lawful limitation. In Kantian terms, state officials may only restrict an individual's freedom, as expressed through rights, as a means of achieving Right, that is, the external freedom for all in the polity.[50]

Putting these two points together, we define Cosmopolitan Right more broadly than many neo-Kantians, as the relations of Right between (i) all persons and (ii) the public officials of states belonging to a federation of republican states, as codified (at least in part) by (iii) one or more applicable charters of rights. The primary mission of any cosmopolitan legal order is to render justice, that is, to give normative content to Cosmopolitan Right, through the enforcement of those charters of rights that are applicable in the federation. In particular, all judges are placed under a duty to evaluate the reasons given by public officials in justification of acts that would burden rights, and to proclaim violations when such justifications are deemed inadequate. Chapter 3 is devoted to defending these claims.

[48] Kant distinguishes between "innate freedom" (which is virtually unlimited in a state of nature) (MM, 6: 237–8), and "outer" (or "external") "freedom" within a Rightful condition (MM, 6: 380; PP, 8: 354; and PP, 8: 350, Kant's Note *). For detailed discussion, see chapter 2.

[49] "[T]here is connected with Right . . . an authorization to coerce someone who infringes upon it. . . . Right and authorization to use coercion . . . mean one and the same thing." MM, 6: 231–2. See, more generally, Ripstein (2009).

[50] Chapter 2.

TRANSFORMATION IN EUROPE

The steady transformation of European law and politics since the Second World War neatly fits Kant's model. Before 1950, Western Europe was the epicenter of two recent and catastrophic world wars. After 1950, it became the fount of a "new constitutionalism,"[51] which spread across the Continent with successive waves of democratization. The basic formula, of (i) an entrenched, written constitution establishing parliamentary democracy, (ii) a charter of rights, and (iii) a mode of constitutional judicial review to protect those rights, was replicated in virtually all new European constitutions adopted since 1950.[52]

At the international level, Western Europe became a full-fledged security community,[53] in alliance with the US and Canada, through the North Atlantic Treaty Organization (NATO). In the NATO regime, each member pledges to defend every other member in the event of an attack, that is, an attack on any one is to be considered an attack on all.[54] NATO membership expanded from twelve members in 1949, to twenty-eight states today; twenty-two other European states are "partner countries." The European Coal and Steel Community (1952), followed by the establishment of the European Community (1958, six members), and then the European Union (EU) (1993) grounded the construction of market federalism, a supranational regulatory system, and a multi-level legal system capable of enforcing EU law and individual rights.[55] The EU now trades more with the rest of the world than does any other member of the World Trade Organization;

[51] Chapters 2 and 3.

[52] The extant exception is the Constitution of the French Fifth Republic (1958) which did not contain a charter of rights. Beginning in 1971, the Constitutional Council began incorporating rights into the constitution, and this process was completed by the end of the 1970s (Stone (1992)).

[53] See Morgan (1993). For NATO's "constitutional" connotations, see Stone (1994: 465–6).

[54] Art. 5 of the North Atlantic Treaty (1949).

[55] Stone Sweet (2004).

and each of its twenty-seven member states exports more to markets within the EU than to all global markets combined. The Council of Europe, founded by ten states in 1949, completed negotiations over the European Convention on Human Rights (ECHR) in 1950, and the Convention entered into force in 1953. With ECHR Protocol no. 11 (1998), all of the High Contracting Parties accepted the right of individuals to petition the Strasbourg Court, as well as the compulsory jurisdiction of the Court to adjudicate these claims.[56] Today, the ECHR regime is truly pan-European, now covering forty-seven states with a population exceeding 820 million people.

Kant's model is dynamic, generating structural change through the complex interaction effects of the three variables—democracy, international organization, and human rights—over time. Thus, as rights-based constitutional democracy spread from Germany, Italy, and Austria to states in Southern Europe (1970s and 1980s), and then across Central and Eastern Europe after the collapse of communism (1990s), membership in NATO, the EU, and the ECHR expanded. The consolidation of rights-based constitutionalism at the national level also influenced the construction of European institutions. As early as 1969,[57] the Court of Justice of the European Union (CJEU) began to invoke, in the guise of general principles of law (derivable from "the constitutional traditions common to the member states" and the ECHR) an enforceable corpus of rights.[58] For their parts, NATO,[59] the EU,[60] and the ECHR[61] have powerfully influenced democratic transitions in Southern, Central, and Eastern Europe. To take just two obvious examples of feedback, many post-communist states modeled

[56] Keller and Stone Sweet (2008).

[57] *Stauder*, CJEU 29/69, 1969. In 1989, the Court secured the power to review the acts of the member states for rights violations; *Wachauf*, CJEU 5/88, 1989.

[58] In December 2000, the member states produced a codified Charter of Rights, which finally entered into force with the Lisbon Treaty on December 1, 2009. For an analysis of the development of human rights in the EU, see De Búrca (2011).

[59] Gheciu (2005); Jacoby (2004).

[60] Grabbe (2006); Sadurski, Czarnota, and Krygier, eds. (2006); Vachudova (2005).

[61] Buyse and Hamilton, eds. (2011); Sadurski (2009).

their bills of rights on the Convention, and their market regulations on the EU's rules. As the ECHR regime evolved into a CLO, its impact on national politics, and the content and dispositions of national and international law, has steadily grown.[62]

To repeat, none of these outcomes were preordained. Kant recognized that his theory could not "foretell the future,"[63] and was largely indeterminate with regard to the substantive content of Public Right in any specific context.[64] Outcomes would depend upon wise leadership of the "moral politician,"[65] the design of effective institutions, the robustness of the mechanisms he theorized, combined with adaptive learning and socialization.[66] Indeed, in the last paragraph of *Perpetual Peace*, Kant warned us that the process might not be a linear one.[67] Nonetheless, in the *Metaphysics of Morals*, Kant reiterated that it was the duty of every individual and state official, "to work toward" peace under a Rightful condition:

> [T]he question is no longer whether perpetual peace is something real or a fiction, and whether we are not deceiving ourselves in our theoretical judgment when we assume that it is real. Instead, we must act as if it is something real, though perhaps it is not; we must work toward establishing perpetual peace and the kind of constitution that seems to us most conducive to it (say, a republicanism of all states, together and separately) in order to bring about perpetual peace and put an end to heinous waging of war . . . And even if the complete realization of this objective always remains a pious wish,

[62] See Keller and Stone Sweet (2008); Hammer and Emmert, eds. (2011), and chapters 3–6.

[63] PP, 8: 368. [64] For example, PP, 8: 370–5. [65] PP, 8: 376.

[66] Cederman (2001); Kleingeld (1999).

[67] "It is a duty to realize a condition of Public Right, and if there is a well-founded hope that this can be attained, even if only in a form of an endlessly progressing approximation of it, then the perpetual peace . . . is not an empty idea, but rather a task which, carried out gradually, [might] steadily [move] towards its goal (since the periods in which . . . advances are made will hopefully grow shorter and shorter)." PP, 8: 386.

> still we are certainly not deceiving ourselves in adopting the maxim of working incessantly towards it. For this is our duty . . . [68]

Although humanity must struggle to achieve Right, Kant also counseled that we should expect setbacks and reversals along the way.

Indeed, given what Kant characterizes as the "natural" and "continual antagonism among [a community's] members,"[69] we have every reason to expect that any meaningful progress toward achieving Public Right, at any level of governance, will be full of hard contestation. Contemporary history testifies to the instability of constitutional democracy, the fragile political legitimacy of judicial review and rights protection, and the contingent status of cosmopolitan sensibilities. Nonetheless, Kant proclaimed, human beings could fully develop their "natural capacities"[70] only by undertaking the arduous task of constructing a Rightful condition.

CONCLUSION

This chapter focuses on *Perpetual Peace* as an entry point into this book's topic: the development of a cosmopolitan legal order in Europe. Kant's ideas, as reconstructed by Doyle and tested by political scientists, provide a theory for why liberal states do not go to war with one another. In Europe, the three definitive articles map onto a massive transformation of legal, political, and economic institutions that combined to enable the CLO to emerge. While Kant argues forcefully to his conclusion that all state officials, indeed all human beings, bear a moral duty to work to achieve peace and a Rightful condition, he tells us virtually nothing of substance on issues of how a legal system—whether of a republican state, or of a federation of

[68] MM, 6: 354–5.
[69] *Idea for a Universal History with a Cosmopolitan Purpose* (Kant [1784] 8: 22).
[70] Brown (2009: 40).

states—should be configured. A focus on this question requires a deeper philosophically-oriented engagement with Kantian constitutional theory than social scientists have undertaken. In the next two chapters, we develop an account of a Kantian-congruent "system of constitutional justice," focusing on the legal norms, structures of public authority, and techniques of rights adjudication that—we claim—will optimize progress toward achieving a Rightful condition.

2

A Kantian System of Constitutional Justice

*With Eric Palmer**

> A constitution allowing the greatest possible human freedom in accordance with laws which ensure that the freedom of each can coexist with the freedom of all . . . other[s], is at all events a necessary idea which must be made the basis not only of the first outline of a political constitution but of all laws as well.
>
> —Kant, *Critique of Pure Reason*[1]

INTRODUCTION

Kant insisted that human beings and states were under a moral obligation to seek to instantiate a Rightful condition under a constitution, which he linked in various ways to the protection of rights. Notwithstanding the force of these arguments, the philosopher had remarkably little to say about how public authority ought to be organized to meet this obligation. Kant gestures toward separation of powers and other features of the "republican state," as we have seen.[2] But these musings typically appear in the form of vague, sometimes inconsistent generalities.[3] He left open the crucial institutional

* This chapter is partly based on Stone Sweet and Palmer (2017).

1 3: 247. 2 Chapter 1.

3 *The Metaphysics of Morals* (6: 311–23) (hereinafter MM).

question: what types of arrangements are most likely to help a community govern itself according to the principle of Right? This gap is hardly surprising, given that Kant wrote before any mature system of constitutional justice had been established anywhere in the world. By *system of constitutional justice*, we mean those arrangements—rights provisions, procedures, and judicial review—whose purpose is to express and protect fundamental rights.[4] The institutional indeterminacy of Kant's constitutional theory motivates this chapter. Our ambition is to fill gaps in ways that make his theory directly relevant to contemporary constitutional practice and to the jurisprudence of the most powerful rights-protecting courts.

Our account of a Kantian system of justice is sequenced as follows. First, rights ground a system of reciprocal freedom for all in positive constitutional law. The system authorizes reliance on state coercion, but only in so far as coercion ensures that each person may exercise her freedom consistently with the freedom of others, that is, according to the Universal Principle of Right (UPR). "Omnilateral lawmaking"—state measures taken on behalf of everyone, rather than by or for an individual or discrete group—is the basic mechanism for achieving a Rightful condition. Second, constitutional rights establish positive requirements of any valid act of public authority. Public officials—agents of the People—are charged with creating and maintaining a Rightful condition in law.[5] Third, the People, by enacting a rights-based constitution, place their freedom in trust. They thereby generate justiciable obligations, borne by all officials, to fulfill these requirements.

Although our fourth point is only implicit in Kant, an effective system of rights protection requires a constitutional organ possessing strong powers of judicial review. It is the duty of this *trustee court*, to supervise the rights-regarding acts of all other state officials, when

[4] For an overview of the evolution of systems of constitutional justice, see Stone Sweet (2008 [4th revised edition, 2017]).

[5] MM, 6: 311.

such officials make and enforce laws.[6] As the caretaker of the system, the court's primary mission is to evaluate the reasons officials give to justify acts that burden the exercise of a right, and to invalidate acts when it judges those reasons to be inadequate. In Kantian terms, the court supervises the incremental process through which Public Right is constructed, through enforcing the will of the constitutional lawmaker: the People. Fifth, Kant's constitutional theory strongly implies that some rights must be expressed in absolute terms, but that most rights can be limited under the UPR. Modern charters reflect these logics, in that most rights are expressly "qualified" by a "limitation clause." Taking a cue from contemporary practice, we argue that the trustee court can do no better than to adopt the proportionality principle[7] to adjudicate qualified rights, so long as the tests are applied in defensible ways. In fact, the world's most powerful courts have adopted proportionality, in large part due to the neat "fit" between it and the structure of qualified rights.[8]

Our most important conclusions are guided by, but not directly derivable from, Kantian ideas. It is a brute fact that Kant's constitutional theory is largely indeterminate when it comes to the operational details of rights protection, and to the substantive content of rights doctrine. Although some of the moves we make are open to challenge, we have taken care to ensure that they do not violate Kantian precepts. Further, the philosopher's arguments proceed functionally, and he routinely posits the "necessity" of further stages of social and institutional development from the prior establishment of moral principles and obligations. This chapter extends this style of reasoning, as Zylberman and others have,[9] with respect to a modern system of

[6] *Toward Perpetual Peace among States* (8: 381–6) (hereinafter PP).

[7] Discussed below and in chapter 3.

[8] On the emergence and diffusion of the proportionality principle, see Stone Sweet and Mathews (2008); and Barak (2012a: ch. 7).

[9] Zylberman (2014: 38), for example, stresses that: "Kant argues that public institutions are *necessary* to a system of rights. . . . Public institutions are not necessary simply in order to enforce fully determinate rights. [They] are also necessary in a

justice. Put differently, our objective is to identify those arrangements that are most likely to resolve the commitment problems that beset any attempt to realize a Rightful constitutional condition.

BASIC ELEMENTS

The central thrust of Kant's constitutional theory is to explicate the necessary constraints that individuals and states must accept in order to fulfill their obligation to leave the "lawless state of nature," and to enter into a "Rightful" civil condition.[10] What must they do to secure their own freedom in community? Two principles are foundational, in that they constrain how the system must be constructed. The *Internal Duty of Rightful Honor* prohibits one from consenting to social arrangements that would permit one to be used as a mere means for others.[11] And the UPR limits the state's "authorization to coerce" to those acts that meet the demands of Right.[12] Kant defined Right as "the sum of the conditions under which the choice of one can be united with the choice of another in accordance with a universal law of freedom."[13] He conceptualized Public Right as an inherently constitutional order:

> Public Right is . . . a system of laws for a people, that is, a multitude of human beings, or for a multitude of peoples, which, because they affect one another, need a rightful condition under . . . a constitution . . . so that they may enjoy what is laid down as Right.[14]

All rational beings are required to set and pursue ends in light of the freedom of every other rational being. They may not withhold their

non-instrumental sense: they are necessary to [the process of] articulating the *content* of rights." [Emphases in the original.]

[10] PP, 8: 354. [11] MM, 6: 236. [12] MM, 6: 231.
[13] MM, 6: 230. [14] MM, 6: 311.

consent from law that conforms to the UPR. Public law constitutes the civil condition, on which every person's external freedom *constitutively* depends.[15] The state—a set of linked, "omnilateral" organs through which officials make, interpret, and enforce law, as agents of the sovereign People[16]—is authorized to coerce individuals for the purpose of realizing Right, but coercion is forbidden for any other purpose.[17]

Box 2 contains selected commentary by Kant on these and other core concepts, the implications of which we discuss in each of the sections to come. We begin where Kant does, with the concept of freedom.

Box 2 **Kant's Constitutional Theory: Principles and Concepts**

Kant elaborated his most important constitutional ideas in part I of *The Metaphysics of Morals* [1797], the Doctrine of Right (6: 229–378) [emphases in original]. In this chapter, we treat these concepts as the micro-foundations of a Rightful constitutional order.

(The Internal Duty of) Rightful Honor

Rightful honor consists in asserting one's worth as a human being in relation to others, a duty expressed by the saying, "Do not make yourself a mere means for others but be at the same time an end for them."[MM, 6: 236]

Innate Freedom

An innate right is that which belongs to everyone by nature, independently of any act that would establish a right; an acquired right is that for which such an act is required.[MM, 6: 237]

There is only one Innate Right. *Freedom* (independence from being constrained by another's choice), insofar as it can coexist with the freedom of every other in accordance with a universal law, is the only original right belonging to every man by virtue of his humanity.[MM, 6: 237]

This principle of innate freedom already involves the following authorizations . . . : innate *equality*, that is, independence from being bound by

[15] MM, 6: 316. For an extended constitutive account of freedom under public law, see Zylberman (2016).

[16] MM, 6: 313–18.

[17] MM, 6: 231.

others by more than one can in turn bound them; hence a human being's quality of being *his own master* . . . , as well as being a human being *beyond reproach* . . ., since before he performs any act affecting rights he has done no wrong to anyone; and finally, his being authorized to do to others anything that does not in itself diminish what is theirs . . . [MM, 6: 237-38]

Public Right and the Universal Principle of Right

Right is . . . the sum of the conditions under which the choice of one can be united with the choice of another in accordance with a universal law of freedom.[MM, 6: 230]

The sum of the laws that need to be promulgated generally in order to bring about a Rightful condition is *Public Right*.[MM, 6: 311]

The Universal Principles of Right: "Any act is *Right* if it can coexist with everyone's freedom in accordance with a universal law, or if on its maxim the freedom of choice of each can coexist with everyone's freedom in accordance with a universal law."[MM, 6: 230]

If then my action or my condition generally can coexist with the freedom of everyone in accordance with a universal law, whoever hinders me in it does me *wrong*, for this hindrance (resistance) cannot coexist with freedom in accordance with a universal law.[MM, 6: 230-31]

[C]oercion is a hindrance or a resistance to freedom. Therefore, if a certain use of freedom is itself a hindrance to freedom in accordance with universal laws (i.e., wrong), coercion that is opposed to this (as a *hindering of a hindrance to freedom*), is consistent with freedom in accordance with universal laws, that is, it is Right.[MM, 6: 231]

The Idea of the Original Contract and the State

The act by which a People forms itself into a state is the *original contract*. Properly speaking, the original contract is only the idea of this act, in terms of which alone we can think of the legitimacy of the state.[MM, 6: 315]

[T]he *spirit* of the original contract . . . involves an obligation on the part of the constituting authority to make the *kind of government* suited to the idea of the original contract. Accordingly, even if this cannot be done all at once, it is under an obligation to change the kind of government gradually and continuously, so that it harmonizes *in its effect* with the only constitution that accords with Right, that of a pure republic, in such a way that the old (empirical) statutory forms, which serve merely to bring about the *submission* of the people, are replaced by the original (rational) form, the only form which makes *freedom* the principle and indeed the condition for any exercise of *coercion*, as is required by a Rightful constitution of the state in the strict sense of the word. Only it will finally lead to what is literally a state. This is the only constititution of a state that lasts, the constitution in which law itself rules, and depends on no particular person.[MM, 6: 340-41]

[I]t is only in conformity with the conditions of freedom and equality that [the] people can become a state and enter into a civil constitution.[MM, 6: 315]

The Omnilateral Lawmaker

[A] will that is *omnilateral*, that is united not contingently but *a priori* and therefore necessarily . . . is the only will that is lawgiving.[MM, 6: 263]

The legislative authority can only belong to the united will of the people. . . . [O]nly the concurring and united will of all, insofar as each decides the same thing for all and all for each, and to only the united general will of the people, can be legislative.[MM, 6: 313-314]

Publicity

[Publicity] is implied in any legal claim, since without it there would be no justice (which can only be thought of as *publicly proclaimable*), and thus no Right, since Right can be conferred only by justice.[PP, 8: 381]

Any legal claim must be capable of publicity.[PP, 8: 381]

This principle is to be understood as being not only *ethical* . . . but also *juridical* (as concerning the rights of humans).[PP, 8: 381]

The *transcendental formula* of Public Right: "All actions that affect the rights of other human beings, the maxims of which are incompatible with publicity, are unjust."[PP, 8: 381]

Kant argues that external freedom—"independence from being constrained by another's choice" is "the only one innate right," possessed by "every man by virtue of his humanity."[18] The scope of freedom is subject to the UPR: the external independence of any person is to be recognized "only insofar as it can coexist with the freedom of every other in accordance with a universal law."[19] Freedom is innate in that its existence does not depend on any affirmative act on the part of an agent or the state, unlike the "acquired rights" that form the substance of contract and property law, for example. Kant supposes that a person's means-based capacity is conceptually prior to the setting of ends. In the absence of such capacity, one can only wish for an end; but one cannot make it one's purpose to set about achieving that end. It follows that every person must possess certain inherent powers if they are to be free.

The concept of external freedom is relational.[20] A person is independent only if she is able to exercise her capacity to set and pursue ends without being subject to the coercive or controlling authority of

[18] MM, 6: 237. [19] MM, 6: 237. [20] Ripstein (2009: 15).

another person.[21] Person X is not independent from Y, if Y has a power to interfere with X's capacity to choose, even if Y foregoes the exercise of that power. Slaves whose master declines to interfere with their decisional autonomy are nonetheless subject to the master's relational authority.[22] For Kant, actual non-interference is not a sufficient condition for freedom, since it can coexist with another person's entitlement to interfere, as in the case of the benign slaveholder. Most important for our purposes, Kant takes pains to argue that *coercive* interference with the independence of each person is defensible only when it is necessary to secure the "external" freedom of all in a Rightful legal order.[23]

Innate Right begets the principle of Rightful Honor, which is expressed through the maxim: one may not allow oneself to be used as a mere means for others.[24] The duty is categorical, admitting to no exception. At first glance, this requirement looks out of place in the Doctrine of Public Right, which concerns social interactions and arrangements. But the internal duty of Rightful Honor is also relational: it operates to restrict a person's exercise of freedom, by barring them from entering into legal relationships that are inconsistent with their own status as free and equal persons.[25] Reciprocal relations among free persons must respect the Innate Freedom—ones inalienable, means-based capacity—not undermine or destroy it.

The notion of freedom as an innate attribute of personhood means that all individuals are entitled to pursue their chosen ends, so long as they do not violate Rightful Honor along the way. We can, on these grounds, distinguish freedom from other justifications of coercive public authority, including welfare maximization. An agent may always ask—why should I accept that reason for coercion? The Kantian response is stark and unyielding: the only acceptable justification for restricting the freedom of a rational agent is the need to instantiate the collective freedom of everyone.[26]

[21] Hodgson (2010: 793).
[22] Kant speaks to the issue of slavery in MM, 6: 330.
[23] Zylberman (2016: 109). [24] MM, 6: 236.
[25] See also Ripstein (2009: 37).
[26] MM, 6: 316. For commentary, see Hodgson (2010: 799); Korsgaard (2009).

A civil condition is Rightful to the extent that public laws conform to the UPR. Kant defined the UPR as follows:

> [A]ny action is Right [that is, *just*] if it can coexist with everyone's freedom in accordance with a universal law, or if on its maxim the freedom of choice of each can coexist with everyone's freedom in accordance with universal law.[27]

Thus, considered in terms of institutional design, Rightful Honor restricts the purposes for which legislative powers can be delegated and held by state organs. And the UPR constrains how officials are to exercise their powers to make, and coercively enforce, the law. State coercion to promote an end other than the construction of Public Right is categorically forbidden, no matter how worthwhile that end might seem to be, or how many might value it.

Looking forward, what are the structural implications of these arguments for contemporary constitutional law and practice? First, the principle of Rightful Honor means that no person may justifiably accept any binding arrangement that abrogates her basic entitlements to freedom.[28] Put positively, in a Rightful constitutional condition, every person possesses an *inalienable entitlement to justiciable rights*. In modern constitutional jurisprudence, Kant's ideas are embedded in what has gradually become a kind of constitutional meta-norm, that of *dignity*. As Weinrib puts it, human dignity converts independence into "the right to interact with others on terms of equal freedom,"[29] an entitlement that is derivable from Kant's account of "hospitality" in *Perpetual Peace*.[30] Second, in any Rightful condition, a person's independence is subject to justifiable limitations. Kant, after all, connects the UPR to a public lawmaker's "authorization to coerce" at the outset of the *Doctrine of Right*.[31] Public law articulates the scope and content of each person's external freedom to act purposively

[27] MM, 6: 230–1.

[28] A point forcefully made by Zylberman (2014).

[29] Weinrib (2016: 7).

[30] See chapter 1; Brown (2010).

[31] MM, 6: 230–1.

within society, insofar as that law meets the demands of the UPR. As Zylberman puts the point, "one is externally free not only when one is independent from the constraining choice of others but primarily when one's actions are in agreement with or depend on a universal law relating one to others in a rightful manner."[32] Third, public law *constitutes* the external freedom of all. As elaborated further below, a charter of rights does not merely give concrete expression to freedom, but grounds the construction of the Rightful constitutional condition. Indeed, qualified rights explicitly authorize officials "to hinder any hindrance" to freedom,[33] in order to realize the external freedom of all under a system of law.

THE STATE AND OMNILATERAL LAWMAKING

Suppose that two persons, X and Y, attempt to interact on conditions of equal freedom in the absence of authoritative legal institutions. If X makes any territorial claim—even through moving from point A to point B—the effect of X's action will be to place Y under an implied duty: to refrain from moving to point B or otherwise interfering with X's purpose for doing so.[34] By what authority does X impose this obligation on Y? Prior to X's decision to walk from point A to point B, Y enjoyed an equal entitlement to move to point B. X's move eviscerates Y's entitlement, while impliedly shackling Y with new obligations. Given the principles of Rightful Honor, X could not possess the capacity to unilaterally subjugate Y's freedom to X's purposes. Y may not allow the private will of X to determine Y's purposes. Self-abnegating deference to the unilateral determinations of others conflicts, more generally, with the dictates of independence and of Rightful Honor.

[32] Zylberman (2016: 109). [33] MM, 6: 231.

[34] The fact that the world is round is a crucial underpinning of Kant's theory of property and, ultimately, of his Doctrine of Public Right; MM, notably 6: 311, and 6: 352–3. As Flikschuh (2000: 179) puts it: "Kant's image of the earth's spherical surface is that unavoidable constraint of nature within the limits of which finite rational beings must resolve conflicts of external freedom and justice."

Simplifying a complex argument, even when people do succeed in freely negotiating rules to govern their relations, these arrangements can only be provisional. In a pre-legal condition, Kant famously insisted,[35] binding legal entitlements cannot exist, because no private person has a power to bind another to act in accordance with duties of Right.

The dilemma Kant diagnoses is one of *unilateral authorization*: Y is never required to accept X's attempts to assert, unilaterally, any entitlement that would limit Y's freedom. X possesses no legitimate authority to compel Y to do anything. The solution requires delegation of powers to an *omnilateral* lawgiver—an institution authorized to make UPR-compliant law in the collective interest—to create a Rightful condition.[36] Public acts are omnilateral insofar as they are choices taken on behalf of all citizens, rather than the choices of one or a group of particular persons. Omnilateral acts are those that seek to create or preserve the formal conditions under which persons can rule themselves, that is, to be externally free in community, under the UPR.[37]

Omnilateral lawmakers establish determinate boundaries on the zone of freedom in which individuals interact. At the same time, the UPR constrains the exercise of public authority.[38] Thus, with respect to tensions that may result from a territorial clash between X and Y, the omnilateral state regulates. The law may: (i) demarcate the spatial zones in which X and Y may act without being liable in trespass; (ii) establish conditions for claiming title; or (iii) turn the land into a public park; and so on. Officials can realize Public Right through myriad means. It is crucial, however, to stress that omnilateral lawmaking has the capacity to construct new *normative* conditions that can not be fully comprehended in terms of a priori moral reasoning;

[35] MM, 6: 256–317. [36] MM, 6: 263.

[37] MM, 6: 263. Required is "a will that is omnilateral, that is united not contingently but *a priori* and therefore necessary, and because of this is the only will that is lawgiving."

[38] MM, 6: 313–14. See also Ripstein (2009: 145–81).

only the principles of Public Right, which are given content through lawmaking, can be known a priori. Thus, nothing in Kantian theory tells us what types of meanings people may invest in a public park, or how such meanings may influence subsequent disputes about its use.

Tellingly, Kant defines the state as "a union of a multitude of human beings under laws of Right," whose legislative powers "can belong only to the united will of the People."[39] He characterizes deputies in parliament as both representatives of the People, and "the guardians of its freedom and rights."[40] The next step comes naturally: all state officials, agents of the people, are under a duty to make, interpret, and apply law in a manner consistent with the UPR. That is, their basic function is to maximize Public Right. While we will specify these duties with more precision below, at this point it is enough to repeat that the delegation of lawmaking authority to public officials is a functional necessity, given the incapacity of individuals to realize Public Right on their own.[41]

RIGHTS AS POSITIVE REQUIREMENTS OF LEGALITY

What little Kant tells us about delegation and the creation of the state is filtered through *the idea of the original contract*:

> In accordance with the original contract, everyone . . . gives up his external freedom in order to take it up again immediately as a member of the commonwealth, that is, of the people considered as a state. . . . [O]ne cannot say: the human being in a state has sacrificed part of his innate outer freedom for the sake of an end, but rather, *he has relinquished entirely his wild lawless freedom in order to find*

[39] MM, 6: 313. [40] MM, 6: 319. [41] See also Ripstein (2009): 192–3.

> *his freedom as such undiminished, in a dependence upon laws, that is, in a Rightful condition, since this dependence arises from his own lawgiving will.*[42] [Emphasis added.]

Kant characterized the "idea" as a necessary *theoretical* construct; it does not depend upon the facts of how any state actually emerged or operates. The construct contrasts with classical contractarian accounts of political authority, which link the legitimacy of state coercion to a datable act of voluntary agreement or authorization in which persons cede powers to the state. Presupposing the original contract sets the stage for an elucidation of the demands imposed by the UPR on the exercise of public authority.

Kant wrote before any state, as he defined it above, had been established.[43] He was also silent on many crucial issues of constitutional design. He did not develop a full-fledged theory of rights, or specify the mechanisms for their protection. Kant illustrates his arguments with reference to a small handful of rights; and he provides little guidance to a polity that commits itself to compliance with the UPR. In response to these gaps, we propose a structural account of constitutional justice that is both Kantian-congruent and consistent with the basic facts of contemporary, rights-based constitutionalism. We thus confront the following question: what components of a system of constitutional justice would optimize a community's capacity to achieve Public Right?

The first step is to conceptualize constitutional rights as *positive requirements of legality*. Rights—substantive limitations on the exercise of public authority, along with standing and due process requirements—are justiciable commands. Every official owes a duty to make and enforce laws in a manner consistent with the UPR, and

[42] MM, 6: 315–16.

[43] Kant was, however, well versed in natural law discourse on the political legitimacy of the state, and kept a sharp eye on the French and American revolutions, for example.

to refrain from subjecting individuals under their authority to coercive rules that are inconsistent with the UPR. And every individual has a right to defend her rights in a lawsuit.

Conceived in Kantian terms, rights formally express external freedom in law for individuals, however imperfectly realized or under construction. Rightful Honor restricts the consent of the People in ways that limit rights provisions. Kant, himself, derived the content of a few rights from Rightful Honor, including freedom of expression, religious liberty,[44] and the presumption of innocence.[45] An expansive notion of freedom of expression, for example, is linked to the right to be one's "own master."[46] Limiting expression is appropriate to prevent one person from depriving another of her own capacity as a free and honorable agent; thus, one may not impugn another's reputation, or deprive another of choice and Rightful means through fraudulent inducement.[47] The right to the presumption of innocence is also rooted in the foundational principles: to be treated, presumptively, as "a human being beyond reproach."[48] And Kant bluntly states that "no human being in a state can be without any dignity," before explaining why slavery must be categorically forbidden.[49]

The principles of Innate Freedom and Rightful Honor imply that certain rights, such as freedom from being enslaved, are absolute insofar as no legitimate, UPR-compliant reasons can be given for their infringement. Absolute rights are those that are required to secure one's place as a juridical person in a system of equal freedom writ large. Most rights in modern constitutions, however, are not expressed in absolute terms, but are "qualified" by limitation clauses. Qualified rights command the omnilateral lawmaker to secure the reciprocal freedom of all in law. In Kantian terms, such rights recognize the individual's entitlements to set and pursue ends, while providing

[44] Kant, *An Answer to the Question: What is Enlightenment?*, 8: 39.
[45] MM, 6: 238. [46] MM, 6: 238. [47] Ripstein (2009: 210).
[48] MM, 6: 238. [49] MM, 6: 329–30.

reasons for officials to restrict the scope of those same entitlements, in order to realize Public Right.

The distinction between an absolute and a qualified right will not always be obvious. Consider the right to life and the prohibition of slavery.[50] The latter is an absolute right, because it amounts to a complete deprivation of a person's entitlement to freedom. There are no UPR-compliant reasons that could justify imposing this status—a denial of juridical personhood—on anyone. By contrast, the right to life has an absolute dimension, in that it safeguards a person's purposiveness as such. But there may well be UPR-compliant reasons licensing the state to take someone's life. The state might kill person X, for example, in order to prevent X from depriving Y of life. The maintenance of a system of equal outer freedom may, at times, depend on the use of lethal force when there is no alternative means of protecting the freedom of others or all. Under this view, only a core of the right to life—a right against being arbitrarily put to death, or killed for the sake of private ends—is absolute.

We can now begin to sketch a picture of a charter of rights as the foundational norms of justice in law. Again, the key is to consider the UPR as a legal obligation binding on the exercise of state authority. The idea of the constitutional contract places officials under a duty, owed to every person subject to their authority, not to make or enforce law in ways that are inconsistent with their rights. When it comes to qualified rights, the legitimacy of the justification for the limitation of one's freedom will turn on its consistency with the UPR. Further along, we will propose a way of conceptualizing the proportionality framework as an analytical procedure for arriving at answers to precisely this type of question. Before doing so, we need to bring judicial review into the picture.

[50] Kant, *Theory and Practice*.

THE CONSTITUTIONAL COURT AS OMNILATERAL TRUSTEE

We have argued that an enumerated bill of rights deserves pride of place in a Kantian constitutional order. The rights-based constitution converts the idea of the original contract into positive constitutional law, while delegating to officials the authority to secure Public Right. Kant insisted that it was the cardinal duty of every official to give effect to the normative principles extrapolated and defended in the *Doctrine of Right*, without which a just constitutional order could never be realized. Enforcing the charter of rights would, in effect, operationalize the UPR as the basic criterion of law's legitimacy. In this constitutional order, some rights will be expressed in absolute terms, but most will be qualified by limitation clauses that authorize lawmakers to infringe on freedoms, but only when necessary to achieve Public Right.

We now take on the task of describing a Kantian-congruent system of constitutional judicial review, a topic on which he wrote virtually nothing. Our claim is that Kantian theory requires a "constitutional court," which we define as an apex, omnilateral organ of governance whose mission is to supervise compliance with the UPR. The court (i) evaluates the rights-regarding acts of all other public officials, (ii) issues authoritative interpretations of the content, scope, and application of the charter, (iii) certifies that officials act according to the UPR, and (iv) invalidates acts that violate rights.

Delegation theory is directly relevant to this situation.[51] Kant elaborates an abstract, functionalist claim: the move to omnilateral governance *must* take place if the polity is to progress toward a Rightful civil condition. The written constitution, a formalized act of delegation by the sovereign People, authorizes public officials to make and enforce law in order to realize a Rightful civil condition. In

[51] Scholars have standardized the theory, as a general approach to delegated governance, in the guise of Principal-Agent models; see Thatcher and Stone Sweet (2002).

pursuing this tack, one confronts an obvious agency problem: how do the People hold officials accountable, ensuring that officials will act according to the UPR?

Rights-as-freedom will be illusory unless each person subject to the state's authority is entitled to challenge state action. For Kant, a right is a moral power held by each citizen, a juridical title to act or be in a condition. But qualified rights are more than that: they provide officials with a title to coerce. It follows that Innate Freedom, once given positive expression in explicit constitutional guarantees, entails that individuals possess a legal power to constrain wrongful acts on the part of state officials.

If no one possesses an individualized title to require the state to comply with the terms of the UPR, then no one holds a genuine right, and compliance with the UPR—which grounds the legitimacy of the legal system—can not be assured. The power to coerce state officials into compliance with the UPR cannot be operationalized through private acts of resistance, on pain of rendering the omnilateral will of the state subject to the unilateral say-so of each person. Put differently, if Innate Freedom transmutes into a sequence of justiciable positive rights held by each person, then each person must also possesses the power to constrain officials from wrongful interference with that freedom.[52] The constitutional court is the institutional solution to this accountability dilemma.[53]

Once activated, the constitutional court determines the scope and application of a pleaded right; its ruling will not be based on the unilateral judgment of the claimant, but on the constitution itself, the foundational act of the will of the People. No other institution could perform this crucial, adjudicative function. In a system of parliamentary sovereignty, notwithstanding the commitment of the legislature to respecting rights (an empirical issue, not a juridical state of affairs),

[52] The mechanism is a lawsuit brought by an individual rights claimant. We take no position on any other grant of authority to a constitutional court here.

[53] For a compatible view, see Weinrib (2016: ch. 5).

individuals possess no entitlement to demand legislative compliance with the UPR. Rather, such a system is deficient in that it recognizes only a *collective* power to hold the legislature accountable, through voting and public deliberation.[54]

A split-the-difference system—the so-called "new commonwealth model" of constitutionalism[55]—purports to reconcile legislative supremacy with rights protection. This type of system features (i) a charter of rights, (ii) some form of judicial power to review legislation and other government acts for consistency with the charter, which is trumped by (iii) a legislative "final word" that will determine whether law judged to be inconsistent with a right provision will nonetheless remain in force. While the model gives standing to individuals to challenge wrongful state action, the legislature can choose to maintain a statute that violates rights. This is a version of what Kant called despotism: "the state executes, on its own authority, law that it has itself made."[56] In such a situation, "the public will" expressed in the constitution is "treated by the monarch as his individual will."[57] A majority within the legislature, rather than pre-existing constitutional rules, determines the resolution of the conflict.

As a practical matter, the capacity of the constitutional court to render justice will depend upon an extensive grant of power and jurisdiction. The authority to review the conformity of statutes with rights and the UPR is required. Prohibited are arrangements that (i) restrict the binding authority of legal statements in judicial opinions to the parties of the judgment; (ii) ascribe to the legislature the competence to make determinations regarding the scope and content of rights, but withhold them from the judge; or (iii) require judges to defer to non-judicial officials in rendering such determinations. Rights must be justiciable with respect to all public acts. In a system designed to achieve Public Right, the court will oversee, and therefore participate in, the omnilateral lawmaking process. But it does so in order to settle disputes that arise from the omnilateral lawmaking of officials,

[54] Weinrib (2014). [55] Gardbaum (2012). [56] PP, 8: 352.
[57] PP, 8: 352.

ensuring that the latter respect the charter of rights, a product of constitutional legislation. Put in the language of delegation theory, although the court is an "agent" of the People, the situation is one of *trusteeship*.[58]

In sketching a simple model of trusteeship, we can express more formally the role to be played by the constitutional court.[59] By legislating a rights-based constitution, the People have placed the ultimate value—their freedom—in trust. The constitution confers judicial review powers on the court, for the purpose of enforcing rights as positive requirements of legality. It places officials under the constitutional obligation to act according to the UPR, as a means of constructing Public Right; and it tasks the constitutional court with monitoring their compliance with this obligation. The court can only properly perform its mission if it possesses the authority to invalidate any public act that violates a rights provision, and its decisions are effectively insulated from override on the part of the public officials whose decisions it controls.[60]

We recognize that this part of our argument—that Kantian imperatives generate a powerful functional demand for the structural supremacy of a "trustee court"—will be controversial. The claim, however, does not conflict with Kant's own pronouncements, spare as they are, on legislative power and justice. As noted, Kant defined the state as a "union of a multitude of human beings under laws of Right,"[61] and asserted that "it is only in conformity with the conditions of freedom and equality that [the] people can become a state and enter into a civil constitution."[62] Under this constitution, the people govern themselves collectively:

> The legislative authority can only belong to the united will of the people. . . . [O]nly the concurring and united will of all, insofar as

[58] Thatcher and Stone Sweet (2002: 7).

[59] On the concept of the trustee court, see Stone Sweet (2002, 2012a); and Stone Sweet and Brunell (2013).

[60] As a matter of institutional design, a court that meets these criteria is a trustee.

[61] MM, 6: 313. [62] MM, 6: 315.

> each decides the same thing for all and all for each, and to only the united, general will of the people, can be legislative.[63]

Today, we no longer have to understand the idea of an "original contract," and the omnilateral lawmaker, as necessary theoretical constructs. The People typically manifest themselves when they enact new constitutions, say, through a referendum; and the rights-based constitution delegates lawmaking authority to various organs and officials, while the charter of rights constrains the exercise of that authority. Given a conflict between a rights provision and any legislative act, the former prevails.[64]

In such a situation, neither parliamentarians nor executives are principals in relation to the constitutional court; instead, they are agents of the People, and the People have commanded the court to supervise the decision-making of all officials. Kant himself equated judicial authority with *justice*:

> A Rightful condition is that relation of human beings among one another that contains the conditions under which alone everyone is able to *enjoy* his rights, the formal condition under which this is possible in accordance with the idea of a will giving laws for everyone is called public justice. . . . [A] court is itself called the *justice* of the country, and whether such a thing exists or does not exist is the most important question that can be asked about any arrangements having to do with rights.[65] [Emphases in the original.]

[63] MM, 6: 314–15.

[64] Put differently, Kantian constitutional theory is capable of embracing rights-based, constitutional democracy, despite Kant's own "failure" to adequately theorize a "democratic sovereign" (Hanisch (2016)).

[65] MM, 6: 305–6. In this passage, Kant is discussing "the possession of objects," in a section of MM concerning Private Right. Nonetheless, he expressly speaks to "public justice," and the fundamental role of the courts in supplying it.

Today, when it comes to rights-based constitutionalism, the People, as primary lawmakers, have legislated judicial supremacy. Parliamentarians are secondary lawmakers, agents of the People, and subject to the decisions of the trustee court, which holds them accountable to the terms of the trust. Constitutional judges are caretakers, stewards, of the regime.

It should be obvious that a system that features the supremacy of an authoritative constitutional court fatally undermines the usual presumptions of delegation theory, which are exemplified by the simpler Principal-Agent models common in social science. In "agency-control" models, a unified Principal possesses the means to control the acts of her Agent on a continuous basis. A trustee, however, is a special type of agent. In this instance, the court is entrusted with promoting the value placed in reserve by the People: their freedom. The People, as the constituent legislative power, are also the beneficiaries of the trust going forward. The constituent power alone possesses the authority to alter the terms of the trust, which it may do by revising the constitution.[66]

Trust law offers further analogies that are appropriate to our argument, notably in its emphasis on fiduciary duties. Because both citizens and officials are vulnerable to the trustee court's judgments, the judges are bound by a set of robust obligations. The most important of these fiduciary duties—typically formalized as (i) *loyalty*, (ii) *accountability*, and (iii) *deliberative engagement*—apply to the trustee judge.[67] As Leib et al. argue, loyalty refers to the judge's duty to protect rights in ways that ensure that public officials act in accordance with the UPR. They stipulate that the duty of accountability requires the court to justify its rulings with reasons.[68] And the obligation of deliberative engagement requires the judge "to engage in dialogue" with those

[66] Stone Sweet (2012a: 820–5).
[67] Leib, Ponet, and Serota (2013); Stone Sweet and Brunell (2013).
[68] Trustees in private law trusts, however, are not typically subject to a reason-giving requirement.

who are subject to her rulings, which includes both rights claimants and officials. The latter entails, Leib et al. emphasize, "an authentic effort to uncover preferences rather than a mere hypothetical projection of what beneficiaries might want."[69]

In Kantian terms, a robust fiduciary construction of trusteeship will underwrite the reasons individuals have to accept the state's "authority to coerce." Each person retains the right to challenge any decision that would infringe upon their rights, and every official is placed under a duty to justify acts under review in terms that are comprehensible under the Doctrine of Public Right. In our view, the *right to justification*[70] cannot be optional. Instead, it comprises a meta-rule that commits the polity to procedures that are conducive to the construction of Public Right. Arguably, the right is derivable from the Kantian principle of "publicity," about which Kant asserted short but important remarks in *Perpetual Peace*:[71]

> [Publicity] . . . is implied in any legal claim, since without it there would be no justice (which can only be thought of as publicly proclaimable), and thus no Right, since Right can be conferred only by justice. Any legal claim must be capable of publicity.[72]

Kant then pronounces a "transcendental formula of Public Right," according to which "all actions that affect the rights of other human beings, the maxims of which are incompatible with publicity, are unjust."[73] Scholars differ on how best to interpret Kant's insistence on the principle of publicity.[74] For present purposes, we understand it as presumptive support for a right to justification (held by all citizens) and its corollary, a reason-giving requirement (binding on officials). More generally, a reason-giving requirement is a functional

[69] Leib et al. (2013: 699).
[70] For a broader account of the "right to justification," see Forst (2011).
[71] Laursen (1986). [72] PP, 8: 381. [73] PP, 8: 381.
[74] See Davis (1991); Laursen (1986).

necessity for any system of constitutional justice, if it is to perform its accountability function, and develop effectiveness.[75] In any event, the right to justification must be reflected in rules of adjudication, including standing (access to justice), the fiduciary duties of the trustee court (deliberative engagement), and in constraints on the exercise of public authority by officials (reason-giving, as disciplined by the UPR).

In this same spirit, we now address the question of why the trustee court ought to embrace the proportionality principle, or some (currently unknown) principle that performs better than proportionality, if it is to fulfill its mission.

THE NEW CONSTITUTIONALISM AND THE PROPORTIONALITY PRINCIPLE

Since 1950, the gradual consolidation of rights-based constitutionalism has transformed the global political and legal landscape. The precepts of this "new constitutionalism" can be simply stated:

(i) state organs are established by, and derive their authority from, a written constitution;

(ii) the constitution assigns ultimate power to the People by way of elections or referenda;

(iii) the exercise of public authority, including legislative, is lawful only insofar as it conforms with the constitutional law;

(iv) the constitution provides for a catalogue of rights and a mode of judicial review to defend those rights; and

(v) the constitution is entrenched, specifying how it may be revised.

[75] See Stone Sweet (2012b).

As an empirical matter, virtually every new constitution adopted over the past three decades established systems of justice in line with this template.[76] These developments make Kant's theory of Public Right directly relevant to constitutional practice.

One can treat our model of Kantian justice as an ideal type for heuristic comparative purposes. The model bears more than a surface resemblance to the most important domestic systems of justice operating in the world today; in these, certain norms and stipulations are treated as necessary determinants of more specific rights, and of constitutional legality itself. Well-known examples include the case of the right to dignity in the German Basic Law,[77] the requirements of "equal citizenship" in "a free and democratic society" found in the Canadian Charter of Rights and Freedoms,[78] or the values of "human dignity, equality, and freedom" that are synthesized in the Constitution of the Republic of South Africa.[79] These formulations come before the listing of more specific rights and, in most contemporary constitutions,[80] the catalogue of rights comes before the establishment of state organs. In post-Second World War constitutions,[81] almost all rights are qualified by limitation clauses, yet another Kantian gloss. Omnilateral lawmaking organs operate under a continuous obligation to generate

[76] The data set on written constitutions compiled by Christina Andersen and Stone Sweet contains information on 194 states, 191 of which have written constitutions. The constitutions of 183 states establish a charter of rights. Of 106 constitutions written since 1985, and on which there exists reliable information, all contain a catalogue of rights. The last constitution to exclude a charter of rights was the racist 1983 South African constitution. Of these 106 constitutions, all but five established a form of constitutional review to protect rights, the exceptions being North Korea, Vietnam, Saudi Arabia, Laos, and Iraq (in its 1990 constitution). Data reported in Stone Sweet (2017).

[77] German Basic Law, Art. 1(1).

[78] *Canadian Charter of Rights and Freedoms*, s. 1, Part I of the Constitution Act, 1982.

[79] *Constitution of the Republic of South Africa* (Act 108 of 1996), s. 7; s. 1.

[80] The Canadian Charter of Rights, a standalone text that applies to the 1867 British North America Act, being a notable exception.

[81] Note that, in many post-Second World War systems, where provisions establishing qualified rights impose an implied duty of dynamic interpretation on judges, an originalist approach is broadly compatible with "living constitution" notions.

a determinate legal ordering that conforms to rights; and a trustee court ensures the constitutional lawfulness of that ordering.

Under the Doctrine of Public Right, law's legitimacy is subjected to the dictates of an overarching principle—the UPR—which, in turn, is rooted in the principles of Innate Freedom and Rightful Honor. Indeterminacy is built into both rights provisions and the UPR. The fraught question—"under what circumstances does an absolute right apply?"—bedevils even the most refined systems of constitutional justice. Qualified rights are indeterminate, incomplete norms by definition and design. Whether officials have abused powers delegated to them by a derogation clause is a question that cannot be settled by referring to a dogmatic conception of the right or the public interest that lawmakers pursue. Further, because the limitation clause incorporates the public interest into the right, the usual conflict rules are useless. One cannot appeal to hierarchy or the primacy of the right or the public interest in the abstract, since both parties are, in fact, pleading the same norm. Applying the *lex posteriori derogat legi priori* rule[82] is also prohibited, since the adoption of any new statute would automatically eviscerate the rights claim, the basis of which dates from the adoption of the constitution. In a situation in which a rights claim comes into conflict with a legitimate public interest, the best constitutional judges can do is to embrace proportionality analysis (PA).[83]

In fact, over the past fifty years, the world's most powerful constitutional courts have institutionalized PA as the dominant, "best-practice" doctrinal framework for adjudicating qualified rights.[84] PA belongs at the very center of a Kantian system of constitutional justice, for three interrelated reasons. First, it permits judges to give broad scope to any qualified right being pleaded, mirroring Kant's argument

[82] In the case of a conflict, the most recently enacted law trumps any earlier law.
[83] Stone Sweet and Mathews (2008); Kumm (2004, 2010); Barak (2010, 2012a).
[84] Stone Sweet and Mathews (2008). For the U.S. as a partial exception, see Mathews and Stone Sweet (2011).

that all positive rights held against public officials give concrete expression to a single unitary right to Innate Freedom, rather than a succession of discrete rights whose scope might, in principle, be quite limited. Most contemporary rights-based constitutions proclaim a general right to liberty, to which the qualified rights give specific content. The trustee court, in accepting the validity of a *claim* based on a qualified right, does not thereby resolve the case but, rather, requires the official to *justify* the act that has burdened the claimant.[85] Second, PA commits judges to the systematic evaluation of such justifications. Under PA the crucial question is always, as Kumm puts it, "whether a public action can be demonstratively justified by reasons that are appropriate in a liberal democracy,"[86] given the paramount importance of rights in modern constitutionalism. Third, a trustee court that deploys PA consistently and in good faith will fulfill the fiduciary duties discussed above of loyalty (to constitutional values), accountability (through reason-giving), and deliberative engagement (with rights-holders and officials).[87] PA thus gives procedural structure to the right to justification, strongly implied by Kant himself, "in terms of public reason."[88]

We now provide a brief summary of PA, and sketch how a Kantian trustee court would deploy it.

PROPORTIONALITY AND QUALIFIED RIGHTS

PA is tailor-made for resolving disputes that involve a conflict between a rights claim and a public act whose constitutional legality,

[85] "In institutional terms, these features of human rights practice require a recharacterization of what courts do when they assess whether public authorities have violated rights. Courts are not simply engaged in applying rules or interpreting principles. They assess justifications. Call this *the turn from interpretation to justification*." Kumm (2010: 144).

[86] Kumm (2010:142).

[87] Stone Sweet and Brunell (2013: 69).

[88] Kumm (2010: 144, 150).

officials alleged, is covered by a limitation clause. In this paradigmatic situation, the analysis proceeds step by step, as follows. In a preliminary phase, the judge considers whether a prima facie case has been made to the effect that a government act burdens the exercise of a right. By convention, the judge will use this occasion to discuss the jurisprudential theories that underpin the pleaded right, as well as prior rulings and other legal materials that will bear upon the court's determination of the right's scope and application in the case at hand. In its most developed form, PA then proceeds through a sequence of four tests: (i) "legitimacy," or "proper purpose"; (ii) "suitability"; (iii) "necessity"; and (iv) balancing in the strict sense. A government measure that fails any one of these tests violates the proportionality principle and is therefore unconstitutional.[89]

The first stage of PA mandates inquiry into the "legitimacy" of the measure under review: the judge confirms that the constitution authorizes the government to take such a measure, typically under a limitation clause (express or implied). In most jurisdictions, judges effectively treat the proper purpose prong of PA in the style of a threshold inquiry: if the constitution has not authorized the state to pursue such a purpose, then the rights claimant must prevail. In the second step—"suitability"—the government must show that a rational relationship exists between the *means chosen* and the *ends pursued*, such that the former is "suitable" to achieving the end (which, the first test has already confirmed, constitutes a legitimate public purpose). In most systems, few laws are struck down on grounds that the official purpose is illicit (per se illegitimate), or that the act is irrational or arbitrary (the means being unsuitable).[90]

The third phase—"necessity"—has far more bite than the suitability inquiry. At its core is a least-restrictive-means (LRM) test,[91] through

[89] For more detailed expositions see Alexy (2002); Barak (2012a).

[90] Some versions of PA collapse legitimacy and suitability into one stage.

[91] Canadian and American judges consider LRM under, respectively, a "minimal impairment" and a "narrow tailoring" requirement.

which the judge ensures that the measure under review does not curtail the right being pleaded more than is necessary for the government to achieve its declared purpose. In practice, most PA-adept courts insist that policymakers have a duty to consider a range of reasonably available alternatives, and to refrain from selecting the more restrictive among them. These courts also typically require, as a pleading matter, that the rights claimant identify less restrictive alternatives; and the judges will never strike down a law as unnecessary without comparing it to at least one reasonably available alternative.

An act that fails either the legitimacy or suitability tests is one that contributes nothing to the realization of Public Right. Ends must meet the dictates of the UPR, and any limitation of a right through means that are not rationally connected to a legitimate end must constitute a per se infringement of freedom. These same considerations suggest that the use of means other than those that are least restrictive on freedom must also qualify as a violation of the UPR: no official possesses the authority to restrict freedom further than is necessary to secure the external freedom of all. Thus, irrespective of the importance of the end being pursued, a public act that fails a LRM test is one that cannot be justified under a system of Public Right.

In the proportionality world, the analysis cannot end with necessity. If it did, a law that imposed an unjustifiable burden on the rights-holder, but was nonetheless narrowly tailored, would prevail. A fourth stage, balancing in the strict sense, is required. In Kantian terms, the court assesses, in light of the facts or policy context, the act's marginal addition to the realization of Public Right against the marginal injury incurred by infringement of the right. Judges that rely heavily on this stage (e.g., members of the German Federal Constitutional Court (GFCC) and the Israeli Supreme Court), also emphasize that balancing allows them to "complete" the analysis, in order to check that no factor of significance to either side has been overlooked in previous stages.[92]

[92] Grimm (2007: 393–5); Mathews and Stone Sweet (2011: 106–8).

Consider, by contrast, the US Supreme Court's ruling in *United States v. O'Brien* (1968).[93] Mr. O'Brien had burned his draft card, in violation of federal statutes, while protesting the Vietnam War and military conscription. The Court took no firm position on the question of whether O'Brien's "wordless" act was protected by the First Amendment; the answer to that question was left incomplete in comparison to what is required under PA. Instead, the Court formulated the following test:

> [A] government regulation is sufficiently justified if it is within the constitutional power of the Government; if it furthers an important or substantial governmental interest; if the governmental interest is unrelated to the suppression of free expression; and if the incidental restriction on alleged First Amendment freedoms is no greater than is essential to the furtherance of that interest. [94]

On the basis of this test, the Court upheld O'Brien's conviction, since the draft card fulfilled various administrative functions. The judgment, however, concluded in deafening silence on the question of the relative importance of the government's interest and O'Brien's "alleged" speech right. Under PA, the judge would have been required to give an answer to that question in the balancing stage. The US Supreme Court, however, marched through the test just announced—which embodies the first three stages of PA—while saying virtually nothing about the First Amendment. It is worth emphasizing that O'Brien still may have lost the case under a full-fledged version of PA. But an additional layer of reasons would have been added, thereby completing the analysis.

It makes little sense to discuss the balancing stage without invoking the formulations of Robert Alexy[95] and Aharon Barak.[96] Alexy,

[93] 391 U.S. 367 (1968). [94] 391 U.S. 367, 377 (1968).

[95] Alexy (2002). [96] Barak (2010, 2012b).

synthesizing the jurisprudence of the GFCC, proposed the *Law of Balancing*:[97]

> The greater the degree of non-satisfaction of, or detriment to, one principle, the greater must be the importance of satisfying the other.

For his part, Barak elaborates the *Rule of Balancing*:[98]

> As the importance of avoiding the marginal limitation on the constitutional right and the likelihood of the limitation coming to pass increase, so do the required importance of the marginal benefit of the public interest or the competing private right and the required likelihood of that benefit being realized.

Barak insists that the balancer must take into account the significance of the right in context:

> The weight that is attached to the side of the rights on the scale is derived not only from the importance of the right but also from the extent of its limitation, its intensity, and its dimensions. A limitation nearing the margins of the right differs from a limitation nearing its core. A temporary limitation is less severe than a permanent one. Thus, consequences of limitation of a human right and its effect on those entitled to the right affect the weight of the right itself.[99]

Both formulations stress the duty of the judge to engage in relational analysis of the values in tension, but in the context of a specific dispute. And both will drive the judge toward an answer to the

[97] See Alexy (2002: Postscript, 390–425).
[98] Barak (2012b: 746).
[99] Barak (2010: 10).

dispositive question: does the law under review burden liberties too much, given our constitutional commitment to rights?

A Kantian reading would convert these formulations into strictures for ensuring that the law can be justified under the UPR.[100] As Barak suggests, "balancing" is only a metaphor for what judges do at this stage:[101]

> To speak of "balancing" is to speak metaphorically, but the mode of thought is normative. It is based on legal rules that determine when a proper purpose may be realized despite the limitation on a constitutional right.

Balancing in the strict sense bears no relation to cost-benefit analysis in a crude utilitarian sense which, in our view, would be anathema to a Kantian approach. Proportionality balancing involves assessing the relationship between the most important requirements of the constitutional order, both of which are Kantian values: (i) the freedom of every individual, embodied in the individual right at issue, and (ii) the duty of state officials to achieve Public Right, to be (partially) effectuated through the realization of the governmental purpose at stake. In the Kantian model, these requirements are not strictly incommensurate: both are subsumed by the UPR, that is, by the concept of freedom within a Rightful civil condition. Balancing

[100] A skeptic might deny that (i) balancing and (ii) the progressive elaboration of rights can have any place in a Kantian system of justice. If, as Kant famously claimed, the fundamental content of morality is given a priori, then why do we need judges to fill out rights, across time, through judicial elaboration? Our response is two-fold. First, Kant follows a larger natural law tradition in understanding the a priori component of morality (or natural legality) as inherently abstract and indeterminate, when considered alongside concrete cases; see Stone (2011). The very purpose of public law, the philosopher insists, is to constitute a Rightful condition, by giving those a priori standards determinate content; MM 6: 312. Second, Kant explicitly recognizes that abstract norms do not interpret and apply themselves in the myriad contexts that could give rise to a legal conflict, while arguing that neither a legislator nor head of state should be the judge of its own law. See also Brown (2009: 79).

[101] Barak (2012b: 745).

comprises a holistic evaluation of whether, given the circumstances and our constitutional commitments, officials are justified in taking a measure, given their duty to create a system of reciprocal constraints on freedom.

The "balancing" inquiry evaluates a particular means of advancing public interests—of constituting Right—not a consequentialist operation of weighing interests against one another. Rather than relying on a metric of evaluation exogenous to the system of Right, or attributing atomistic weights to principles, the Kantian account we have developed considers all dimensions of importance within a single universal system of freedom. A law that is judged to be proportional comports with the UPR, and can thus be credited as a contribution to Public Right. A law that is disproportionate makes no such contribution, and is therefore invalid.

Kant insisted that a system of Public Right could only be produced through a sustained process of practical reasoning, to render the determinable more determinate, not to discover absolute answers beyond the realm of reasonable disagreement.[102] In Barak's formulation, the judge's task is to determine whether a law falls within *a zone of proportionality*; in Kantian terms, the question is whether the law can be justified under the UPR, which is *coterminous with that zone.* The outcome will depend on an assessment of the severity of the infringement in context, whether the activity or condition covered by the right falls within the right's core or periphery, and the availability of alternative measures, all of which demand sensitivity to empirical circumstances as they change over time.[103] We find Barak's exposition of balancing adaptable to a Kantian-congruent legal system. The function of balancing is to adjust rights and regulation (issuing from a presumptive authority to coerce) in relation to one another, on an ongoing basis, so that they fit together into a coherent whole.

[102] PP, 8: 366–7, 386; and MM, 6: 230–1, 317–20, 340–9, 354–5.
[103] Barak (2012b).

PA has many critics. Some see potential dangers: judges may use PA as a cover for deferring to legislators and executives, or for balancing rights away. Others see PA as being too restrictive of policy discretion, inevitably casting judges as masters of the policy processes under review. Proponents defend proportionality against attacks from both sides.[104] It is important to emphasize that PA is an *analytical procedure*. PA does not, in itself, produce substantive outcomes; and it does not tell judges the importance of any two contending values and interests. Instead, PA organizes the systematic review of justifications for government measures that would burden the exercise of a right. Judges also use PA to build secondary doctrine: the argumentation and justification frameworks that will govern adjudication (and hence policymaking) in any domain covered by a specific right. As we argued in the last section, a meta-rule—melding the entitlement to justification and the reason-giving requirement—is a necessary component of any effective system of constitutional justice. Adopting PA places this meta-rule at the very heart of adjudicating rights, and the enforcement of the UPR.

EXCLUDED REASONS AND ABSOLUTE RIGHTS

PA neatly fits the demands of the UPR and structures how judges will fulfill their fiduciary obligations. Yet, with regard to the first stage of the framework—legitimate purpose—Kant's ideas arguably point away from necessity analysis and balancing, and towards a mode of decision-making in which the judge's principal task is to exclude *illegitimate* justifications for limiting freedom, thereby determining the scope of the right.

As noted, when adjudicating qualified rights, most skilled judges treat the legitimacy prong of PA in the style of a threshold inquiry: if

[104] Stone Sweet and Mathews (2008); Mathews and Stone Sweet (2011).

the constitution has not authorized the state to pursue such a purpose, then the claimant prevails on the basis of little more than a prima facie demonstration that a right is in play. Except in the most egregious cases, the law under review will pass this prong of PA without much ado. After all, the competence to regulate is conferred on officials by the rights provision itself, through a limitation clause. Without further contextual clarification, the outcome conforms to Kantian dictates: officials may hinder the freedom of any rights-holder, but only to secure the external freedom of all. If a system contains a general right to liberty, then officials may act only to secure this liberty.[105] Further, officials may also claim that the act under review had been designed to protect or fulfill another right, thrusting the court into a balancing posture. In the proportionality world, judges and scholars typically downplay the importance of proper purpose inquiry, deploying it most often to pay their respects to officials' good faith efforts in pursuit of valid public interests, saving any censure for later stages.

This *de facto* insouciance deserves more scrutiny. Simplifying a complex issue, a more robust, sustained inquiry into legitimate purpose could well subsume the types of reasoning found in subsequent stages. Concrete constitutional guarantees can only be limited for the sake of freedom; and ends that are exogenous to the system of Right are impermissible bases for restricting freedom. Because the Kantian judge is under a clear duty to filter out such ends, one should ask why the legitimate purpose test is not sufficient in itself, that is, why supplement it with three subsequent stages?

If judges focused more attention on proper purpose, treating the legitimacy prong as a general test of legality, then it would likely evolve

[105] In a widely copied formulation, the German Basic Law announces a general right to liberty in the guise of "the right to freely develop one's personality" (Art. 2.1 GG) which, the GFCC insists, covers virtually anything an individual would want to do. The leading case is *Elfes*, 6 BVerfGE 32 at 36 (1957), which affirms a right to a "general human freedom of action" that encompasses all activities consistent with the rights of others.

as the privileged site for the elaboration of categorical, means-based restrictions. As it is, suitability and necessity analysis (both of which also help courts "smoke out" illicit motives), and balancing (through which courts assess the proportionality of marginal benefits and harms) do the work that, arguably, could be done in proper purpose analysis. In the proportionality world, one typically asks whether a purpose is constitutionally legitimate in the sense that the aim pursued can be subsumed under a legal power that state officials rightfully possess. But one could also wonder if a purpose is constitutionally legitimate only once the judge finds that the end is itself a sufficient reason for restricting a right in the first place. The latter situation requires categorical reasoning, not just *pro forma* box ticking.

To bring the point into focus, consider the well-known trolley problem, which involves two scenarios.[106] In the first, a runaway trolley will kill five people unless a bystander switches the trolley onto another track where, foreseeably, it will kill only one person. In the second, a runaway trolley will kill five people, unless a bystander pushes an enormous man in front of it as a means of triggering the emergency break. The standard intuition associated with this pair of cases is that diverting the trolley is permissible, but pushing the man in front of the trolley is impermissible.[107]

A robust legitimate purpose test would ask whether saving the lives of the five could constitute a legitimate reason for violating the right of the man against being used as a means. On the Kantian view, the answer to this question is clearly "no": each person possesses an entitlement to be one's own master, and not to be used for another's ends. This secures the man's right against being conscripted into the purposes of the five, no matter how urgent their situation. The crucial point is that the analysis proceeds by way of categorical reasoning, not through assigning weights to benefits and harms, and then balancing.

[106] Jarvis Thomson (1985).

[107] Cushman, Young, and Hauser (2006).

One powerful defense of PA, however, rests on the distinction between absolute and qualified rights.[108] Once the constitution or judge classifies a right in absolute terms, it is removed from the domain governed by the proportionality test. Famously, the GFCC refuses to apply PA to full-fledged dignity cases, on grounds that are strikingly Kantian. In the *Life Imprisonment Case* (1977), adjudicating whether life imprisonment is lawful under the banners of retribution and deterrence, the Court held that:

> It is contrary to human dignity to make the individual the mere tool (*blosses Objekt*) of the state. The principle that "each person must always be an end in himself" applies unreservedly to all areas of the law; the intrinsic dignity of the person consists in acknowledging him as an independent personality.[109]

The GFCC sidesteps the issue raised here—whether the policy reflects an improper purpose—by categorizing the dispute as directly involving the individual's dignity, which prohibits PA altogether. In another full-fledged dignity ruling, *Aviation Security* (2006), the GFCC invalidated, on dignity grounds, a statute that would have authorized the interior minister to shoot down an airliner that had been hijacked by terrorists with the intention of using it as a weapon against the population.[110] The Court's rationale is overtly neo-Kantian: to allow an official to intentionally terminate the lives of the innocent persons on board would convert those persons into objects of the state.[111] In

[108] A second defense would emphasize the advantages of "as-applied" review: judges are often called upon to judge statutes in light of circumstances that the legislature had not fully contemplated. In such situations, it would be needlessly provocative to assert that legislature had pursued an improper purpose. In proportionality-based systems, courts typically run each case based on new facts and circumstances through PA; past acts and decisions are typically treated as relevant but not dispositive.

[109] *Life Imprisonment Case*, 45 BVerfGE at 228.

[110] BVerfGE, 1 BvR 357.

[111] This is not to say that the GFCC reached the conclusion that Kant would have reached in either case. We do not offer a general excursis on the casuistic side of Kant's legal philosophy.

cases in which dignity is directly and fully implicated, the German Court does not apply PA.

The issue of whether courts should develop a more robust application of the legitimate purpose test deserves more consideration. In the proportionality world, however, no court has moved in this direction in any consistent way. Such a move might very well lead to the migration of balancing considerations into deliberations on proper purpose, a type of "hydraulic effect."[112] While the US Supreme Court sometimes adopts a categorical posture, for example, it often engages in balancing to produce the categorical rule.[113] Put in terms of PA, balancing and necessity reasoning would likely flow into the analysis of proper purpose. Such an outcome would undermine transparency, as well as the tribunal's capacity to express respect (and condemnation) for officials precisely where it is due.

PROPORTIONALITY AND JUDICIAL SUPREMACY

The mission of the Kantian trustee is to supervise the rights-regarding acts of all other officials, to assess the reasons officials give when they burden any right, and to invalidate laws when these reasons are insufficient. The extent to which the court's rulings are insulated from override—by those over whom the court exercises authority—is an important determinant of the system's effectiveness.[114]

Judicial supremacy raises well-worn legitimacy concerns, including the so-called "counter-majoritarian difficulty": the capacity of the trustee to generate policy outcomes that elected officials would not have produced on their own, but which are difficult or impossible

[112] Hydraulic dynamics emerge when a court shifts burdens within balancing frameworks. As Han (2014: 1716) puts it, "legal doctrine is often hydraulic in nature; whenever the rigidness in one doctrinal area exerts pressure on courts' decisionmaking, that pressure often seeks release in other areas of the doctrine."

[113] Aleinikoff (1987); Mathews and Stone Sweet (2011).

[114] Stone Sweet (2017).

to reverse. Under such conditions, the override or revision of important rulings on constitutional rights is, in practice, only possible through subsequent rounds of adjudication (to the extent constitutional amendment is an impossibility, in practice).[115] The court that adopts PA—a highly intrusive standard of review—makes its formal supremacy a mundane fact. Indeed, the necessity and balancing prongs position a trustee court to exercise direct authority over the lawmaking of all other officials; it does so through enforcement of the will of the constitutional legislator—the People—who have commanded as much.

While we recognize that supremacy raises deep normative issues, Kantian theory is largely immune to the counter-majoritarian objections.[116] Kant gives freedom—rights—pride of place, not the will of a transient, political majority. For Kant, representation and accountability demands more than occasional consultation of the People as an electoral body. It requires accountability to the People considered *as individual citizens*, whose entitlements to rights is unimpeachable, and to the People as constitutional legislators. To the extent that the People have legislated supremacy, placing the parliament under the control of a constitutional court, normative arguments grounded in the dogmas of legislative sovereignty are beside the point. We have not argued that courts are the repository of some type of special wisdom when it comes to enforcing rights. We do claim that trusteeship—supremacy constrained by robust fiduciary obligations—will optimize the polity's capacity to progress in its goal of achieving a Rightful constitutional condition.

As an empirical matter, modern systems of constitutional justice are, in fact, characterized by judicial supremacy.[117] How effective systems of constitutional justice actually operate should bear on the

[115] Stone Sweet (2012a).

[116] For example, those marshaled by Waldron (2004, 2006), and by those who worry that supremacy institutionalizes the so-called "majoritarian difficulty," a preoccupation surveyed by Friedman (1998).

[117] Stone Sweet (2012a).

normative debate. Three points, each of which is based on strong empirical findings, deserve emphasis. First, the most effective constitutional courts are those that are able to draw other policymakers, and at times the citizenry, into the discourse they constitute and curate as a jurisprudence of rights.[118] If officials and citizens ignore or conspire to undermine the consequences of its rulings, then trustee courts will fail. Second, the ongoing use of PA creates an interface for deliberative engagement between the constitutional court and all other officials who make and enforce law.[119] Successful trustee courts use PA not to bludgeon officials into submission, but to construct (often intricate) "dialogues" with legislatures, executives, and the ordinary courts concerning the respective scope of their lawmaking authority. These same courts have strongly embraced PA, an operating system for dialogue, which shapes the evolution of policy and the content of the rights-based constitution.[120] Third, legislatures and executives are unlikely to render a charter of rights effective on their own, without having their decision-making placed in the shadow of a trustee court. This last point firmly applies to the new commonwealth model.[121]

[118] Stone Sweet (2000). [119] Stone Sweet and Mathews (2008: 104–60).

[120] Stone Sweet (2000: chs. 3–5); Hiebert (2011).

[121] The main proponent of the argument to the contrary is Waldron (2004), who rests his case on one UK episode, involving the regulation of abortion. In contrast, compare the situation under the Canadian Charter of Rights (1982–present) with that under the Canadian Bill of Rights (1960–1982). As Gardbaum (2012: 99) puts it: "the Canadian Bill of Rights is almost universally thought to have been ineffective because of the courts' tendency to interpret its impact and their power through the traditional lens of parliamentary sovereignty, thereby limiting the scope and effectiveness of the rights protected." Under the "New Commonwealth Model," the legislator is given the "final word" when it comes to the enforceability of any statutory provisions that supreme courts declare to violate the Charter of Rights (Canada), or to be incompatible and/or inconsistent with human rights statutes (New Zealand, the UK). Gardbaum and Hiebert have undertaken the most intensive empirical research on the effects of these new rights instruments. Gardbaum (2012: 172–3) argues that "there is consensus that rights have been better protected" in these countries "since adopting the new model and abandoning traditional parliamentary sovereignty." But he also states that the "record suggests that judicial supremacy is not necessary for such protection," insofar as there is "no significant sacrifice" of rights protection to pay for democratic legitimacy. Leaving aside the indeterminacy of "significant sacrifice" standard,

CONCLUSION

This chapter develops an account of a Kantian system of constitutional justice, the persuasiveness of which will depend on the acceptance of an interlocking set of claims:

(i) that the People have placed their freedom in trust, in the form of a charter of rights;

(ii) that rights provisions instantiate, as positive law, the foundations on which the external freedom of all persons may be constructed;

(iii) that public officials are under a duty to make and enforce law in ways that fulfill the rights of persons that come under their authority;

(iv) that an omnilateral trustee, a constitutional court, supervises the lawmaking activities of officials, through the enforcement of the UPR; and

(v) that the UPR, as operationalized through the proportionality principle, lays down the basic criterion for the legitimacy of all positive law.

These are the features, we have argued, that will maximize a polity's capacity to achieve a Rightful condition.

this type of argument is not available in a Kantian system; either a statute complies with the UPR or it does not. Hiebert, who has focused on the capacity of parliament to debate rights meaningfully on their own, sums up the empirical record as follows (2011: 61): "Research in all three jurisdictions suggests that the legal costs [the risk of judicial censure] are more persuasive than parliamentary criticism when encouraging governments to take rights seriously . . . Unless parliamentary pressure is sufficient to threaten defeat of a bill, governments have generally been unwilling to amend bills." With regard to the UK Human Rights Act (HRA), Hiebert (2012: 44) concludes that, "the idea of [the HRA] facilitating a culture of rights, at least as it pertains to Westminster, is likely wishful thinking."

Looking forward, our model of constitutional justice is directly relevant to the development of a cosmopolitan legal order. Kant developed his notions of Right beyond the state from micro-foundations laid in the Doctrine of Public Right[122] and, we will argue next, a system of cosmopolitan justice cannot emerge unless and until each state within the federation has committed itself to achieving justice at the domestic level. Chapter 3 considers in detail the structural requirements of a transnational and multi-level system of rights protection.

[122] See chapter 3; Flikschuh (2000: 170).

3

Constitutional Pluralism and Transnational Justice

INTRODUCTION

This chapter develops an account of a Kantian-congruent system of transnational justice, extending the constitutional theory presented in chapter 2 to rights protection beyond the state.[1] Kant, we have emphasized, did not prescribe a determinate set of legal arrangements to meet his command to achieve a Rightful condition. Instead, he developed universal, a priori, principles of justice meant to establish robust criteria for law's legitimacy.[2] States, he insisted in *Perpetual Peace*, could only achieve Right in the international realm through freely associating with one another in a federation; and, Kant counseled, the league's organs (at least in the first stages of the enterprise) should not be empowered to exercise direct authority *within* domestic legal orders.[3] The philosopher understood that only a massive transformation in law and politics—at both the national and federative levels—would

[1] Our account is therefore vulnerable to the same types of criticisms raised in the conclusion to chapter 2.

[2] Brown (2009: 78).

[3] There exists a lively and important debate concerning how to understand Kant's evolving views on the importance of establishing a world state to achieve Right. We do not directly engage these debates, but see Brown (2009: ch. 3); Corradetti (2016); Flikschuh (2010); Kleingeld (2004; 2011); Raponi (2014).

A Cosmopolitan Legal Order: Kant, Constitutional Justice, and the European Convention on Human Rights. Alec Stone Sweet and Clare Ryan. Published 2018 by Oxford University Press.

permit the construction of a treaty-based legal system capable of rendering constitutional justice. But, again, he provided scant detail on how this process would unfold. What conditions would have to be fulfilled, through what stages, and how?

This chapter responds to these questions, providing a structural account of a rights-based system of justice beyond the state: a cosmopolitan legal order (CLO).[4] As we proceed, we push well beyond the strictures of Kant, refining the concept of the CLO, identifying the crucial transition points of systemic construction, and providing empirical content in light of the European experience.

THE MULTI-LEVEL STRUCTURE OF RIGHT

The precision of Kant's notion of Right rests on its fidelity to a set of stable first principles that enable him to produce variations on the idea. Right, Public Right, International Right, and Cosmopolitan Right share common micro-foundations, and each comprises a conceptually related solution to the same generic problem.[5] That problem concerns how to constitute the external and reciprocal freedom of communities—individuals, nations, states—given that, as people interact on territory that is limited and spherical, the threat of domination between persons will be continuous and conflict inevitable. Flikschuh puts the point neatly:

> Kant does not share the widespread view that we can turn our attention to the issue of cosmopolitan Right only *after* we have settled the matter of domestic justice. The grounds of cosmopolitan

[4] We will describe any treaty-based legal order that confers rights upon individuals on the basis of their status as human beings as "transnational" and "cosmopolitan" which, for such purposes, are synonyms.

[5] "[T]hese principles should not only be the concern of domestic constitutions, but also a requirement of all laws, which should ultimately culminate in a cosmopolitan constitution," Brown (2009: 67).

> justice are identical with those of domestic justice: both follow from the claim to external freedom of each other under conditions of unavoidable empirical constraints. Instead of distinguishing between different theories of justice for the domestic and international contexts, Kant refers to different *levels* of institutionalizing his cosmopolitan conception of Right.[6] [Emphasis in original.]

The implication for any system of constitutional justice, as we have defined such a system in chapter 2, should be clear: for all "human relations,"[7] at every level of governance, the Universal Principle of Right (UPR) embodies the foundational, constitutional criteria of the legitimacy of law.

The UPR lies at the core of any Rightful condition for two reasons. First, it complies with, and flows outward from, even more primordial principles. The notions of Innate Freedom and the Internal Duty of Rightful Honor, respectively, enable and restrict human agency, including the building of institutions capable of achieving Public Right. Second, Kant casts the UPR as a meta-norm, whose constitutional function is to constrain the exercise of the omnilateral (legislative) will. All officials are under a duty to make, interpret, and apply law in conformity with the UPR. Acts that conform to the UPR command the obedience of both citizens and their agents: public officials. In Hart's terms,[8] the UPR embodies a cluster of secondary rules—constitutional criteria of legal validity—that take primacy over any other rules.

As discussed in the first two chapters, Kant acknowledged that the pathways through which perpetual peace and a Rightful condition could be achieved were likely to be complex, non-linear, and fraught with political obstacles. As Kant often noted, Williams reminds us, "the human race does not progress the easy way. It only adopts rational principles for governing its social relations after a hard and

[6] Flikschuh (2000: 170). [7] Williams (2015). [8] Hart (1994: 92–4).

frequently violent struggle with itself and its worst characteristics."[9] Nonetheless, Kant presciently identified certain necessary conditions for the development of Right, as well as mechanisms capable of propelling the process forward. We will focus here on three building blocks: (i) peace among states; (ii) the commitment to the UPR as foundational of rights-based constitutionalism; and (iii) the relationship between domestic and international institutional arrangements.

Box 3 contains Kant's statements on some of the core concepts and issues we consider in this chapter.

Box 3 Cosmopolitan Right: Principles and Concepts

Kant considered the concept of Right beyond the state primarily in *Toward Perpetual Peace*[8: 343–60] and *The Metaphysics of Morals*.[6: 352–5] In this chapter, we treat these concepts as foundational of a rights-based system of transnational constitutional justice, extending arguments developed in chapters 1 and 2. All emphases are in the original.

The Universal Principle of Right

Any action is *Right* if it can coexist with everyone's freedom in accordance with a universal law, or if on its maxim the freedom of choice of each can coexist with everyone's freedom in accordance with a universal law.[MM, 6: 230]

Peace and Right

[The] non-rightful condition is a condition of war.[MM, 6: 344]

The state of nature *(status naturalis)* is not a state of peace among human beings who live next to one another but a state of war, that is, if not always an outbreak of hostilities, then at least the constant threat of such hostilities. Hence the state of peace must be *established*.[PP, 8: 348–9]

Since a state of nature among nations, like a state of nature among individual human beings, is a condition one ought to leave in order to enter a lawful condition, before this happens any rights of nations, and anything external that is mine or yours which states can acquire . . . are merely *provisional*. Only in a universal association of states (analogous to that by which a people becomes a state) can rights come to hold *conclusively* and a true *condition of peace* come about.[MM, 6: 350]

[9] Williams (2015).

A Congress of States

The rational idea of a *peaceful*, even if not friendly, thoroughgoing community of all nations on the earth that can come into relations affecting one another is not a philanthropic (ethical) principle but a principle *having to do with rights*. Nature has enclosed them all together within determinate limits (by the spherical shape of the place they live in . . .).[MM, 6: 352]

A league of nations in accordance with the original social contract is necessary . . . to protect against attacks from without.[MM, 6: 344–5]

Only by such a congress can the idea of Public Right of nations be realized, one to be established for deciding their disputes in a civil way, as if by lawsuit, rather than in a barbaric way (the way of savages), namely by war.[MM, 6: 351]

[I]t must be an alliance that can be renounced at any time and so must be renewed from time to time.[MM, 6:345]

[T]he political principles directed toward perpetual peace, of entering into such alliances of states, which serve for continual *approximation* to it, are not unachievable. Instead, since continual approximation to it is a task based on duty and therefore on the right of human beings and states, this can certainly be achieved. Such an *association* of several *states* to preserve peace can be called a *permanent congress of states*, which each neighboring state is at liberty to join.[MM, 6: 350]

Public Right and Levels of Governance

Public Right is . . . a system of law for a people, that is, a multitude of human beings, or a multitude of peoples which . . . need a Rightful condition under a will uniting them, a *constitution*, so they may enjoy what is laid down in Right. . . . Since the earth's surface is not unlimited, but closed, the concepts of the right of a state and of a right of nations lead inevitably to the idea of *a right of all nations* (*jus gentium*) or *Cosmopolitan Right* (*ius cosmopoliticum*). So if the principle of outer freedom limited by the laws is lacking in any one of these three possible forms of Rightful condition, the framework of all the others is unavoidably undermined and must finally collapse.[MM, 6: 311]

It can be said that establishing universal and lasting peace constitutes not merely a part of the doctrine of Right but rather the entire final end of the doctrine of Right within the limits of reason alone; for the condition of peace is the only condition in which what is mine and what is yours are secured under laws for a multitude of human beings living in proximity to one another and therefore under a constitution. But the rule for this constitution . . . must . . . be derived a priori by reason from the ideal of a Rightful association of human beings under public laws as such.[MM, 6: 355]

[W]e must work toward establishing perpetual peace and the kind of constitution that seems to us most conducive to it (say, a republicanism of all states, together and separately) in order to bring about perpetual peace . . . And even if complete realization of this objective always remains a pious wish, still we are certainly not deceiving ourselves in adopting the maxim of working incessantly towards it. For this is our duty . . . [MM, 6: 354–5]

> [A]ny juridical constitution, with regard to the persons that are subject to it, takes one of the following forms: 1. one based on the right of *Citizens of a State* governing the individuals of a people (*ius civitatis*); 2, one based on *International Right* governing the relations of states among one another (*ius gentium*), 3. one based on *Cosmopolitan Right*, to the extent that individuals and states, who are related externally by the mutual exertion of influence on each other, are to be regarded as citizens of a universal state of humankind (*ius cosmopoliticum*).[PP, 8: 349]
>
> [T]he idea of Cosmopolitan Right . . . is a necessary supplement to the unwritten code of Constitutional and International Right, for Public Human Right in general, and hence for perpetual peace. Only under this condition can one flatter oneself to be continually progressing toward perpetual peace.[PP, 8: 360]

Readers will recall that Kant proposed that perpetual peace could be achieved once a group of "republican" states joined together in a league, and insofar as the rights of "hospitality" were recognized (chapter 1). We argued that the basic template for the charters of rights that undergird contemporary conceptions of justice could be derived from the synergistic development of liberal democracy, international organization, and hospitality.[10] Clearly, the absence of war is not the only end that matters; rather, the construction of perpetual peace and progress toward Right are symbiotic processes on one another. Kant defined the non-Rightful condition at the inter-state level as one of war, and its ceaseless preparation. Only through joining a "congress of states," he stressed, could "the idea of Public Right of nations be realized, one to be established for deciding their disputes in a civil way, *as if by lawsuit*, rather than in a barbaric way (the way of savages), namely by war."[11]

[10] In some of his writings, including *Toward Perpetual Peace among States* (8: 358) (hereinafter PP) and *The Metaphysics of Morals* (6: 352) (hereinafter MM), Kant developed a relatively restrictive notion of hospitality and Cosmopolitan Right, based on a presumptive right to travel and to engage in commerce across borders. We adopt more expansive notions for reasons discussed in chapter 1.

[11] MM, 6: 351 (emphasis added). The statement mirrors a claim made with reference to individuals in the state of nature, which Kant characterizes as "devoid of justice" since, "when rights are in dispute, there [is] no judge competent to render a verdict having Rightful force." MM, 6: 312.

Kant conceives of Right, both within and beyond the state, as entailing moral obligations whose existence does not depend upon states, but which nonetheless bind officials. Those institutional arrangements capable of achieving a Rightful condition are inherently "constitutional":[12]

> Public Right is . . . a system of law for a people, that is, a multitude of human beings, or a multitude of peoples which . . . need a Rightful condition under a will uniting them, a *constitution*, so they may enjoy what is laid down as Right.[13]

In the same passage, he linked levels of governance to a common fate:

> Since the earth's surface is not unlimited, but closed, the concepts of the right of a state and of a right of nations lead inevitably to the idea of *a right of all nations* (*jus gentium*) or *Cosmopolitan Right* (*ius cosmopoliticum*). So if the principle of outer freedom limited by the laws is lacking in any one of these three possible forms of Rightful condition, the framework of all the others is unavoidably undermined and must finally collapse.[14] [Emphases in original.]

In Brown's terms, the cosmopolitan constitution is a set of "normative and juridical principles of . . . Cosmopolitan Right."[15] We understand these principles, once codified in law, as a code for universal justice that states must establish if they are to realize their own external freedom, as well as that of all persons coming under their jurisdiction. The UPR, we claim, governs how that code is to be interpreted and enforced. And state officials, whenever and wherever they exercise authority, are under fiduciary duties to protect the rights of all that come under their jurisdiction.

[12] Also PP, 8: 349 (Box 3). [13] MM, 6: 311. [14] MM, 6: 311.
[15] Brown (2006: 674).

Finally, Kant pointed to the dynamic relationships—interactive, "feedback" effects—of the different levels of Right. These effects could "undermine" progress toward a Rightful condition, and might even lead the process to "collapse." But they could also reinforce it. Once formerly despotic states become republican, others might choose to follow, as the benefits of doing so become apparent.[16] And the emergence of a Rightful condition at the transnational level could help support the consolidation of Public Right at the domestic level. Indeed, Kant imagined the establishment of "a republicanism of all states, together and separately."[17] Yet the viability of republicanism could never be taken for granted:

> The *republican* constitution is . . . the most difficult constitution to establish, and even more so to preserve, and to such an extent that many assert that it would have to be a state of *angels*, because human beings would be incapable of a constitution of such a sublime nature, given their selfish inclinations.[18]

Kant would likely be impressed by the process through which rights-based constitutionalism has gradually become the dominant form of the republican constitution since 1950 (chapters 1 and 2).

Now consider a multi-level regime for the protection of rights. In the last chapter, we argued that a domestic system of constitutional justice must contain an apex, constitutional court whose purpose is to enforce the UPR. The mission of this "trustee court" is to supervise the rights-regarding activities of all other public officials, to assess the reasons officials give when they burden a right, and to invalidate laws when such justifications are judged to be insufficient. Extending these arguments to a transnational system of rights protection is relatively straightforward. Upon entering into a federation, the states (whose powers "can only belong to the united will of the People"[19]), place

[16] PP, 8: 356; chapter 1. [17] MM, 6: 354–5. [18] PP, 8: 366.
[19] MM, 6: 313–14.

the supreme constitutional value—freedom—in trust, in the form of a judicially enforceable charter of human rights.[20] The Contracting States, acting jointly, embody the constitutional legislator, a functional equivalent of the People at the domestic level. As Kant stressed (chapter 1), the league should not exercise direct, coercive authority *within* the states that make up the federation, at least during the foundational period. However, in order to maximize the effectiveness of the cosmopolitan constitution, states may constitute and empower a trustee court for three overlapping purposes: (i) to ensure compliance with the UPR, (ii) to render authoritative interpretations of the code, and (iii) to supervise performance of the fiduciary duties that bind all state officials when they make and enforce the law. But the transnational court need not possess the power to invalidate national laws that conflict with the code, as domestic constitutional courts do. Instead, the regime's trustee court governs through the persuasive authority of its rulings; and national officials decide how to give those judgments effect.

We have defined a Kantian-congruent CLO as a multi-level, transnational legal system in which all public officials, at every level of governance within the treaty regime, bear an obligation to fulfill the fundamental rights of every person within their jurisdiction, without respect to nationality or citizenship. A CLO only emerges once (i) rights, given expression through the UPR, constrain the exercise of all public authority; (ii) rights are justiciable and enforceable in the courts; and (iii) a transnational trustee court is positioned to supervise how all officials, including judges, discharge their fiduciary obligations at each level of governance within the regime. The CLO will therefore exhibit a peculiar institutional architecture: charters of rights found at the domestic and transnational levels overlap; all courts are involved in enforcing rights; and separate trustee courts will monitor how they do so. We call the resulting structure one of

[20] As Williams (2015) stresses, Cosmopolitan Right, just as is Public Right more generally, flows from first principles, including that of Innate Freedom.

"constitutional pluralism."[21] In the rest of the chapter, we discuss the arduous process through which European states overcame structural obstacles to meeting these criteria. The most important barriers to full realization of the CLO were those domestic doctrines associated with legislative sovereignty. Before turning to the empirics, we define and discuss key concepts.

CONCEPTS

By *rights cosmopolitanism*, we mean the commitment to those institutional arrangements that enable a treaty regime to render justice under a multi-level, cosmopolitan constitution. At the domestic level, a trustee court must be positioned to supervise compliance with the UPR by all other officials, including judges. Anathema to a Kantian system of constitutional justice are rules or doctrines that (i) prohibit judicial review of public authorities' acts or (ii) establish formalized deference doctrines that block judges from reviewing such acts, including statutes, on the merits (chapter 2). In Europe, domestic legal systems have gradually abandoned such doctrines. At the transnational level, a trustee court must be positioned to monitor domestic systems of justice and to fill gaps in domestic protection when necessary.

Constitutional pluralism is a structural feature of a transnational system of rights protection that is produced when two situations are combined.[22] The first is "source pluralism." Within a domestic constitutional order, the term describes a situation in which two or more autonomous sources of judicial-enforceable rights coexist in the same legal field. In many European legal systems, three such

[21] For broader discussions of constitutional pluralism, see chapter 6; Walker (2002); Halberstam (2012); Stone Sweet (2013).

[22] As Corradetti (2016) has argued, constitutional pluralism is also congruent with ideas of the multi-level structure of governance Kant elaborates in *Perpetual Peace* and other writings.

sources—national constitutional rights, EU rights, and the European Convention on Human Rights (ECHR)—overlap. Often, individuals have a choice of which source to plead and judges can choose which to enforce. These choices have consequences, for instance when national judges prefer to apply European rights, rather than their own constitution law, as a means of raising domestic standards of protection.[23] The fact that the Convention maps onto rights found in national systems undergirds the notion of multi-level constitutionalism:[24] no act taken by any public authority, at any level of governance, can be considered lawful if it violates rights.

The second situation is "jurisdictional pluralism." The structure of authority within this regime is pluralistic, in that the system is comprised of discrete hierarchies, represented by national and treaty-based apex courts capable of asserting their own respective autonomy and legitimacy, on the basis of separate legal instruments. With Protocol no. 11 of the European Convention (1998), individuals have an unfettered right to petition the European Court of Human Rights, once national remedies have been exhausted. As the regime's trustee, the Strasbourg Court benefits from this crucial strategic position, but it has no authority to invalidate national law that conflicts with the Convention. As we show, source and jurisdictional pluralism can also develop *within* any domestic legal system that features multiple apex courts.

The instantiation of a CLO in Europe is a momentous outcome, given legacies of the past. Across the Continent, traditional models of the juridical state[25] are grounded not in notions of legal pluralism, but its supposed antithesis: *sovereignty*.[26] These models depict the legal

[23] For doctrinal-empirical studies of these dynamics, see Stone Sweet and Stranz (2012) for the EU, and Bjorge (2015) for the ECHR.

[24] Kumm (2009); Petersmann (2009); Stone Sweet (2009a); Walker (2002; 2015: ch. 3).

[25] Dyson (1980).

[26] We define *sovereignty* in narrow, juridical terms, as the formal capacity to make and enforce legal norms. In the international system, states are sovereign in that they

order as hierarchically organized, with one apex organ positioned to defend the norms and principles at the top of this hierarchy. This organ is portrayed as the repository of *centralized sovereignty*, to the extent that it possesses a monopoly on the authority to resolve certain legal questions. In the archetypal cases, a constitutional court (under rights-based constitutionalism) or a parliament (under a regime of legislative sovereignty) is assumed to have the "final word" on questions involving the validity of legal norms, as well as jurisdictional conflicts between organs that make and enforce the law.

The multi-level and pluralist nature of a CLO means that rights will be enforced by a "decentralized sovereign." Sovereignty is not hierarchically constructed[27] with one jurisdiction positioned to definitively settle questions of legal interpretation and validity. Instead, rights claims will beget multiple pronouncements, many of which will be authoritative with respect to any particular case, brought before any particular apex court. What makes the system "constitutional" is an overarching normative structure: the code of rights and principles, such as the UPR, that all public officials are under fiduciary obligations to promote and respect.

In Europe, the drafters of treaties and constitutions, high courts, and legislators have distributed sovereignty so as to entrench judicial authority to protect rights across arenas and levels of governance. Each of these nodes has defensible claims to autonomy as a matter of

are capable of entering into binding agreements with other states, thereby incurring duties under international law. Domestically, sovereignty refers to the authority to make and enforce legal norms within the jurisdictional boundaries of the state. The constitutions of liberal states distribute sovereignty among governmental organs, specify procedures for making and enforcing law, and stipulate restrictions on the exercise of public authority through rights. Treaties of the kind discussed in this chapter "pool" state sovereignty in order to achieve common purposes. In the EU and the Council of Europe, states have conferred on the CJEU and the Strasbourg Court compulsory jurisdiction to review state compliance with rights found in EU law and the Convention respectively. Williams (2015) describes such pooling as one in which each state's "sovereignty" is "interlocking with the sovereignty of other states."

[27] "[D]ecentralized sovereignty is 'polyarchical,'" Smith (2008: 423) explains, "in that there is no single hierarchy that encompasses the entire political order, but instead a series of related hierarchies."

formal law. Yet the cosmopolitan order exists only to the extent that officials, in particular judges on apex courts, credit their roles in a common project: to enforce the UPR and to render rights effective. Insofar as they do, a system of "judicial polyarchy"—a highly institutionalized form of decentralized sovereignty—will be the result.[28] In the European CLO, these nodes of judicial authority are coordinated through the judgments of the trustee court of the regime, sitting in Strasbourg.

A system of decentralized sovereignty suffers from two generic coordination problems that centralized sovereignty purports to resolve.[29] The first concerns the underlying basis for systemic order. As Kant does, we presuppose a constitution from foundational principles:[30] the overarching framework of rights that underpins rights-based constitutionalism within and beyond the state, and the fiduciary obligations that underwrite the legitimacy claims of public authority. The second problem is one of overlapping competences: each high court in the CLO is under a duty to resolve disputes within the same domain, that of the cosmopolitan constitution. Part II of this book is devoted to this issue. At this point, it is enough to emphasize that in the CLO overlapping competences will count as a good[31] in so far as individuals (i) have multiple points of access to the decentralized sovereign; (ii) gaps in right protection that materialize in one jurisdiction are filled by a court in another; and (iii) healthy competition among nodes of authority serves to upgrade, rather than reduce, a collective commitment to rights protection.

JUDICIAL REVIEW AND ITS PROHIBITION

In a CLO, every public act must be capable of being reviewed by a court for its conformity with rights. To the extent that this

[28] Sabel and Gerstenberg (2010). [29] Smith (2008: 427–9).
[30] See also Gardbaum (2008); De Wet (2006); Stone Sweet (2013).
[31] At least for those who see value in the enhancement of rights protection.

requirement is fulfilled, the system is relatively *complete*, that is, there are no gaps in rights protection. In Europe, a formalized, colossal gap in protection—the prohibition of judicial review of statute, a corollary of legislative sovereignty—presented the most important obstacle to the emergence of a CLO. In 1950, when the Convention was signed, Ireland was the only High Contracting Party which had any meaningful experience with judicial review under a charter of rights. The constitutions of Belgium, France, Luxembourg, the Netherlands, and the UK either did not contain a bill of rights, or constitutional separation of powers doctrines prohibited the judicial review of statutes, or both. The new German and the Italian constitutional courts were still being designed. It is thus not surprising that, in the original treaty, a majority of states rejected proposals to grant individuals a right of petition and to make the jurisdiction of the European Court compulsory (which began operation only in 1959). With Protocol no. 11 (1998), states fundamentally altered the regime, embracing robust rights protection through the delegation of compulsory jurisdiction, which could be activated by any individual applicant.

Three major factors are crucial to understanding why they did so. First, after 1950, Western Europe became the epicenter of a "new constitutionalism"[32] that spread across the Continent, and then globally, through successive waves of democratization. Nearly all new constitutions adopted since 1985 contain a charter of rights and a judicial mechanism for protecting rights (chapter 2). Second, in Western Europe, the development of the EU's legal system had given national officials a chance to adjust to new forms of judicial power within an earlier form of constitutional pluralism. Third, and of the most immediate importance, the Soviet bloc collapsed. In the 1990s, with constitutional reconstruction in full swing, the EU and the Council of Europe offered admission to post-Communist states on the basis of certain conditions, including a commitment to rights protection.

[32] Shapiro and Stone Sweet, eds. (1994); see also chapter 2.

Locking them into the ECHR, and harnessing the supervision of its Court, was an obvious means of securing that commitment. In Kantian terms, expansion to the Baltics and the Balkans, and across Central and Eastern Europe, widened the project of achieving Right within a pan-European zone of peace.

We now turn to the process through which the dogmas of legislative sovereignty were undermined, principally through the impact of European law. A new form of multi-level constitutional pluralism first materialized with the consolidation of the doctrines of the *direct effect*[33] and *supremacy*[34] of EU law, announced by the Court of Justice of the European Union (CJEU) in the 1960s, and refined in the 1970s.[35] As a massive scholarly literature has demonstrated, the gradual acceptance of these doctrines by national courts integrated the EU and national systems in complex ways, "constitutionalizing" the regime in all but name.[36] The Treaty of Rome (1959) contained no supremacy clause and the member states did not provide for the direct effect of treaty provisions or directives. Yet, the CJEU held, individuals could directly plead entitlements found in the treaties and in directives (EU statutes that member states are obliged to "transpose" into national law) before national courts. The doctrine of supremacy requires that national judges resolve any conflict between domestic law and EU law with reference, and deference, to the latter. The CJEU justified these moves, and subsequent "constitutional" rulings, as necessary to secure the treaty's effectiveness.

Supremacy challenged the prohibition of judicial review because it required judges to refuse to apply any national norm, including

[33] Following from *Van Gend en Loos*, ECJ 26/62 (1963), and *Van Duyn*, ECJ 41/74 (1974).

[34] Following from *Costa*, ECJ 6/64 (1964), and *Simmenthal II*, ECJ 106/77 (1978).

[35] For an overview of the evolution of these doctrines, see Stone Sweet (2004: 65–96).

[36] The scholarly literature on this question proceeds from two seminal articles, of Stein (1981) and Weiler (1991). In the 1990s, the impact of the so-called constitutionalization process on both the domestic and supranational levels of governance has been the focus of extensive empirical research. For a survey of this literature, see Stone Sweet (2010).

statutory provisions, found to be in conflict with EU law. By 1989, every high court in the EU had accepted supremacy, and the courts of new member states quickly joined them. The result: all judges acquired the authority to review statute, albeit only in areas governed by EU law. Prior to this process, most high courts in the EU were denied this power under domestic constitutional law. In systems in which a specialized constitutional court enforced a domestic charter of rights, the CJEU's case law undermined the presumed monopoly of constitutional judges (only Germany and Italy in the 1960s) to determine the conditions under which statutes could be disapplied by the ordinary (non-constitutional) courts.[37]

The judicial politics of supremacy involved significant conflict.[38] The CJEU had placed no limits on the doctrine's scope: the most banal provision of an EU directive would trump every conflicting statute, as well as the most sacred of constitutional provisions. Under a regime of supremacy, however, each extension of EU law would potentially create a gap in rights protection, wherever a system of domestic constitutional justice existed. In 1974, the German Federal Constitutional Court (GFCC) reacted, declaring that it would review (for conformity with German constitutional principles) the implementation of directly effective EU law, upon referrals from the ordinary courts and individuals, "so long as the integration process has not progressed so far that Community law also possesses a catalogue of rights . . . of settled validity, which is adequate in comparison with a catalogue of fundamental rights contained in the [German] constitution."[39] Meanwhile, the CJEU had begun to develop such a catalogue, in the guise of (unwritten, judge-made) general principles of law.[40] These general principles, the CJEU announced, were rooted in

[37] Following from *Simmenthal II*, ECJ 106/77 (1978).
[38] Slaughter, Stone Sweet, and Weiler, eds. (1998); Alter (2001).
[39] *Solange I*, BVerfGE [1974] 34: 269.
[40] For an analysis of this process and its effects, see De Búrca (2011).

the ECHR, the charter of rights of Europe, and "the constitutional traditions common to the member states."[41] In 1986, the German Court withdrew its objections "so long as . . . [the CJEU] generally ensures an effective protection of fundamental rights."[42] These "constitutional dialogues,"[43] and those that followed, did not destroy supremacy; rather, they served to upgrade standards of protection and the authority of courts at both the national and EU levels of governance. On the other hand, they undermined domestic prohibitions of judicial review.

While it may be argued that the supremacy doctrine constituted a sovereignty claim on the part of the CJEU, no national constitutional court has accepted supremacy as the EU court understands it. The CJEU, in effect, holds that all national judges are agents of the EU legal order, not the national order, whenever they act in domains that fall within the scope of EU law. The CJEU further asserts that it alone has the "final word" when it comes to determining the compatibility of EU law—as well as national law that implements EU law—with rights.[44] For their part, most national high courts have asserted that EU law—including rules issuing from the CJEU's pronouncements—only enter into national law through the domestic constitution, and thus cannot deprive them of their own "final" authority to control the constitutionality of EU acts. This "jurisprudence of constitutional conflict,"[45] is a manifestation, probably permanent, of the pluralistic structure of EU law.

On the ground, most ordinary courts, including supreme civil and administrative courts, routinely behave as faithful agents of the EU order when they adjudicate EU law.[46] That is, the jurisprudence,

[41] Pre-*Solange I*, see *Internationale Handelsgesellschaft*, ECJ 11/70 (1970), and *Nold*, ECJ 4/73 (1974); post-*Solange I*, see *Rutili*, ECJ 36/75 (1975).

[42] *Solange II*, BVerfGE [1987] 73: 339.

[43] Stone Sweet (1995).

[44] *Foto Frost*, ECJ 314/85 (1987).

[45] Kumm (2005).

[46] With the enormous expansion of EU law over the past forty years, national legal autonomy has been all but extinguished in many important policy domains (see Kelemen (2010)).

and daily practice, of constitutional cooperation between courts is far deeper than that of conflict.[47] Moreover, national courts routinely partner with the CJEU in order to expand their own authority, and to subvert that of the domestic constitutional order. In the area of workplace discrimination, for example, the German Supreme Labor Court (an apex court in its own right) successfully engaged the CJEU in a joint effort to raise national standards of rights protection, not least, by requiring proportionality review of such disputes. The GFCC, which had consistently chosen not to confront aggressively discrimination based on sex and age (preferring a type of rational basis test to proportionality), lost these skirmishes. The GFCC was forced to adapt, along with every other domestic court that had been left behind.[48] Today, across Europe, rights emanating from the EU level are a more important source of non-discrimination law than are national constitutional provisions, an outcome produced by the dynamics of inter-court dialogue under conditions of pluralism.

Although elected officials have at times sought to constrain the courts, these efforts have failed to block the expansion of judicial power. In the end, governments too adapted. With the Maastricht Treaty on European Union (1993), the member states revised the Treaty of Rome, echoing the Court's seminal case law: "the Union shall respect fundamental rights as guaranteed by the European Convention on Human Rights . . . and as they result from the constitutional traditions common to the member states as general principles of Community law." In 2009, EU member states promulgated a Charter of Rights through the Lisbon Treaty. They also accepted (for the first time) the basics of the

[47] We do not mean to underestimate the extent of resistance to the CJEU, and its creative rulings, which routinely takes place across a broad range of domains. See Conant (2002); review of literature in Stone Sweet (2010: 29–33).

[48] Stone Sweet and Stranz (2012).

supremacy doctrine,[49] and committed to accession of the EU to the ECHR.[50]

The accession of the EU to the ECHR would consolidate the various systemic elements of the European human rights regime under the Convention and the tutelage, if not the formal primacy, of the Strasbourg Court. In 2013, EU member states published a draft treaty of accession, which was referred to the CJEU for a binding, advisory opinion on its compatibility with EU treaty law. In a long and complex ruling,[51] the CJEU strongly criticized the draft agreement, invoking a list of faults concerning technical issues of internal EU law, the most important of which express concerns for the fate of its own constitutional authority if the EU were to recognize, in the terms of this book, the trustee status of the Strasbourg Court. Among other issues, the ruling raises knotty procedural questions, including the extent to which accession would enable individuals and national judges to bypass the CJEU, by going directly to Strasbourg with claims. In a nutshell, the CJEU blocked accession, unless and until its own procedural and substantive primacy with respect to EU law and the EU Charter of Rights could be guaranteed to its satisfaction. Thus, the accession agreement—the product of delicate compromises in the first place—will now have to be negotiated, signed, and ratified by all forty-seven signatories of the Convention, and then "agreed upon unanimously by the EU's Council of Ministers and ratified by the European Parliament."[52]

[49] While the CJEU's fundamental rights jurisprudence remains in place, rights-oriented litigation under the Charter is likely to increase substantially.

[50] The CJEU reject the draft treaty of accession in December 2014. Opinion 2/13 *Accession of the European Union to the European Convention for the Protection of Human Rights and Fundamental Freedoms* ECLI:EU: C:2014:2454.

[51] *Opinion Pursuant to Article 218(11) TFEU*, CJEU Case C-2/13 (18 December 2014); Halberstam (2015) provides analysis from the standpoint of constitutional pluralism within Europe.

[52] Peers (2015: 217–18).

INCORPORATION OF THE CONVENTION

The development of rights and constitutional pluralism within the EU weakened the prohibition of judicial review by creating an ever-expanding domain of exceptions in which judges were required to review statutes. The incorporation of the Convention obliterated the prohibition, with transformative effects.

The incorporation of the ECHR refers to the process through which the Convention is converted into national law, as a judicially enforceable charter of rights. The domestification of the Convention proceeded via different routes:[53] express constitutional provision (Austria, many post-Communist states); judicial interpretation of constitutional provisions related to treaty law generally (most states in Western Europe); or special statutes (UK, Ireland, and Scandinavian states). All members of the Council of Europe have incorporated the Convention. As a result, individuals can plead the ECHR at national bar against any act of public authority. Judges are under a duty to identify statutes that conflict with Convention rights, to interpret statutes in light of the ECHR, and to avoid conflicts whenever possible. And virtually all courts may refuse to apply statutes that conflict with Convention rights, with the notable exception of those in the UK and Ireland.

The process subverted centralized sovereignty within domestic orders, while provoking the construction of a pluralistic, multi-level system of constitutional justice. In Europe, domestic legal orders had been organized under one of two systems of centralized sovereignty. In legislative supremacy systems, parliament held the "final authority" when it comes to settling legal conflicts. In constitutional rights-based systems, an apex court performed this function. In systems that featured a specialized constitutional court—the majority in Europe today—the "ordinary" (that is, non-constitutional) supreme courts,

[53] Documented in Stone Sweet (2012b: Appendix 1).

such as the supreme civil and administrative courts, could refuse to apply statutes only when expressly authorized to do so by the constitutional court, or once the latter had invalidated them. Incorporation, by placing all judges under a presumptive duty to enforce Convention rights, is gradually extinguishing the supposed primacy of the constitutional courts when it came to judicial review and the enforcement of rights. As we will see, some constitutional courts continue to assert and jealously defend their prerogatives, but the dynamics of constitutional pluralism has meant they now share rights-protecting responsibilities with the ordinary courts.

With incorporation, the Convention developed into a "shadow," or "surrogate," constitution[54] in states that did not possess their own judicially enforceable charter of rights, including Belgium, France, the Netherlands, Switzerland, and the UK. Finland, Norway, and Sweden enacted new Bills of Rights, closely modeled on the ECHR, in order to fill gaps in their own constitutions. In those states that possessed, at least on paper, relatively complete systems of constitutional justice, incorporation provided supplementary protection. We find this latter situation in Germany, Greece, Ireland, Italy, Portugal, Spain, Turkey, and in the post-Communist countries.

In many domestic systems, constitutional courts have been central to the incorporation process. The Spanish Constitutional Tribunal, for example, began enforcing Convention rights as quasi-constitutional norms even before the entry into force of Protocol no. 11. The Tribunal will strike down statutes that violate the Convention as per se unconstitutional. It interprets Spanish constitutional rights in light of the ECHR wherever possible and it has ordered the ordinary courts to abide by the Strasbourg Court's jurisprudence as a matter of *constitutional* obligation, including case law generated by rulings not involving Spain. If the judiciary ignores the Court's jurisprudence, individuals can appeal directly to the Tribunal for redress,[55] a

[54] Keller and Stone Sweet, eds. (2008).

[55] Candela Soriano (2008).

procedural innovation that enhances the Tribunal's control over the ordinary courts. At the same time, the Tribunal insists that in the event of an irreconcilable conflict between the ECHR and the Spanish Constitution, national law will prevail—a common position among constitutional courts.[56] In many post-Communist states, as well, constitutional judges routinely enforce the case law of the Strasbourg Court, not least, to enhance their own status as rights protectors domestically.[57]

Strikingly, some states give the Convention constitutional rank (e.g., Albania, Austria, Slovenia); and, in the Netherlands, the ECHR enjoys supra-constitutional status. The Lithuanian Constitutional Court decided that the national constitution and the Convention are, presumptively, in harmony with one another. The Belgian Constitutional Court has determined that the ECHR possesses supra-legislative but infra-constitutional rank, whereas the Belgian Supreme Court holds that the ECHR possesses supra-constitutional status, thereby enhancing its own autonomy vis-à-vis the Constitutional Court.

One could continue in this vein, but the basic point has been made. The incorporation of the ECHR generated constitutional pluralism and inter-judicial competition *within* national legal orders.[58] It destroyed the doctrines that underpinned centralized sovereignty, including legislative supremacy, and undermined the dominance of constitutional courts with respect to rights review. It created a fluid system that continues to evolve as domestic judges negotiate their

[56] In systems in which such doctrines hold sway, a model of centralized sovereignty can usually be constructed from the internal perspective of the national constitutional court.

[57] Hammer and Emmert, eds. (2011).

[58] The most obvious cases of internal constitutional pluralism are systems in which one finds both (i) a constitutional court which, as a matter of national constitutional law, alone possesses the authority to invalidate statutes that conflict with constitutional rights, and (ii) one or several supreme courts which may refuse to apply statutes in conflict with rights found in EU law or the Convention. Today, classic distinctions between the constitutional and ordinary courts, themselves derived from traditional models of legislative sovereignty, are on the verge of extinction. See Garlicki (2007); Stone Sweet (2013).

respective relationships, and as national high courts deepen their dialogues with Strasbourg.

TRANSFORMATION

Incorporation radically expanded the authority of the judiciary vis-à-vis legislative and executive power. With few exceptions, all judges are now expected to refuse to enforce any act of public authority that conflicts with the Convention; at the same time, they are rapidly abandoning traditional methods of statutory interpretation. Rather than prioritizing legislative intent (as faithful agents of the parliament), judges increasingly favor the purposive construction of statutes in light of an evolving jurisprudence of rights. In systems in which multiple, functionally differentiated, high courts coexist (the majority of states in the Council of Europe), pluralism means that the supreme courts of ordinary jurisdiction may assume the mantle of *de facto* constitutional courts whenever they review the lawfulness of domestic statutes under the Convention. Stated in the most general terms, incorporation means that all judges are positioned to become active participants in enforcing rights.

France, which for two centuries famously embraced and propagated the dogmas of the General Will (legislative sovereignty and the prohibition of judicial review), and did not accept the compulsory jurisdiction of the Court pursuant to individual petitions until the 1980s, is now a robust example of pluralism.[59] From the point of view of a rights claimant, the Supreme Civil Court (*Cour de Cassation*) and the Council of State (the supreme administrative court) function as the "real" constitutional courts; and litigants and judges treat the Convention as the "real" charter of rights. The outcome is dictated by the fact that individuals have no direct access to the Constitutional

[59] Lambert Abdelgawad and Weber (2008).

Council,[60] while they can directly petition Strasbourg. And it is the European Court, not the Constitutional Council, which supervises the bulk of the rights-protecting activities of the civil and administrative courts. Today, three autonomous high courts protect rights on an ongoing basis; and there is no formal means of coordinating rights doctrine, or of resolving conflicts, among these courts. Without revising the Constitution or exiting the ECHR, French officials are now locked into a pluralist system of justice within its own borders.[61]

Some of the most powerful states in Western Europe have had the greatest difficulty adjusting to the incorporation of the ECHR, insofar as it requires the courts to enforce Convention rights against conflicting statutes. In legal terms, the structural problem concerns the fact that in so-called "dualist" systems—including original signatories, Germany, Ireland, Italy, Sweden, Norway, and the UK—constitutions confer upon treaty law the same rank as statute in the hierarchy of norms. In such systems, conflicts between statutes and treaty provisions are typically resolved according to the rule, *lex posterior derogat legi priori*. This rule, too, is anathema to a CLO, since it would make legislation adopted after the transposition of the ECHR into national law immune from review under the Convention. What is critical for the emergence of the CLO is that, in these states, the rule has been relaxed or overridden altogether.

In Italy, at least until the late 1960s, the courts "refused to apply the Convention, considering its provisions to be merely programmatic."[62] In the twenty-first century, Italian courts reversed course and incorporated the Convention, destroying the *lex posterior* rule and producing a pluralist order. In 2004, the Supreme Court (*Cassazione*) began treating the Convention as directly applicable, while in 2007,

[60] In 2008, the French Constitution was revised to permit the Supreme Court and the Council of State to refer laws to the Constitutional Council for review, in the context of ongoing litigation. One of the motivations for the amendment was to "renationalize" rights protection, in the context of Protocol no. 11; see Fabbrini (2008).

[61] Lasser rightly analyzes the result as a set of "judicial transformations" (2009).

[62] Candela Soriano (2008: 405).

the Italian Constitutional Court (ICC) struck down a statute as unconstitutional on the grounds that it violated a right guaranteed by the Convention.[63] In its decision, the ICC held that Italian judges are required to interpret national law in light of the ECHR and, when a conflict is unavoidable, to refer the matter to the ICC. The ICC insisted that no statute could be disapplied by any other Italian judge without its explicit authorization. Some judges have chosen to ignore this jurisprudence. In 2008, for example, a court of appeal decided on its own authority to refuse to apply a controlling statute on grounds that it was incompatible with the Convention.[64] The situation has given rise to a fierce debate: does the ECHR enjoy, as a matter of judicial practice at least, supra-legislative but infra-constitutional rank (the ICC's position) or constitutional status (the position of some civil and administrative courts, as well as scholars)? This is yet another example of constitutional pluralism in action, taking place at the domestic level.

In Germany, overcoming the *lex posterior* rule has been tortuous.[65] Not until 1987 did the GFCC directly confront the problem, holding that German statutes, regardless of their date of adoption, must be "interpreted and applied in harmony" with the Convention.[66] In its *Görgülü* decision (2005),[67] the GFCC repudiated the "traditional theory" according to which the Strasbourg Court's judgments did not bind the domestic organs of government, including the courts.[68] The ruling establishes a strong presumption that judges are to apply the Court's jurisprudence when it is on point, except in "exceptional" circumstances, namely, when ignoring Convention law "is the only way to avoid a violation of the fundamental principles contained in the Constitution."[69] As important, the GFCC's ruling expanded the

[63] Candela Soriano (2008: 405–6).
[64] Reported in Andenæs and Bjørge (2011: 37–8).
[65] Lambert Abdelgawad and Weber (2008).
[66] BVerfGE 74, 358 (370).
[67] *Görgülü*, BVerfGE 111, 307.
[68] Hoffmeister (2006: 728–9).
[69] *Görgülü*, BVerfGE 111, 307 para. 35.

constitutional complaint procedure. As in Spain, individuals can now challenge (as a violation of their *national* constitutional rights) any judicial ruling that ignores or fails to properly take into account the European Court's case law. While *Görgülü* significantly bolstered the domestic status of the ECHR, the GFCC warned, unsurprisingly, that it would settle any conflict between the Basic Law and the ECHR in terms of the former.

In 2011, the GFCC declared that the ECHR and the European Court's case law comprise interpretive "aids for the determination of the contents and scope of the fundamental rights and of rule-of-law principles enshrined in the Basic Law." [70] Like *Görgülü,* the GFCC's *Preventive Detention* ruling ended a convoluted saga involving a direct conflict between the German courts and the European Court. In 2009, in *M. v. Germany*, the Strasbourg Court had held that German law allowing the further detention of convicted criminals after they had served their prison sentences violated the ECHR.[71] The GFCC had upheld the constitutionality of the relevant statute in 2004, in so far as such detention was deemed necessary to protect public security. When the GFCC appeared reluctant to change its position following the *M.* judgment, the European Court issued a series of rulings finding the same violation. In *Prevention Detention*, the GFCC overturned its 2004 ruling, on the grounds that the Strasbourg Court's case law had constituted a significant "change in the legal situation." The Court then went on to ground the Basic Law's "openness" to the Convention in Article 1.2 of the Basic Law, which recognizes human rights as foundational principles. As a result, all organs of the state are under a duty "not only to take into account" the ECHR in their decisions, but "to avoid conflict" between it and national law. "The openness of the Basic Law," the GFCC stated, "expresses an understanding of

[70] *Preventive Detention, no. 2* BvR 2365/09 (4 May 2011).
[71] *M. v. Germany* (17 December 2009).

sovereignty that not only does not oppose international and supranational integration, it presupposes and expects [integration]."[72]

By formally recognizing the overlapping nature of fundamental rights in Europe, the GFCC has taken a more cosmopolitan-constitutional position. In *Görgülü*, the GFCC had already declared that its own rights-protecting role is exercised "indirectly in the service" of the Convention, an engagement that both protects Germany from findings of violations and "contributes to promoting a joint European development of fundamental rights."[73] In *Preventive Detention*, the GFCC acknowledged a dialogic relationship with the Strasbourg Court, without abandoning its position on the primacy of the Basic Law: "The fact that the German constitution has the final word is not incompatible with an international and European dialogue between courts, rather it [comprises the dialogue's] normative foundation."[74] In June 2011, two months after *Preventive Detention*, the European Court responded favorably, finding no violation in a related case, *Mork v. Germany* (2011). "In its judgment," the Strasbourg Court noted, "the GFCC stressed that the fact that the Constitution stood above the Convention in the domestic hierarchy of norms was not an obstacle to . . . dialogue between the courts," and that "in its reasoning, [the GFCC] relied on the interpretation . . . of the Convention made by this Court in its judgment in the case of *M. v. Germany*."[75] The outcome illustrates one basic mechanism—formal dialogue among autonomous courts—through which rights are enforced by the decentralized sovereign.

[72] *Preventive Detention*, para. 89.
[73] As characterized by the GFCC in *Preventive Detention*, para. 61.
[74] *Preventive Detention*, para. 89.
[75] *Mork v. Germany* (9 June 2011). In *Schmitz v. Germany* (9 June 2011) para. 41, the Court noted that the GFCC had reversed its earlier case law and declared that it "welcomes the [GFCC's] approach of interpreting the provisions of the Basic Law also in the light of the Convention and this Court's case-law, which demonstrates that court's continuing commitment to the protection of fundamental rights not only on national, but also on European level."

In two states—Ireland and the UK—the *lex posterior* rule has also been relaxed, although no judge is authorized to set aside legislation conflicting with the Convention.[76] Pursuant to the ECHR Act (2003), Irish officials are under a duty to respect and enforce the Convention, and individuals can plead it against all acts of public authority, except those of Parliament and the courts. This is one of the few formal gaps in protection one finds in the CLO. Under the UK Human Rights Act (1998), individuals may challenge all acts, including Parliamentary legislation; if a Parliamentary statute is found to be incompatible with the ECHR, the high courts are obligated to issue a ruling of incompatibility, but they may not set aside the offending legislative provisions. Declarations of incompatibility are addressed to the Parliament, which must then indicate what remedial legislation, if any, will be proposed.[77] In Ireland, the high courts may also issue rulings of incompatibility, although Parliament is not obliged to respond to them.

In Norway and Sweden,[78] which incorporated the ECHR through human rights statutes in the 1990s, the courts must give primacy to the Convention when in a conflict with legislation.[79] In the past decade, Norwegian courts in particular have positioned themselves to become active participants in the development of Convention rights.[80]

While the dynamics of incorporation are heavily mediated by constitutional provisions and domestic doctrine, important strategic interests have been catalysts. In the 1990s, incorporation constituted a formal means for post-Communist states to signal their commitment

[76] Besson (2008).

[77] Although a surface commitment to parliamentary sovereignty survives, constitutional pluralism nonetheless emerged. The (pre-Brexit) courts must apply EU law, including EU fundamental rights and the Charter, against conflicting legislation; the Parliament, however, may choose not to harmonize legislation with the Convention in the face of a declaration of incompatibility.

[78] Scandinavia possesses some of the oldest systems of judicial review in the world (Husa (2000)), although no court in the region used review authority to any effect. Indeed, even today, these courts do little *domestic* constitutional judicial review of any political consequence, and deference to the legislature is the rule (Husa (2000); Hirschl (2011)).

[79] Wiklund (2008).

[80] Andenæs and Bjørge (2011: 15–17).

to the massive institutional reforms demanded by Western states. And Western European officials understood that peace on the Continent would be furthered by the development of effective systems of justice across Europe. As a growing scholarly literature has shown, the ECHR has played a crucial role in democratic transitions after 1989.[81] New bills of rights were modeled on the ECHR, with an eye toward future membership in the EU and the Council of Europe; and some states even signed the ECHR prior to ratifying new constitutions (including Albania, Armenia, Azerbaijan, Georgia, Poland, Slovakia, and Ukraine).

For the core states of Western Europe, folding the post-Communist states into the ECHR also fulfilled important strategic interests. Protocol no. 11 reconstructed the regime, making it an extraordinarily efficient mechanism for monitoring domestic politics, and the course of democratization, in regions that could pose serious threats to peace and stability. For Western states, the cost of Protocol no. 11 was stronger supervision of their own systems of rights protection, which they have thus far been willing to pay.[82]

TRUSTEESHIP

Protocol no. 11 and the incorporation of the Convention into national law combined to instantiate the European CLO, a transnational system of justice as defined above. Incorporation made the Convention binding on public officials, and placed the courts under the duty to enforce the Convention. Judges do so, most commonly, in synergy with their obligations under domestic charters of rights

[81] Sadurski, Czarnota, and Krygier, eds. (2006); Buyse and Hamilton, eds. (2011); Hammer and Emmert, eds. (2011); Motoc and Ziemele, eds. (2016).

[82] In December 2016, Prime Minister May announced that she would campaign, in part, on a promise to withdraw the UK from the ECHR; and in May 2017, she declared that the UK would remain a member of the regime; *Independent*, December 29, 2016, and May 18, 2017.

(where such exist). Protocol no. 11, in turn, made the decisions of national judges, and every other domestic official, reviewable by the European Court. The CLO is, therefore, a relatively complete, multi-level system of rights protection.

The European Court is the trustee court of the regime (chapter 4). In the international context, a court can be considered a trustee if it meets three criteria: (i) it is recognized as the authoritative interpreter of the regime's law, which it applies to resolve disputes concerning state compliance; (ii) the court's jurisdiction, with regard to state compliance, is compulsory; and (iii) it is virtually impossible, in practice, for contracting states to reverse the court's important rulings.[83] The charge of a Kantian trustee is to defend the value placed in trust—freedom—as expressed by a charter of rights (chapter 2). The third criteria means that the court's rights jurisprudence is likely to be "sticky" and path dependent: outcomes produced will be relatively resistant to change except through subsequent rounds of adjudication. International trustee courts have a powerful interest in eliciting compliance with their decisions because compliance is intimately connected to the fulfillment of their mission, not because they fear override.[84] In fact, no important ruling of the European Court has ever been overridden through treaty revision, an unsurprising result given that the decision rule for treaty amendment is unanimity (of the High Contracting Parties). At the same time, unlike national constitutional courts, the Strasbourg Court does not possess the authority to invalidate national law. Instead, its effectiveness depends upon the capacity to persuade domestic lawmakers and apex courts to comply with its rulings.

From a Kantian perspective, the basic systemic features of the European CLO should now be in view. First, the regime is a multi-level, transnational system of constitutional justice, the purpose of which is to enable the construction of a Rightful condition under a code of

[83] Stone Sweet and Brunell (2013).

[84] Stone Sweet and Brunell (2013).

rights. Second, this code is enforced by a decentralized sovereign: a community of courts who are networked through the Convention and its incorporation as domestic law. While the "code" metaphor is Kant's,[85] senior European judges have echoed this language when describing constitutional pluralism. A former Lord Chief Justice of the UK, for example, has stated that national judges are "called upon to administer an international code of human rights largely laid down by the European Court in Strasbourg."[86] Third, the system is pluralist. One can chart and assess the dynamics of constitutional pluralism not only at the regime level, wherein the European Court interacts with national courts and other state officials, but also within domestic legal systems. Fourth, the European Court is a constitutional court among constitutional courts, but it also occupies a crucial strategic position. As a trustee court of the regime, the Strasbourg Court supervises the activities of all national officials, including the judges on domestic apex courts. That point made, pluralism means that the latter are likely to recognize the primacy of the Strasbourg Court only insofar as they can do so voluntarily, through purposive interpretation of their own domestic constitutions.

PROPORTIONALITY

The rest of the book explains how the European CLO functions, and with what effects on standards of rights protection. We focus, in particular, on specific mechanisms of coordination between courts. These mechanisms are embedded in highly structured "constitutional dialogues," which are facilitated by the consolidation of a common approach to rights protection: proportionality analysis (PA). Chapter 2 discussed the importance of PA to Kantian justice at length, and we will not repeat these arguments. What deserves emphasis here

[85] PP, 8:360. [86] Bingham (2010: 71), discussed in Bjorge (2015: 48).

is that the Strasbourg Court not only embraced the proportionality principle, but required domestic judges to use PA whenever they adjudicated the qualified rights of the Convention. As a result, courts now share a common, relatively stable framework for rights adjudication. This discursive interface gives the regime a *lingua franca* and a doctrinal coherence it would not otherwise have.

As part of the incorporation process, the diffusion of PA also upgraded the regime's completeness and effectiveness by replacing domestic standards of review that required, or strongly encouraged, judges to defer to the policy choices of legislators and executives. By tying PA to Article 13 ECHR—the right to an effective judicial remedy—the Court put a final nail into the coffin of legislative sovereignty. Tellingly, the Court did so in the context of a sustained confrontation with a formal deference doctrine—the so-called *Wednesbury unreasonableness* standard—which was deeply embedded in the UK, the center of gravity for parliamentary sovereignty in Europe.

The Convention proclaims some state obligations in absolute terms, including torture, degrading treatment, and slavery.[87] But most rights are "qualified" by a limitation clause, just as they are in all domestic charters of rights adopted in Europe after the Second World War. The ECHR stipulates that states may only infringe upon the freedom of thought, conscience, religion, expression, assembly, and association, and the enjoyment of rights to privacy and respect for family life, when *necessary* to achieve certain purposes. In the standard formula, states may "interfere with" or "restrict the exercise of" a Convention right (i) when such interferences are "prescribed by law," and (ii) when they:

> are necessary in a democratic society in the interests of national security or public safety for the prevention of disorder or crime,

[87] Arts. 3 and 4 ECHR.

> for the protection of health or morals, or for the protection of the rights and freedoms of others.[88]

For any qualified right, the headings covering permissible derogations are exhaustive: Article 18 ECHR prohibits states from infringing upon rights "for any purpose other than those . . . prescribed." The Strasbourg Court, joining virtually every other powerful constitutional court in the world,[89] assesses compliance with the "necessity" requirement under PA.

The Court's early confrontation with the issue of how to judge "necessity" took place at a time when domestic approaches to judicial review and rights protection varied widely. By the early 1970s, the proportionality framework was routinely used in Germany, and had begun to appear in the EU under the CJEU's tutelage.[90] But PA was virtually unknown in the legal systems of the High Contracting Parties, with the exception of Switzerland. The Court's turn to proportionality[91] was heavily conditioned by its confrontation with cases coming from the UK, where the "Wednesbury unreasonableness" test governed applications for judicial review of administrative acts, while statutes were immune from review altogether.[92] This conflict, between German-style proportionality and UK-style reasonableness, is a deeply structural one, implicating the basic foundations of a legal system wherever it arises. While the UK's accession to the EU led judges to create exceptions to certain core precepts of parliamentary sovereignty, traditionalists could assert that these exceptions were limited, since they only applied to legal domains governed by EU law.

[88] Art. 8 ECHR. [89] Stone Sweet and Mathews (2008).

[90] By the end of the 1970s, PA had emerged as a general principle of EU law with constitutional properties; Stone Sweet and Mathews (2008: 139–45).

[91] Stone Sweet and Mathews (2008: 146–53). The main agent of this development was Professor Jochen Frowein, a member of the Commission on Human Rights (1973–93), and its Vice President (1981–93).

[92] The fount of which is *Associated Provincial Picture Houses Ltd. v. Wednesbury Corp.* [1948] 1 KB 223 (UK).

Convention rights, however, are potentially relevant to every domain of law and policy.

The Court's first serious dealing with a limitation clause came in *Handyside v. the United Kingdom* (1976),[93] a freedom of expression case involving the censorship of a book on public morals grounds. In its ruling, the Court observed that "the adjective 'necessary' [was] not synonymous with 'indispensable,' and neither has it the flexibility of such expressions as . . . 'admissible,' . . . 'useful,' 'reasonable,' or 'desirable.'" Nevertheless, it was up to "national authorities to make the initial assessment of the reality of the pressing social need implied by the notion of 'necessity' in this context."[94] The Court then found that the UK had exercised its "margin of appreciation" properly, but insisted that the use of such authority must "go hand in hand with . . . European supervision."[95] (As discussed in chapters 4 and 5, the *margin of appreciation* is doctrinal jargon that today describes the zone of discretion in which states may determine how a right may be hindered in pursuit of legitimate public policy purposes.) Five years later, in *Dudgeon v. the United Kingdom* (1981),[96] a right to privacy case, the Court declared measures that criminalized homosexual acts to be "disproportionate," having failed a least-restrictive means ("necessity") test (chapter 2). Building on *Dudgeon*, the Court then gradually evolved its own version of PA, which it treated as a general approach to rights protection (chapter 5).

In doing so, the Court became a powerful agent in PA's diffusion into national legal orders. In two more privacy cases rendered after the entry into force of Protocol no. 11, *Smith and Grady v. the United Kingdom* (1999),[97] and *Peck v. the United Kingdom* (2003),[98] the Court strongly criticized UK judges for continuing to be guided by the Wednesbury unreasonableness standard. In *Peck*, the Court noted that

[93] *Handyside v. the United Kingdom* (Plenary, 7 December 1976).
[94] *Handyside*, para. 22. [95] *Handyside*, para. 23.
[96] *Dudgeon v. the United Kingdom* (Plenary, 22 October 1981).
[97] *Smith and Grady v. the United Kingdom* (27 September 1999).
[98] *Peck v. the United Kingdom* (28 January 2003).

UK judges refused to entertain pleadings based on the Convention except where claimants could show that public authorities had acted "irrationally in the sense that they had taken leave of their senses, or had acted in a manner in which no reasonable authority could have acted" (i.e., the Wednesbury test).[99] In both *Smith and Grady* (unlawful discrimination against homosexuals in the armed services) and *Peck* (unlawful broadcasting of closed circuit camera footage), the Court held that the absence of proportionality review by the UK courts constituted a per se breach of Article 13 ECHR: "Everyone whose rights and freedoms as set forth in this Convention are violated shall have an effective remedy before a national authority."[100] In both cases, the Court stressed that UK judges had strongly implied that they would have found for the applicants, but for the Wednesbury restriction.[101] In *Smith and Grady*, judges on the Court of Appeal not only criticized the policy banning homosexuals from serving in the armed forces, but encouraged the claimants to apply to the European Court.[102] Thus, it can be argued that the Court was helping UK judges overcome a restriction that had made it impossible for them to fulfill their obligations under the Convention,[103] thereby closing an important gap in protection.

Anticipating Strasbourg, the UK courts had already begun to embrace a weaker form of reasonableness review (moving away from a plainly absurd or irrational test), when it came to rights claims, in advance of the entry into force of the Human Rights Act. Peck's application for judicial review was rejected by the High Court in 1997, and the European Court's judgment on the merits did not come until 2003. In the meantime, the 1998 Human Rights Act would incorporate the ECHR into UK law, which quickly induced the House of

[99] *Peck*, para. 32. [100] *Peck*, para. 137.
[101] *Peck*, para. 137; *Smith and Grady*, para. 37.
[102] *Smith and Grady*, paras. 38–9.
[103] In *Peck*, the Court implies as much, para. 137.

Lords to adopt a (relatively weak) form of PA.[104] In *Hirst v. the United Kingdom*,[105] a 2005 case involving the voting rights of incarcerated prisoners, the European Court condemned the UK, in part, on the grounds that neither Parliament nor the judiciary[106] had bothered to assess the proportionality of a blanket ban on the right of prisoners to vote.[107] When 2010 elections replaced the Labour Government by a Conservative-Liberal coalition, legislative efforts to comply with *Hirst* were abruptly halted. Nonetheless, the story does not end with the present stalemate. Indeed, in 2012, the UK Supreme Court committed to a proportionality framework that mirrors the form described in chapter 2.[108]

We have gone into detail on the development of PA, not least because it is part and parcel of two broader processes: the demise of legislative sovereignty, and the building of the regime's capacity to render justice. Under the Court's supervision, PA is diffusing into every national legal order in Europe, where it will typically be absorbed as a *constitutional* principle. Failure on the part of a national judiciary to use PA to adjudicate qualified rights is itself an infringement of the Convention right to an effective judicial remedy (Art. 13). In Kantian terms, the proportionality principle operationalizes the UPR as a basic criterion of legality (chapter 2). Last, as discussed in the rest of the book, adopting PA positions all apex courts judges to fulfill their duties as national trustees of the Convention.

[104] In *de Freitas v. Permanent Secretary of Ministry of Agriculture, Fisheries, Lands, and Housing*, 1 AC 69, 80 (PC 1998).

[105] *Hirst v. the United Kingdom*, No. 2 (GC, 6 October 2005).

[106] Writing for the Divisional Court, Lord Justice Kennedy stated: "The European Court also requires that the means employed . . . are not disproportionate, and that is the point at which, as it seems to me, it is appropriate for this court to defer to the legislature"; quoted in *Hirst*, para. 16.

[107] *Hirst*, paras. 79–80.

[108] *Quila & Another* [2011] UKSC 45, [2012] 1 AC 621. For an overview of this process, see Bjorge (2015: 169–73, 175).

CONCLUSION

We have argued that a Cosmopolitan Legal Order was instantiated in Europe through the combined impact of Protocol no. 11 and the incorporation of the Convention into national legal systems as directly applicable law. The crucial empirical claim is that two processes—(i) the evolution of constitutional pluralism at the national level; and (ii) the development of rights protection at the transnational level—are causally connected to one another. The first process undermined traditional models of domestic orders wherein the notions of constitutional unity and centralized sovereignty reinforced one another. The second instantiated a multi-level system of constitutional justice whose effectiveness will depend on the extent to which the European Court is able to induce and sustain the cooperation of domestic courts and officials. The constitutionalization of the proportionality principle, at both the domestic and transnational levels, provided a doctrinal interface for inter-jurisdictional dialogue, and the collective enforcement of the UPR.

The emergence of a CLO, anywhere at any time, should be the cause of some wonderment, as a momentous outcome in itself. In Europe, a number of "transition"[109] points combined to transform the normative foundations of European law. We have emphasized the reconfiguration of domestic legal orders—normative hierarchies, powers, procedures, remedies—so as to position judges to render justice. Of course, the appearance of a CLO does not guarantee its survival. Progress toward a Rightful condition may be halting, and justice may be denied in some or many important cases. In part II of the book, we examine how the ECHR operates, focusing on its impact on the effectiveness of rights protection, and on the development of rights-based constitutionalism beyond the state.

[109] On the importance of identifying such transition points, see Corradetti (2016).

Part II

The European Convention on Human Rights

4

Beyond Individual Justice

INTRODUCTION

In part I, we confronted a series of important lacunae in Kantian theory. In *Perpetual Peace*, Kant proposed a set of necessary conditions that states would be required to meet if they were to overcome the problem of perpetual war. As discussed in chapter 1, political scientists, treating these and other factors as causal variables, have found strong support for the basics of his theory, as applied to the absence of war among liberal states. Yet scholars have hardly addressed the philosopher's own priority: the achievement of Right beyond the state (a constituent component of *Perpetual Peace*). While Kant insisted that citizens, nations, and states were morally obligated to realize Right, he wrote little of substance on how a legal system should be designed to help them do so. At most, he sketched bits of normative scaffolding that, although grounded in a handful of bedrock principles, are largely indeterminate when it comes to the institutional details of rights protection. In chapter 2, we elaborated a Kantian-congruent account of a domestic system of constitutional justice, connecting this model to contemporary constitutional practice. In chapter 3, we extended these ideas to Europe, and argued that Protocol no. 11 and domestic incorporation of the Convention combined to instantiate a cosmopolitan legal order. Protocol no. 11 conferred on individuals an unfettered right to petition the Court after exhausting domestic remedies; and incorporation made Convention rights directly enforceable by national judges, as domestic law. The outcome was not preordained. The cosmopolitan legal order (CLO) would not have emerged, for example, had national officials failed to overcome deeply embedded orthodoxies related to legislative sovereignty and the prohibition of judicial review of statute.

Part II of the book focuses on how the European CLO is configured and operates, paying particular attention to the dynamics of institutional change. This chapter examines the growing capacity of the European Court to fulfill its role as the omnilateral trustee for the regime, in conjunction with state officials and the Committee of Ministers of the Council of Europe. Particularly since the entry into force of Protocol no. 11, the regime has produced a set of inter-related mechanisms of coordination, designed to enhance the regime's effectiveness. Their consolidation registers the growing structural embeddedness among levels and arenas of rights governance.

The process of building effectiveness is ongoing and remains incomplete, yet significant advances have been made. As we will show, since the entry into force of Protocol no. 11, formal and informal amendments to the regime have made the system all but unrecognizable from the standpoint of the Court's powers and responsibilities. It is obvious[1] that the Court could not, on its own, meet the demands of *individual justice*,[2] if by that term we mean that it must provide a remedy to every worthy applicant. Realizing as much, the Court committed to building its own *constitutional* authority as the regime's trustee, not least, with respect to the supervision of domestic systems of justice, which hold primary duties of protection in the regime.

We begin with a brief defense of the view that the European Court serves as a trustee of a multi-level, constitutional legal order. We then discuss the basic determinates of the Court's effectiveness, and assess

[1] Keller and Stone Sweet (2008: 19, 704–5); Sadurski (2009); Stone Sweet (2012b: 76–9); Greer and Wildhaber (2012).

[2] In a foundational sense, justice conceived in Kantian terms is always "individual"; see chapters 2 and 3.

reforms initiated to enhance Strasbourg's capacity to strengthen rights protection at the national level. Box 4 lists the major provisions and rules to be discussed.

Box 4 Major Provisions of the ECHR and the Rules of the Court

Legal Status

The Convention for the Protection Human Rights and Fundamental Freedoms was signed on 4 November 1950, and entered into force on 3 September 1953. The centerpiece of the Council of Europe, the Convention has been ratified by 47 states across Europe.

Purposes

Preamble: [T]he aim of the Council of Europe is the achievement of greater unity between its members and that one of the methods by which that aim is to be pursued is the maintenance and further realisation of human rights and fundamental freedoms. [These rights and freedoms] are the foundation of justice and peace in the world and are best maintained on the one hand by an effective political democracy and on the other by a common understanding and observance of the human rights upon which they depend.

General Provisions on Rights and State Obligations

ART. 1: OBLIGATION TO RESPECT HUMAN RIGHTS

The High Contracting Parties shall secure to everyone within their jurisdiction the rights and freedoms defined in Section I of this Convention.

ART. 13: RIGHT TO AN EFFECTIVE REMEDY

Everyone whose rights and freedoms as set forth in this Convention are violated shall have an effective remedy before a national authority notwithstanding that the violation has been committed by persons acting in an official capacity.

ART. 17: PROHIBITION OF ABUSE OF RIGHTS

Nothing in this Convention may be interpreted as implying for any State, group or person any right to engage in any activity or perform any act aimed at the destruction of any of the rights and freedoms set forth herein or at their limitation to a greater extent than is provided for in the Convention.

ART. 18: LIMITATION ON USE OF RESTRICTIONS ON RIGHTS

The restrictions permitted under this Convention to the said rights and freedoms shall not be applied for any purpose other than those for which they have been prescribed.

ART. 53: SAFEGUARD FOR EXISTING HUMAN RIGHTS

Nothing in this Convention shall be construed as limiting or derogating from any of the human rights and fundamental freedoms which may be ensured under the laws of any High Contracting Party . . .

[For specific rights provisions, see Boxes 5 and 6.]

Jurisdiction and Competences of the Court

ART. 32: JURISDICTION OF THE COURT

1. The jurisdiction of the Court shall extend to all matters concerning the interpretation and application of the Convention and the Protocols thereto which are referred to it . . .
2. In the event of dispute as to whether the Court has jurisdiction, the Court shall decide.

ART. 33: INTER-STATE CASES

Any High Contracting Party may refer to the Court any alleged breach of the provisions of the Convention and the Protocols thereto by another High Contracting Party.

ART. 34: INDIVIDUAL APPLICATIONS

The Court may receive applications from any person, non-governmental organisation or group of individuals claiming to be the victim of a violation by one of the High Contracting Parties of the rights set forth in the Convention or the Protocols thereto. The High Contracting Parties undertake not to hinder in any way the effective exercise of this right.

ART. 41: JUST SATISFACTION

If the Court finds that there has been a violation of the Convention or the Protocols thereto, and if the internal law of the High Contracting Party concerned allows only partial reparation to be made, the Court shall, if necessary, afford just satisfaction to the injured party.

Judgments and their Execution

ART. 45: REASONS FOR JUDGMENTS AND DECISIONS

1. Reasons shall be given for judgments as well as for decisions declaring applications admissible or inadmissible.
2. If a judgment does not represent, in whole or in part, the unanimous opinion of the judges, any judge shall be entitled to deliver a separate opinion.

ART. 46: BINDING FORCE AND EXECUTION OF JUDGMENTS

1. The High Contracting Parties undertake to abide by the final judgment of the Court in any case to which they are parties.
2. The final judgment of the Court shall be transmitted to the Committee of Ministers, which shall supervise its execution . . . .
4. If the Committee of Ministers considers that a High Contracting Party refuses to abide by a final judgment in a case to which it is a party, it may, after serving formal notice on that Party and by decision adopted by a majority vote of two thirds of the representatives entitled to sit on the

committee, refer to the Court the question whether that Party has failed to fulfil its obligation under paragraph 1.

5. If the Court finds a violation of paragraph 1, it shall refer the case to the Committee of Ministers for consideration of the measures to be taken . . .

Important Rules of the Court

RULE 39: INTERIM MEASURES

1. The Chamber . . . may, at the request of a party or of any other person concerned, or of [its] own motion, indicate to the parties any interim measure which [it considers] should be adopted in the interests of the parties or of the proper conduct of the proceedings.

RULE 61: PILOT-JUDGMENT PROCEDURE

1. The Court may initiate a pilot-judgment procedure and adopt a pilot judgment where the facts of an application reveal . . . the existence of a structural or systemic problem or other similar dysfunction which has given rise or may give rise to similar applications.
3. The Court shall in its pilot judgment identify both the nature of the structural or systemic problem or other dysfunction as established as well as the type of remedial measures which the Contracting Party concerned is required to take at the domestic level . . .

CONSTITUTIONAL CONSIDERATIONS

From the perspective of Kantian theory, the regime's constitutional character after Protocol no. 11 and incorporation, is unproblematic. Once an international legal system meets the criteria of a CLO, as such, its constitutional nature is presumed. Kant, after all, defined as inherently "constitutional," any set of stable arrangements capable of helping a community achieve a Rightful condition. Further, as we have argued, a modern Kantian-congruent system of justice must include a judicially enforceable charter of rights and a trustee court, features that are basic to constitutionalism today (chapters 2 and 3).

In addition, since the 1990s, a growing group of scholars have deployed constitutional styles of analysis in their explanations of how treaty-based regimes,[3] as well as private arenas of transnational

[3] Walker (2008b); Stone Sweet (2009a). On the idea of a supranational constitutional court, see Fabbrini and Maduro (2017).

activity,[4] have emerged and evolved. This "constitutional turn" has provoked controversy, precisely because the term *constitutional* is heavily freighted, conceptually and normatively, with idealized representations drawn from the history of the nation state.[5] With regard to the European Convention on Human Rights (ECHR), scholars, judges, and even some state officials are now debating the appropriateness of the label.[6] In our view, the growing intensity of this debate is a robust indicator of the mounting importance of the Convention and its Court within domestic legal systems.

In any event, the European Court performs functions that are unambiguously "constitutional." The Court protects the rights of individuals within and beyond the state: a "justice" function. It supervises the rights-regarding activities of all national officials: a "monitoring" function. And it authoritatively determines the content and scope of convention rights on an ongoing basis: an "oracular," law-creating function. Put in terms of the Kantian theory developed in this book, these are omnilateral responsibilities of trusteeship.[7]

When one considers the combined effects of Protocol no. 11 and incorporation, another set of constitutional features appear. The Court not only confronts cases that would definitively be classified as "constitutional" by domestic judges, Strasbourg is likely to receive most important claims that national apex courts reject. The Court resolves tensions between rights and state interests in light of the proportionality principle, just as the most powerful domestic rights-protecting courts in the world do. It has steadily raised standards with regard to every Convention right; it holds that its precedents bind all national judges in the system; and it routinely indicates how a state must reform its law, within a stipulated deadline, in order to avoid future violations.

The incorporation process, too, provides support for the constitutional view.[8] Virtually all states have integrated the Convention into

[4] Teubner (2004); Pollicino (2018).
[5] Kumm (2009); Walker (2008a).
[6] Stone Sweet (2009b); Greer and Wildhaber (2012).
[7] Chapter 2.
[8] Chapter 3.

national hierarchies of norms, most commonly, at a rank enforceable against ordinary statute. Some domestic systems bestow on the ECHR express constitutional status, and still others a supra-constitutional rank. Domestification of the Convention expanded judicial authority across Europe, while undermining (or obliterating altogether) classic separation of powers doctrines that had long constrained judicial review. From the perspective adopted in this book, incorporation helped to complete, or positively instantiate, domestic systems of constitutional justice. These dynamics are most visible when we observe the evolution of national orders that (i) did not have a native and judicially enforceable bill of rights, and/or (ii) whose courts had been prohibited from enforcing rights against statute. In such situations, the incorporated Convention constitutes the polity's charter of rights, filling the void.

Not everyone will agree that these considerations add up to a defensible case for a constitutional understanding of the Convention and its Court. The most important objection issues from the fact that the judges in Strasbourg—unlike national constitutional judges—do not possess the power to invalidate acts found to be in conflict with the ECHR. Protocol no. 11 fully exposed all state organs, including apex courts, to the supervisory machinery of the ECHR. But states did not give the Court competences to exercise "sovereign" authority within domestic law.[9] On paper, the Court's remedial authority is tightly constrained: if the Court finds a violation, it may order the offending state to pay monetary damages, called "just satisfaction" (Art. 41 ECHR). In the post-Protocol no. 11 context, the absence of authority to invalidate national acts exacerbates an institutional weakness, in so far as one expects the Court both (i) to render retrospective justice in individual cases, and (ii) to ensure the ongoing effectiveness of Convention rights, at the domestic level, across Europe.

[9] A feature consistent with Kant's vision in *Perpetual Peace*.

We see no persuasive reason to deny an *international* court's "constitutional" status on the basis of that court's incapacity to exercise direct authority within *domestic* legal orders. Certainly, Kant would not accept such an argument. As an empirical matter, the more national judges enforce Convention rights, and accept the pedagogical authority of the Strasbourg Court, the less significant the objection. What matters is how decentralized sovereignty works. In the Protocol no. 11 regime, the Court's formal authority to engage in compliance dialogues with national systems has been upgraded and formalized. In the rest of this chapter, we explain why and how this has occurred.

THE CONVENTION AND ITS COURT

In 1950, the new Council of Europe completed its first major venture: drafting the Convention. The treaty was negotiated in the immediate aftermath of the Holocaust and a cataclysmic war, and as part of a reconstruction of European law and politics. This context heavily conditioned the "original intent,"[10] of the fourteen initial signatories of the treaty. In strikingly Kantian terms, the High Contracting Parties jointly committed to rights protection to help them prevent future wars, bolster liberal democracy, and express a common European identity.[11]

The representatives of the founding states, however, were deeply divided on the question of judicial review. In 1950, they agreed to disagree. After voting seven to four against creating a court with compulsory jurisdiction, they made acceptance of judicial authority voluntary, through an optional protocol. The Contracting Parties also made the individual petition optional. They placed an administrative body, the Commission of Human Rights (which began operation

[10] Nichol (2005). [11] See Preamble: Box 4.

in 1954), between applicants and the Court (which opened only in 1959). Until it was abolished by Protocol no. 11, the Commission filtered applications, which would reach the Court only after the former had completed its work and, even then, only under certain conditions.

Today, the European CLO is comprised of four interlocking components. First, all forty-seven members of the regime have incorporated the ECHR. As a result, the Convention can be pleaded by individuals and enforced by national judges, as *domestic* law. Second, through Protocol no. 11, national systems of rights protection are linked directly to a legal realm beyond the state. Every individual, regardless of nationality or citizenship, may petition the European Court, with regard to any public act enforced by a Contracting State, once domestic remedies are exhausted. Third, the ECHR comprises an autonomous source of rights doctrine. The Strasbourg Court treats the Convention as a "living" instrument, which it interprets and applies in order to secure the effectiveness of rights progressively, as European society evolves.[12] States have no lawful means of blocking applications or the Court's rulings, which are final. Fourth, national judges, through incorporation, possess and exercise their own autonomous capacity to interpret and apply the Convention.[13]

In evaluating the Court-as-trustee, the criterion that matters most is its capacity to positively influence standards of rights protection in the regime over time. We label this capacity: "effectiveness." The effectiveness of the Court is a variable. It will vary over time, and across different domains of rights protection at the domestic level, under the influence of myriad—primarily, domestic-level—variables.

Three conditions are necessary for *any* court to accrete influence within the broader legal and political environment in which it is embedded: (i) the institutional competence to determine the law in

[12] Chapter 5. [13] Bjorge (2015); chapter 5.

an authoritative manner; (ii) a steady caseload; and (iii) the development of a minimally robust conception of precedent as binding. In the ECHR, these conditions are not sufficient, since the Court must rely on national officials to give agency to its rulings. It is primarily up to legislators, executives, and judges to determine how to respond to the evolution of the Court's jurisprudence. For the Convention to make a difference domestically, officials must take decisions that credit the Court as an authoritative source of law. That point made, these three factors have blended in ways that have helped to strengthen, over time, the Convention's impact on domestic rights protection.

Powers are a first determinate of influence. The Strasbourg Court is a paradigmatic example of an international trustee court. By definition,[14] a trustee court possesses compulsory jurisdiction with respect to state compliance with their treaty obligations, and the authority to censure them for compliance failures. The Court is the authoritative interpreter of the treaty; and the Contracting Parties have little prospect of overturning rulings they find objectionable.

The core of the Convention is a charter of rights. Article 1 requires all High Contracting Parties "to secure to everyone within their jurisdiction the rights and freedoms" enumerated in the Convention. The Court's mission is to ensure that states meet this obligation, and its authority to do so is largely insulated from the latter's direct control, except by way of treaty revision. Article 32 grants the Court exclusive, final jurisdiction over "all matters concerning the interpretation and application of the Convention," and gives the Court (not states) the competence to determine the limits of its own jurisdiction. Under Article 46, members "undertake to abide by the final judgment of the Court in any case to which they are parties." Article 46 also places states, in the guise of the Committee of Ministers of the Council of Europe, under a collective duty to "supervise [the]

[14] Stone Sweet and Brunell (2013).

execution" of the Court's final judgments, the activities of which we discuss below. States, as a collective body, could overturn an objectionable interpretation of the Court, but only by revising the Convention. The prospect is a virtual impossibility (and has yet to occur), given the decision-rule governing the regime's revision: unanimity of all of its members.

The Court also possesses implied powers of interpretation, which were strongly reinforced by Protocol no. 11. Convention norms, like modern rights provisions more generally, are textually open-ended and incomplete.[15] Few rights are expressed in absolute terms. Article 2 (right to life), Article 3 (prohibition of torture, and inhuman and degrading treatment), and Article 4 (the prohibition of slavery and forced labor) are the major exceptions. In addition, the Court has constructed Article 13 (the right to an effective remedy for the violation of Convention rights) as a master procedural guarantee—of access to justice. Most rights, however, are qualified by a derogation clause, which permits states to restrict their scope under certain conditions (Box 5).

As research on the *travaux préparatoires* shows,[16] the founding states were never able to settle differences concerning the nature and content of the rights they enshrined. They disagreed, for example, about whether the Convention expressed minimum common denominator conceptions of basic rights and nothing more, or if it established a legal foundation for a more expansive evolution of rights. This disagreement necessarily conditioned attitudes toward establishing a mode of judicial enforcement. With Protocol no. 11, the Contracting Parties delegated strong implied interpretive powers on the Court to "complete"—that is, to dynamically construct—rights over time, thereby rendering them more determinate.[17]

[15] Chapters 2 and 5. [16] Nichol (2005).
[17] On incomplete contracting in international regimes, see Stone Sweet (2004); Stone Sweet and Brunell (2013).

In addition to competences, judges must have a caseload. Individual rights claims comprise, almost entirely,[18] the Court's docket. Each petition contains a detailed record of the domestic decisions that have, allegedly, violated the claimant's entitlements under the Convention. Applications open a window onto the internal organization of national systems, through which the Court will review domestic law and practice, in light of Convention requirements.

The Court not only receives a steady stream of cases, the flood of petitions threatens to overwhelm the regime altogether. The European Commission of Human Rights registered 49 individual applications in the entire decade of the 1960s, 163 in the 1970s, and 455 in the 1980s. With enlargement following the collapse of Communism (1990s), and the entry into force of Protocol no. 11 (on November 1, 1998), petitions skyrocketed. In 1999, the Registry received 8,400 complaints, then a record; and the figure exploded thereafter. The Court gathered some 65,800 applications in 2013, and more than 150,000 in the latest three-year period (2014–2016). Although the Registry and judges have made significant progress in reducing arrears, the Court is overloaded. The annual rate of judgments on the merits shows a similar trend. Through 1982, the Court had issued, in its history, only sixty-one full rulings pursuant to applications by individuals. It issued 250 fully reasoned judgments in 1995 and 1,625 in 2010.[19] In the 2001–2016 period, the Court rendered 17,861 such judgments, an average of 1,116 per year,[20] the vast majority of which find at least one violation. In 2016, violations were found in more than 85% of judgments on the merits.[21] Under Protocol no. 11, the

[18] Through 2016, there have been only twenty-two interstate applications, although some of these have resulted in important Court judgments. ECHR: Inter-states Applications (2016).

[19] The source of these data is the annual *Survey of Activities* published by the European Court of Human Rights on its website.

[20] Committee of Ministers: Annual Report (2016: 197). Available at: https://www.coe.int/en/web/execution/annual-reports.

[21] Committee of Ministers: Annual Report (2016: 201).

Strasbourg Court is far and away the most active rights-protecting court in the world. But it is also a victim of its own success: the demand for rights protection sharply exceeds the regime's capacities.

The development of progressive, precedent-based case law is the third factor conditioning effectiveness. Although the drafters widely (but not unanimously) considered the Convention to have established minimal standards, its judges have consistently interpreted rights in a progressive manner. Even prior to the entry into force of Protocol no. 11, the Court had insisted that the ECHR was a "living instrument,"[22] evolving as European society does. In a bold effort to fortify its position as trustee, it declared that the core of its jurisprudence exerted *erga omnes* effects,[23] binding all state parties (discussed below). Alongside a strong teleology of purpose and effectiveness, it also developed an overarching comparative methodology, one that highlights a creative role in the Convention's development. In defining the content and scope of Convention rights, the Court will typically survey the evolution of law and practice in the state parties, and often beyond Europe, in light of its own jurisprudence. Where it finds an emerging consensus on a new, higher standard of rights protection among states, it may move to consolidate this consensus as the new standard binding upon all members. In chapter 5, we examine these dynamics in detail.

Strasbourg judgments have strong, but not rigid, precedential force. The Court's jurisprudence structures the argumentation of applicants and defendant states, and grounds its progressive moves in recursive, self-reinforcing processes. It does so in the name of "legal certainty and the orderly development of [its] case law."[24] The Court will abandon a line of case law in order to correct an earlier error, or

[22] See Letsas (2013) for an overview of the doctrine, and a normative assessment of its institutional legitimacy.

[23] Its authoritative interpretations of the Conventions apply to all states, not just the parties in a particular case.

[24] *Cossey v. the United Kingdom* (Plenary, 27 September 1990), para. 35.

"to ensure that the interpretation of the Convention reflects societal change and remains in line with present day conditions."[25]

This mode of governance raises an empirical issue that lies at the heart of our concern with effectiveness. Convention rights will have impact beyond any individual case only in so far as national officials take into account the Court's judgments in their own decision-making. Incorporation, being generative of legal duties in domestic law, may induce national officials to do so. But the Convention does not formally require incorporation, or the acceptance of the *erga omnes* effects of the Court's rulings. Moreover, national officials, including judges, will normally possess some measure of discretion—called a "margin of appreciation"—with regard to implementing Convention rights and applying the Court's case law. State officials, including judges, may seek to resist the Court, choosing to reject or delay compliance with its rulings. They may choose to ignore the Court's interpretation of the Convention, even when on point, and even where Convention rights have been fully domesticated. Thus, the development of a coherent jurisprudence is a necessary condition, but not sufficient alone or in combination with the other two factors, for the ECHR to exert influence on national legal orders.

In summary, the Court is well positioned to exercise effective trusteeship. On the input side, most important violations of Convention rights will eventually be referred to Strasbourg, by single or multiple applicants. On the output side, the Court has produced a dense and elaborate case law that provides an authoritative construction of Convention rights and, thus, guidance to those national officials who will interpret and apply the Convention on their own. These points made, serious deficiencies in domestic systems have resulted in overload and crisis, threatening the Court's mission in obvious ways.

[25] *Cossey*, para. 35.

OVERLOAD AND REFORM

The vertiginous numbers of applications, rulings, and pending cases tell only part of the story, and nothing about the nature and relative importance of the claims, or of the domestic contexts that generate them. Simplifying a complex set of issues, we can distinguish between quite different situations that the new (post-1998) Court regularly confronts. In a first situation—one of "fine-tuning"[26]—the Court seeks to enhance performance in domestic systems that otherwise possess relatively good records of compliance with the Convention. Applications enable the Court to identify gaps in protection, which it may use to encourage states to raise standards. In this mode, the Court has evolved new protections for discreet communities (e.g., for transgender people or the Roma people) or for specific situations (e.g., hate speech or refugee and asylum claims). In post-Protocol no. 11 Europe, the Court will never want for such opportunities. Once Convention standards begin to rise, the Court can expect to be activated, relatively systematically, by individuals seeking to change domestic law in lower standard states. These dynamics can be accentuated by local politics, as when two domestic apex courts disagree with one another, when tensions between legislators and courts thwart legal change, or when a constitutional court seeks to resist Strasbourg's pedagogical moves. The European Court, in interpreting Convention rights in expansive, open-ended ways, creates pressure for national adaptation, including through the strengthening of those domestic constituencies seeking to raise standards. Every national system is exposed to such dynamics, including high-standard states such as Germany, Ireland, and Spain. In this situation, the Court unambiguously plays the role of an omnilateral lawmaker and external regulator of the internal operations of domestic orders.[27]

[26] Keller and Stone Sweet (2008: ch. 6). [27] Chapter 5.

The Court faces a qualitatively different problem when it encounters failures to protect rights of a deep, systemic nature. Across Europe, for example, many states find it virtually impossible to meet Convention standards under Article 6(1) ECHR, which requires judicial proceedings to be completed in a reasonable time. In this area, floods of clone applications from certain countries, such as Italy, have become chronic.[28] In the early 2000s, the Court flipped the burden of proof, establishing the presumption that Italy had violated Article 6 unless it could justify delays.[29] Italy is not alone. Through 2015, the Court has issued more than 5,000 judgments finding length of proceedings violations, including over 500 judgments against Turkey, and nearly as many against Poland.[30]

With enlargement into Central and Eastern Europe, and into the Balkans, the new Court confronted a third, far more serious, problem: massive failures to provide protection of the most basic rights, including the prohibition of torture and inhuman and degrading treatment. In some states, including Georgia, Moldova, Russia, Turkey, and the Ukraine, political officials and judges regularly fail to uphold principles of rule of law established by their own constitutions. In this situation, the Court functions as a stand-in for ineffective national trustee courts. Recent political challenges to national constitutional courts (and judicial power, more generally) in Hungary and Poland will produce waves of new applications.[31] As the Court well knows, the more ineffective are national apex courts, the greater will be its own burden.

[28] In *Ferrari v. Italy* (GC, 28 July 1999), para. 21, the Court reminded Italy that it had already issued sixty-five judgments, and the Committee of Ministers more than 1,400 resolutions, against the state for excessive length of proceedings.

[29] See Kuijer (2013: 779–80).

[30] ECHR: Statistics by State: Violations by Article and by State 1959–2015. Available at: http://www.echr.coe.int/Documents/Stats_violation_1959_2015_ENG.pdf.

[31] By May of 2017, Hungary's pending application count had already risen to 10,000, putting it in the top three. ECHR: Pending Cases 2017 (updated September 30, 2017). Available at: http://www.echr.coe.int/Documents/Stats_pending_2017_BIL.pdf.

The data show that a small group of defective domestic systems of constitutional justice account for the vast bulk of the Court's docket. At the end of 2016, some 79,750 applications were pending.[32] In the parlance of the Registry, judges and staff had certified these applications as "admissible," and then assigned them to a "judicial formation." The backlog is all the more impressive, since officials typically reject well over 97% received per annum as "inadmissible." Six states—the Ukraine (18,171 pending applications), Turkey (12,575), Russia (7,821), Hungary (8,962), Romania (7,402), and Italy (6,180)—have generated 77% of the backlog. Ten states—adding Georgia (2,077), Poland (1,818), Azerbaijan (1,662), and Moldova (1,283) to the top six—have produced a whopping 85% of all pending cases.[33]

Very early in the life of the new Protocol no. 11 system, leading members of the Court came to the realization that the regime could not survive on the basis of a narrow view of the justice function, one that prioritizes just satisfaction for victims on a case-by-case basis. Saving the regime from collapse[34] required a broader, and necessarily more systemic and constitutional, vision of justice. It would be impossible for the Court to regain control of its docket without a more formal engagement with domestic authorities. These reforms constitutionalized the regime in all but name.

DOCKET CONTROL

Although the Contracting Parties had their own strategic reasons for absorbing the post-Communist states into the ECHR, few if any of the new members were prepared to meet the regime's standards.

[32] Committee of Ministers: Annual Report (2016: 193).
[33] Committee of Ministers: Annual Report (2016: 192).
[34] Hunt (2003: 483).

The Council of Europe set minimal thresholds for the new members, betting that accession to the Convention would contribute to democratization and the consolidation of rights-based constitutionalism. The most intensive scholarship on the question has demonstrated that accession did, in fact, make a positive difference.[35] But it also imposed a crushing burden on the Court.

Under Protocol no. 11, applications skyrocketed, more than doubling in the first five years. By 2009, the Registry found itself with a yearly deficit of more than 21,000 cases: it processed as admissible about 1,800 new applications per month *more* than were being disposed of through judicial decision; and the cumulative backlog of pending applications reached nearly 120,000.[36] By 2009, the delay between application and decision on the merits had exceeded five years. Arguably, the European Court had fallen out of compliance with its own jurisprudence on Article 6 ECHR (right to a fair trial "within a reasonable time").[37] Through a series of procedural innovations, the Court has shrunk the backlog at an astounding rate. By 2016, the number of pending applications had fallen to 79,950 (if up from 64,850 in 2015).[38] Overload, and its underling causes, remains the Court's most significant problem, but the crisis is less acute.

What happened to all of the pending applications? The formal answer is that the Court, supported by the Committee of Ministers, devised new procedures to filter and join cases, such that the vast majority of applications are disposed of without full Court review. The deeper answer is that the Court moved aggressively to reinforce its status as the regime's trustee whose primary purpose is to govern a multi-level system of rights protection, not to provide a remedy for every applicant.

[35] See Motoc and Ziemele, eds. (2016) and the literature cited in chapter 3.

[36] ECHR: Analysis of Statistics (2009). Available at: http://www.echr.coe.int/Documents/Stats_analysis_2009_ENG.pdf.

[37] Donald and Leach (2016: 3).

[38] Committee of Ministers: Annual Report (2016: 191).

Protocol no. 14, which entered into force in 2010,[39] facilitated this transition.[40] It codified a number of filtering mechanisms already in place, and reorganized how the Court would deal with applications once accepted. Petitions could now be rejected as "manifestly ill-founded," or where claimants had suffered "no significant disadvantage."[41] The protocol also introduced two key reforms long advocated by the Court. Proceedings would be organized into formations of one judge, a three-judge committee, a seven-judge chamber, and the seventeen-judge Grand Chamber. Dispositive decisions could now be taken quickly by a smaller number of people. The Court immediately interpreted the reform as conferring virtually unlimited discretion to process applications as its judges and staff—called the Registry—see fit, permitting it to focus on the most important claims. Under Protocol no. 14, the Court has elaborated its own basic rules governing the admissibility process.[42]

Today, less than 3% of all applications will result in a ruling on the merits. The Court will have jettisoned the rest for failure to meet procedural requirements or admissibility criteria, the most controversial of which enable the Court to reject claims when "manifestly ill-founded," or upon a determination that the petitioner has not

[39] The final draft of Protocol no. 14 was produced in 2004, but Russia blocked its adoption until 2010.

[40] It was well understood that Protocol no. 14 fused managerial and constitutional logics. As Thorbjørn Jagland, then the Council of Europe's Secretary General, and Jean-Paul Costa, then President of the Court, put it in a joint statement: "[T]he entry into force of Protocol No. 14 represents a crucial step in improving the effectiveness of the Court and the protection of human rights in Europe. The Convention establishes the foundations of a common legal space across Europe. Protocol 14 will permit the Court to concentrate more on cases that raise important human rights issues, so it can play its role most effectively." Council of Europe Press Release (May 31, 2010). Available at: https://wcd.coe.int/ViewDoc.jsp?p=&id=1628875&Site=DC&BackColorInternet=F5CA75&BackColorIntranet=F5CA75&BackColorLogged=A9BACE&direct=true.

[41] ECHR Protocol no. 14. The final text does not include a much-debated proposal to give the Court certiorari-like powers; see Shelton (2016: 307).

[42] A new Rule 47, which came into force in 2014, tightened application requirements. See the ECHR: *Practical Guide on Admissibility Criteria* (2014). Available at: http://www.echr.coe.int/Documents/Admissibility_guide_ENG.pdf.

suffered a "significant disadvantage."[43] Applications will typically be marked "manifestly ill-founded" if they ask the Court to act, in effect, as an appellate jurisdiction for purposes of interpreting national law (or factual findings—such as guilt), or when they fail to ground allegations in principles derived from the Court's case law.[44] Strasbourg officials apply the "no significant disadvantage" standard somewhat more sparingly, mostly in situations where the damage is financial, and the amount in question small (under 500 euros at present).[45]

Docket control serves another ancillary purpose: the strengthening of the Court's identity as a constitutional organ. The staff and judges rely heavily on declarations of a "well-established case law," for example, to avoid writing full judgments on the merits. Doing so reinforces precedent-based governance. Streamlining admissibility is only one—managerial—component of a wider, and more profound, process through which the Court has actively sought to enhance its authority as the regime's trustee. Underwriting the Court's strategy is the constitutional principle of subsidiarity, which entails relying heavily on national courts to act as "faithful trustees" of the regime at the national level.[46]

SUBSIDIARITY

Any stable legal framework that organizes how discreet systems interact in ways that produce legal effects performs a meaningfully "constitutional" function.[47] Obvious examples include the rules that

[43] De Londras and Dzehtsiarou (2015: 530). [44] *Admissibility Guide*: 83.

[45] *Admissibility Guide*: 90. [46] Bjorge (2015).

[47] In the international realm, the EU underwent a process of "constitutionalisation" with the gradual acceptance, by the national courts, of the basics of the Court of Justice's doctrines of direct effect, supremacy, and other principles (chapter 3). In the world of international arbitration, the 1958 New York Convention requires national courts to acknowledge the autonomy of the arbitral order, and to enforce its awards, subject to certain conditions; Stone Sweet and Grisel (2017: chs.1 and 6).

undergird federations, enabling the federal and state "levels" to govern collectively, even when competences overlap. It is worth noting that the first federal constitutions (the United States and Switzerland, for example) were understood to be compacts among sovereigns. The European Court, too, has been engaged in constructing such a framework for the ECHR. Protocol no. 14 blends managerial and constitutional rationales. In other areas, the Court has generated legal doctrines meant to establish the rules of engagement between Strasbourg and domestic legal orders. Most of these doctrines implicate, or are covered by, the principle of "subsidiarity," which only superficially disguises their centralizing tendencies.

Subsidiarity is a fundamental, constitutional feature of the regime.[48] Some judges and scholars stress that subsidiarity creates a "rebuttable presumption for the local,"[49] shifting the "center of gravity" for primary rights protection towards the domestic level. From the perspective of the CLO, subsidiarity is also product of incorporation: national officials are under an obligation to fulfill the rights of individuals; and the Court supervises how they do so. The Court's own embrace of subsidiarity is predicated on an enhancement of Strasbourg's interpretive authority, and a strengthening of supervisory powers. Far from being a placeholder for deference, subsidiarity has entrenched the Court's constitutional centrality.[50] Primary indicators of this development include the enhancement of the precedential authority of the Court's case law, and the expanding scope of obligations flowing from Article 13 (effective remedy).

[48] Besson (2016: 70); Mowbray (2015: 313). Walker (2015b: 1) describes subsidiarity as "the idea that the more central and encompassing authority or authorities within any multi-level or multi-polar political arrangement, should have a subsidiary or support function, performing only those tasks that cannot be performed effectively at a more immediate or local level."

[49] Føllesdal (2016: 148).

[50] As Besson (2011: 157) puts it: "Subsidiarity requires not only the 'embededdness' of ECHR rights in domestic law, but also the mutual responsiveness between domestic and European interpretations of the Convention."

As we have seen, the Court's capacity to fulfill its subsidiary function relies heavily on domestic incorporation, not just of the ECHR, but also of the Strasbourg Court's jurisprudence. Questions concerning the *erga omnes* effects of the Court's judgments remain in debate within most domestic systems, but the issue is well settled in Strasbourg.[51] As early as 1978, in *Ireland v. the United Kingdom*, the Court asserted its authority to build rights jurisprudence for all, beyond the case at hand:

> The Court's judgments in fact serve not only to decide those cases brought before the Court but, more generally, to elucidate, safeguard and develop the rules instituted by the Convention, thereby contributing to the observance by the States of the engagements undertaken by them as Contracting Parties.[52]

By 2009, it could confidently state that:

> [T]he Court provides final authoritative interpretation of the rights and freedoms . . . [and it] will consider whether the national authorities have sufficiently taken into account the principles flowing from its judgments on similar issues, even when they concern other States.[53]

Not every member has explicitly embraced Strasbourg's interpretive authority, but many have.[54] As discussed in chapter 5, domestic

[51] Although there is no textual grant of interpretive authority in the Convention, the Court has (through its use of precedent) asserted interpretive authority, making its judgments an integral part of the ECHR; a point made forcefully by Besson (2011: 134–5).

[52] *Ireland v. the United Kigndom* (Plenary, 18 January 1978), para. 154.

[53] *Opuz v. Turkey* (9 June 2009), para. 163.

[54] Besson (2011: 141–2) found, that by 2011, Switzerland, the UK, Ireland, Belgium, Spain, the Netherlands, Croatia, and the Ukraine had formally recognized the *erga omnes* effects of the Court's judgments. Motoc and Ziemele, eds. (2016: 4) reports that the Polish Constitutional Court has also done so. The courts of many more states have

judges have a strong interest in recognizing the *erga omnes* effects of the Court's important judgments. In doing do, they enlist a partner in the building of their own competences and expertise, while active resistance would risk censure in Strasbourg.

Of course, the Court's effectiveness partly depends upon its own precedential authority, which recognition of the *erga omnes* effects of its jurisprudence ratifies. As important, the move helps the Court manage its overload crisis, reducing redundant decision-making. The Office of the Jurisconsult within the Court's Registry is tasked with ensuring that the Court's case law is consistent across chambers, leaving it to the Grand Chamber to decide when settled case law ought to be overturned.

The Court has expanded its remedial powers in line with its claim to strong interpretive authority. Although Strasbourg must rely on national courts to set aside national law that is incompatible with the Convention, the Court has asserted its own competence to declare incompatibility. Starting in the early 2000s, the Court began requiring systemic changes to domestic law or practice through the taking of general measures.[55] In *Scozzari and Giunta v. Italy* (2000), the Court held that:

> [A] judgment in which the Court finds a breach imposes on the respondent State a legal obligation not just to pay those concerned the sums awarded by way of just satisfaction, but also to choose . . . the general and/or, if appropriate, individual measures to be adopted in their domestic legal order to put an end to the violation found by the Court and to redress so far as possible the effects.[56]

accepted that the Court's case law is presumptively binding, although the presumption may be overridden under certain circumstances.

[55] Rainey, Wicks, and Ovey (2014: 59–62).

[56] *Scozzari and Giunta v. Italy* (GC, 13 July 2000), para. 249.

The Convention does not confer upon the Court express competences to order general or individual measures. It has nevertheless become common practice.

In 2013, the Court found that a Ukrainian judge had been wrongfully dismissed, in violation of the Article 6(1) right to an independent and impartial tribunal, and the right to privacy guaranteed by Article 8.[57] Assessing the state of judicial independence in the country, the Court determined that both general and individual measures were required to remedy the violation. After gesturing toward the principle that "[Strasbourg] judgments are essentially declaratory in nature and that, in general, it is primarily for the State concerned to choose . . . the means to be used in its domestic legal order to discharge its obligation under Article 46,"[58] the Court declared that, "with a view to helping the respondent State," it would "seek to indicate the type of measure that might be taken in order to put an end to a violation it has found to exist."[59] The Court then ordered the State (i) "to secure the applicant's reinstatement to the post of judge of the Supreme Court at the earliest possible date"[60] (an individual measure), and (ii) to undertake "legislative reform involving the restructuring of the institutional basis of the system"[61] (a general measure).

Consolidation of the Court's interpretive authority has led most states to evolve a host of mechanisms for assessing and implementing the European Court's jurisprudence.[62] In a recent study of parliamentary mechanisms, Donald and Leach identify three types of systems: cross-cutting (no specific human rights committee, but every committee is tasked with addressing human rights issues within their substantive fields); specialized (specific committee tasked with reviewing human rights compatibility); and hybrid (several

[57] *Oleksandr Volkov v. Ukraine* (9 January 2013).
[58] *Oleksandr Volkov*, para. 194.
[59] *Oleksandr Volkov*, para. 195.
[60] *Oleksandr Volkov*, para. 208.
[61] *Oleksandr Volkov*, para. 200.
[62] For an examination of such mechanisms in eighteen states, see Keller and Stone Sweet (2008: chs. 2–10).

committees have certain human rights review functions).[63] The cross-cutting countries include states where every parliamentary committee addresses human rights compatibility (such as the Netherlands and Spain); but in other states, there is no obligatory mechanism for reviewing compliance with Strasbourg (e.g., Sweden and Russia).[64] These categories, too, are not static. The Romanian Parliament did not have an institutionalized mechanism for monitoring implementation of the Court's judgments until 2009, and even now the sub-committee tasked with monitoring is institutionally weak (when first created, its only advisor was not a lawyer).[65]

Coordination mechanisms can be preventative, reactive, or both. The Dutch Parliament acknowledges the immediate, binding nature of the Court's judgments, taken with regard to any situation, in any Contracting Party.[66] The United Kingdom employs a preventative model in which ministries are required to prepare reports on the human rights implications of all legislation.[67] In Scandinavian countries, an Ombudsman typically invokes the ECHR when monitoring the governments' human rights protection.[68] Poland's Ministry of Justice and Foreign Affairs works with the national courts to identify and translate key judgments into Polish, while Germany enlists independent academics to compile annual reports on Strasbourg case law.[69]

Two new draft protocols represent further efforts toward constitutionalization. Draft Protocol no. 15 (Box 4) would codify the concept of margin of appreciation and insert it directly into the Convention, while shortening the deadline for filing claims, and

[63] Donald and Leach (2016: 76).

[64] Donald and Leach (2016: 76–8). Nonetheless, in Sweden, members of legislative committees may raise considerations of compatibility with the Convention of any bill, as can the Law Council, which is composed of judges from the high courts (Wiklund 2008: 209–10).

[65] Donald and Leach (2016: 20).

[66] De Wet (2008: 237).

[67] Besson (2008: 73).

[68] Wiklund (2008: 220).

[69] Donald and Leach (2016: 27).

strengthening the "no significant disadvantage" criteria for inadmissibility.[70] Draft Protocol no. 16 would grant the Court the power to issue advisory opinions. Under this proposal, apex national courts would have discretion to send questions of Convention interpretation directly to Strasbourg.[71] The process, non-binding and non-adversarial, would result in a Grand Chamber ruling on questions of Convention law. If adopted, Protocol no. 16 would strengthen the capacity of national courts to set the agenda in their dialogues with Strasbourg, while providing the Court with the opportunity to enhance the effectiveness of Convention rights without waiting for applications, and without censuring a national court.[72]

PILOT RULINGS

As we have seen, the new Protocol no. 11 regime quickly flooded with applications, tens of thousands of which alleged rights violations of a scale and complexity rarely encountered in Strasbourg.[73] Petitions clustered in ways that starkly revealed problems that states appeared to be unable or unwilling to resolve.[74] Not surprisingly, case-by-case compensatory justice proved to be woefully ineffective: once the Court had awarded compensation in one case, thousands more similarly situated applicants would come forward demanding just satisfaction. By 2003, it was estimated that around 60% of all the Court's judgments

[70] ECHR: Protocol 15 Explanatory Report. Available at: http://www.echr.coe.int/Documents/Protocol_15_explanatory_report_ENG.pdf.

[71] Protocol 15 Explanatory Report.

[72] Giannopoulos (2015: 337–8). Partly for these reasons, the CJEU declared the 2013 Draft Agreement on EU accession to the ECHR to be incompatible with EU law; see Halberstam (2015: 112); chapter 3.

[73] That is not the say that the Court had never confronted serious human rights violations prior to the inclusion of the Central and Eastern European countries. Conflict in Turkey and Northern Ireland, for instance, had given rise to grave rights abuses.

[74] Haider (2013: 3–5).

on the merits concerned repetitive cases.[75] In some countries—where systemic problems ran so deep that they touched, for example, nearly every criminal defendant or every civil litigant waiting for the execution of judicial decisions (Italy), or everyone whose land had been expropriated by a past communist government—the number of clone petitions on virtually identical facts exploded. The Court lacked the personnel and budgetary resources to deal with the situation, and states found themselves exposed to a seemingly unlimited number of claimants.

At the regime level, the Court and the Committee of Ministers partnered to design a first order response—now called the "pilot judgment"—which permits Strasbourg to adjudicate a representative case, or a set of joined cases, while keeping similar claims at bay. Legal systems deal with multi-plaintiff claims in various ways, the American class action model being just one.[76] Prior to its first pilot ruling, in a series of important judgments, the Court had already ordered domestic authorities to revise national legislation in order to fully comply with a ruling.[77] Sadurski rightly finds in these early decisions the seeds of constitutionalization, which have since taken strong root.[78] While pilot judgments vary in the specificity of the stipulated remedies, their defining feature is that they require the state to implement general measures capable of bringing the national system into conformity with the Convention, within a specified time frame.

The first pilot judgment so named, *Broniowski v. Poland* (2004),[79] concerned expropriation of property resulting from the redrawing of international boundaries after the Second World War. The Court had been bombarded by applications arising out of Poland's arrangements

[75] Haider (2013: 5). [76] Sainati (2015: 151).

[77] The origins of the pilot procedure are murky, given that the Court began developing its components before the term was coined. According to Haider (2013: 26), the term "pilot judgment" was used for the first time in 2003 in the Final Report of the Steering Committee for the Committee of Ministers.

[78] Sadurski (2009: 413). [79] *Broniowski v. Poland* (GC, 22 June 2004).

to compensate former property holders, with a potential number of claimants reaching 80,000.[80] Throughout a drawn-out policy process lasting many years, legislators pointedly ignored rulings by the Polish apex courts. In 2002, the Polish Constitutional Court ruled that the arrangements—which had resulted in applicants being awarded only about 2% of the assessed value of their holdings—comprised a "fictional instrument of compensation," and were thus a disproportionate infringement on the right to property. It also gave relatively precise instructions as to how relevant statutes should be revised, not least to meet basic principles of "rule of law," a position echoed by the Supreme Court.[81] The European Court, siding squarely with the Polish judges, held that the compensation scheme violated the right to property under Article 1 of Protocol no. 1,[82] while criticizing legislative authorities for their "obstructive action."[83]

Pilot rulings position the Strasbourg Court to don the mantle of a supplementary, domestic constitutional court. In *Broniowski*, the Court held that Poland's responsibility under the Convention required statutory and administrative reform:

> [I]n view of the systemic situation which it has identified, the Court would observe that general measures are . . . called for in execution of the present judgment, measures which must take into account the many people affected. Above all, the measures adopted must be such as to remedy the systemic defect . . . so as not to overburden the Convention system with large numbers of applications deriving from the same cause. . . . In this context the Court's concern is to facilitate the most [timely] and effective resolution of a dysfunction established in national human rights protection.[84]

[80] Yildiz (2015: 84).

[81] The next year, the Polish Supreme Court held that subsequent changes, which had done nothing to resolve the problem, "cannot be accepted in a democratic State governed by the rule of law and applying the principles of social justice. . . .," *Broniowski*, paras. 110, 175.

[82] *Broniowski*, paras. 186–7.

[83] *Broniowski*, para. 181.

[84] *Broniowski*, para. 193.

The move succeeded. Poland adopted new legislation in 2005, which established a compensatory regime that the European Court later found "to be effective in practice," leading it to strike more than 200 adjourned applications off the Court's rolls in 2007 and 2008.[85]

Today the procedure is codified as Rule 61 of the Rules of the Court. Once a pilot case is designated, clone applications are "adjourned," an act that suspends their adjudication pending the results of domestic reform. The Court monitors the process, seeking assurance that: (i) the reform will stop the flow of repetitive applications at its source, a systemic gap in national rights protection; and (ii) that domestic courts are able to provide an "effective remedy" for those whose applications have been adjourned. The procedure gives a constitutional gloss to Article 13, the right to an effective remedy; and it formalizes a caretaker (trusteeship) role for the Court, that of monitoring national systems of justice. At the same time, it eliminates the possibility for every (otherwise eligible) individual to be given justice in Strasbourg.[86]

Here again, one sees the importance of subsidiarity as a constitutional principle.[87] Pilot rulings starkly reveal Strasbourg's dependence on domestic legislators and judges to eliminate the defect and to furnish an appropriate remedy for past and future violations. When they do so, the Court's effectiveness—ultimately a function of the effectiveness of rights protection at the domestic level—is positively affirmed. National authorities that refuse to do so threaten the regime. Not surprisingly, the record is mixed.

To date, the Court has initiated twenty-five pilot rulings with respect to situations in fifteen states. The list includes six original signatories

[85] ECHR Factsheet: Pilot Judgments (November 2016: 12). Available at: http://www.echr.coe.int/Documents/FS_Pilot_judgments_ENG.pdf .

[86] Yildiz (2015: 86).

[87] The Court has emphasized the dual role of the pilot procedure: "on the one hand, it is intended to assist respondent States in remedying an identified defect arising from a widespread or systemic problem; on the other, it aims to ensure the effective treatment of follow-up cases"; *Greens and M.T. v. the United Kingdom* (23 November 2010), para. 117.

(Belgium, Germany, Greece, Italy, Turkey, and the UK), and ten post-Communist members (Albania, Bosnia and Herzegovina, Bulgaria, Hungary, Moldova, Romania, Russia, Serbia, Slovenia, and the Ukraine).[88] Of these, we count eleven successes,[89] in that the Court has either certified that reforms undertaken had resolved the problem identified, or has rejected pending or subsequent applications, holding that adequate domestic remedies were now available, at least in principle. Pilot proceedings are ongoing in the remaining fourteen cases,[90] five of which are clear failures. We counted as a "failure" those situations in which officials of the target state have (i) repeatedly declined to undertake reform, (ii) missed multiple deadlines, and/or (iii) refused to take further action after the Court dismissed reforms undertaken as inadequate.[91]

[88] ECHR Factsheet: Pilot Judgments (November 2016).

[89] Pilot ruling proceedings counted as successes: *Broniowski v. Poland* (inadequate compensation for expropriation); *Hutten-Czapska v. Poland* (GC, 19 June 2006; inability of landlords to make a profit); *Olaru and Others v. the Republic of Moldova* (28 July 2009; non-enforcement of social housing judgments); *Suljagic v. Bosnia and Herzegovina* (3 November 2009; inability to convert former Yugoslavian currency); *Rumpf v. Germany* (2 September 2010; excessive length of judicial proceedings and lack of remedy); *Maria Atanasiu and Others v. Romania* (12 October 2010; inadequate compensation for expropriation); *Athanasiou and Others v. Greece* (21 December 2010; excessive length of judicial proceedings and lack of remedy); *Dimitrov and Hamanov v. Bulgaria* and *Finger v. Bulgaria* (10 May 2011; excessive length of judicial proceedings and lack of remedy); *Michelioudakis v. Greece* (3 April 2012) and *Glykantzi v. Greece* (30 October 2012; excessive length of judicial proceedings); *Kurić and Others v. Slovenia* (GC, 26 June 2012; failure to recognize citizenship and lack of remedy); and *Torreggiani and Others v. Italy* (8 January 2013; detention conditions).

[90] Ongoing pilot ruling proceedings (not counted as failures): *Ananyev and Others v. Russia* (10 January 2012; detention conditions); *Manushaqe Puto and Others v. Albania* (31 July 2012; non-enforcement of compensation for expropriation); *M.C. and Others v. Italy* (3 September 2013; remedy for blood contamination); *Ališić and Others v. Bosnia and Herzegovina, Croatia, "the former Yugoslav Republic of Macedonia", Serbia and Slovenia* (GC, 16 July 2014; recovery of former Yugoslavian currency); *Neshkov and Others v. Bulgaria* (27 January 2015; detention conditions); *Varga and Others v. Hungary* (10 March 2015; detention conditions); *Rutkowski and Others v. Poland* (7 July 2015; excessive length of judicial proceedings); *Gazsó v. Hungary* (16 July 2015; excessive length of judicial proceedings); and *W.D. v. Belgium* (6 September 2016; detention conditions for mentally ill).

[91] Ongoing pilot ruling procedures counted as failures: *Greens and M.T. v. the United Kingdom* (23 November 2010; prisoners' right to vote); *Ümmühan Kaplan v. Turkey* (20 March 2012; excessive length of judicial proceedings); *Burdov v. Russia*

Two of these failures are of heightened importance because they involve incapacities of national apex courts. In *Burdov v. Russia, no. 1* (2002), the Court confronted a refusal to enforce judgments rendered against Russian state officials. Mr. Burdov, having suffered the effects of radioactivity contamination during cleanup efforts following the explosion at the Chernobyl nuclear plant, filed suit to obtain social security benefits to which he was legally entitled. He prevailed in a judicial ruling of 1997, but government officials refused to abide by it, claiming a budgetary shortfall. Burdov received his payments in arrears only after the European Court had accepted his application. The Court declared a violation of the right to a fair hearing (Art. 6) and of property (Art. 1, Protocol no. 1), taking pains to emphasize the importance of enforcing judicial rulings in a timely manner, and the insufficiency of the pleaded defense.

The Court's judgment proved prescient. After *Burdov no. 1*, the problem of non-enforcement of judgments became, in Leach et. al.'s terms, "the most significant systemic human rights problem" confronting Russia; it is also one that would, in itself, fatally undermine *any* domestic system of justice. Within five years of the ruling, "such cases comprised about 40% of all admissible applications" emanating from Russia.[92] Before the Court decided to activate the pilot ruling procedure, it had already issued "more than 200 judgments concerning the Russian authorities' failure to execute judicial decisions against the state."[93] Russian officials acknowledged the weight of the problem. In 2005, the Constitutional Court—citing to *Burdov no. 1*—declared that year's budget to be unconstitutional, on the grounds that the legislature did not provide compensation for the absence of timely enforcement of judgments. In 2008, before an assembly of the Russian

no. 2 (15 January 2009; non-enforcement of judgments); *Yuriy Nikolayevich Ivanov v. Ukraine* (15 October 2009; non-enforcement of judgments); and *Gerasimov and Others v. Russia* (1 July 2014; non-enforcement of judgments).

92 Leach, Hardman, and Stephenson (2010: 348).

93 Leach, Hardman, and Stephenson (2010: 348).

Council of Federation Judges, President Medvedev admitted that budgetary limitations affected some 50% of all such judgments issued each year. That same year, the Supreme Court ordered Parliament to rectify the situation through statute. When lawmakers treated these decisions as "non-compulsory recommendations," the Supreme Court itself submitted a draft law to Parliament, which subsequently dismissed the proposal as "unnecessary."[94]

In the meantime, payments to Mr. Burdov stopped, provoking further court judgments in his favor and, ultimately, a return to Strasbourg. In its pilot ruling, *Burdov v. Russia, no. 2* (2009), the Court ordered Russia to redress the situation within six months of the verdict, which led Parliament to adopt two statutes. To test the effectiveness of the new arrangements, the Court sent new applicants back to Russian courts.[95] Two years later, the Court declared the reforms a failure, tersely noting that: "an application [to Strasbourg is] the only means by which . . . applicants [may] . . . obtain effective redress for the clear violations of their Convention rights."[96] Russian authorities have ignored the problem since.

A second major failure of a pilot judgment followed from the reaction of UK officials to *Hirst* (2005),[97] a saga we discussed in chapter 3 with respect to the evolution of the proportionality principle. In that case, recall, the Court found that the UK's blanket denial of the right to vote of convicted prisoners violated Article 3 of Protocol no. 1, insofar as the legislature had not given reasons capable of satisfying the proportionality principle. *Hirst* did not require the UK to permit all prisoners to vote, but it did suggest that Parliament was under an obligation to justify restrictions on prisoners' rights to vote, in particular, when applied to those convicted of minor offenses. The ruling rapidly became a central element of the UK's fraught domestic politics

[94] Leach, Hardman, and Stephenson (2010: 356).

[95] *Nagovitsyn and Nalgiyev v. Russia* and *Fakhretdinov and Others v. Russia* (23 September 2010).

[96] *Ilyushkin and Others v. Russia* and *Kalinkin and Others v. Russia* (17 April 2012).

[97] *Hirst v. the United Kingdom, No. 2* (GC, 6 October 2005).

concerning membership in European organizations, freezing the situation. Five years later, in the wake of some 2,500 new applications, the Court activated the pilot ruling procedure. In *Greens and M.T.* (2010), it held that "[t]he only relevant remedy is a change in the law,"[98] and gave the UK until November 2012 to table appropriate reform legislation. Softening the bite, the Court rejected the applicants' claims for compensation and costs, while promising to suspend consideration of registered (and future) applications on the evidence of a good faith effort to redress the situation.

In its ruling in *Scoppola v. Italy* (2012), the Court upheld a ban on voting for prisoners serving sentences of three years or more, while maintaining its position on *Hirst*, emphasizing that the Italian rule was neither automatic nor indiscriminate. *Scopolla*, addressed as much to the UK as Italy, demonstrated how easily UK authorities could settle the matter. When the latter refused to budge, the Court announced (September 2013) that it would rescind the adjournment of 2,281 petitions filed by UK prisoners. In *McHugh and Others v. the United Kingdom* (2015), it found a violation of the right to vote affecting more than 1,015 applicants. Again, the Court chose not to award damages and legal costs.[99]

Meanwhile, on the UK front, steadfast governmental intransigence blocked what little progress has been made. After months of deliberation on a draft bill, a special Joint Committee of the Parliament concluded (December 2013) that there were good reasons for changing the electoral law, stressing that securing compliance would require only a minor adjustment (invoking *Scoppola*, among other judgments). The Joint Committee proposed that prisoners subject to less than twelve months incarceration be allowed to vote. The government ignored the report, and the country's highest court simply

[98] *Greens and M.T. v. the United Kingdom* (23 November 2010), para. 118.

[99] *McHugh and Others v. the United Kingdom* (10 February 2015). See also *Firth and Others v. the United Kingdom* (12 August 2014), which involved ten prisoners.

abdicated its role as a "faithful trustee" of the Convention.[100] In *Chester v. Ministry of Justice* (2013), the UK Supreme Court refused to declare existing law incompatible with the Convention, holding that it was the function of the legislative authority to respond to the Court's pilot ruling. In December 2015, after the UK missed further deadlines, the Committee of Ministers again called upon the state to move forward; the UK disingenuously replied that it was engaged in an ongoing "dialogue" with Strasbourg. Addressing Parliament that same month, Michael Gove (then Lord Chancellor and Secretary of State for Justice), not only strongly criticized the Court, but declared that "parliamentary sovereignty and our traditions have been a more effective bulwark over time for individual rights than almost any other constitutional arrangement of which I can think." The pilot ruling has clearly failed, at least for now.

Greer and Wildhaber characterize the pilot ruling procedure as "the [Court's] boldest attempt to tackle the problem of defective national legislation," while stressing that it has not been a "panacea."[101] As we have seen, some pilot judgments have failed, whether due to official resistance or a lack of capacity, but in most cases, the member state in question has funneled considerable resources into meeting its obligations.[102] In any event, the Court typically certifies a pilot case only once earlier rulings have identified systemic problems, in a context that combines a compliance failure with a rising number of repetitive claims.[103] For their part, national officials have not mounted sustained opposition to pilot rulings, and many appear to welcome the Court's efforts and guidance. At the High Level Conferences on the Future of the European Court of Human Rights in 2011 (Izmir) and 2012 (Brighton), states expressed strong support for Rule 61 and encouraged its further development.

[100] Bjorge (2015). [101] Greer and Wildhaber (2012: 671).
[102] Cases cited in note 89; Factsheet: Pilot Judgments (November 2016).
[103] Haider (2013: 38).

INTERIM MEASURES

The Court possesses an autonomous capacity to develop its own procedures, which is has used to enhance the effectiveness of trusteeship. A dramatic instance concerns Rule 39, which permits it to issue "interim measures": injunctions that prohibit state officials from taking certain actions pending the resolution of a case on the merits.[104] Although the Convention itself is silent on pre-judgment injunctive orders, under the Commission's procedures, that body could recommend interim measures that it deemed "desirable in the interest of the parties."[105] But in *Cruz Varas and Others v. Sweden* (1991), the Court concluded that, because such powers were not to be found in the Convention, a state could disregard such orders without breaching its obligations.[106] A Grand Chamber took a U-turn in 2005:

> The notion of an effective remedy under Article 13 of the Convention requires . . . preventing the execution of measures that are contrary to the Convention and whose effects are potentially irreversible. [U]nder the Convention system, interim measures . . . play a vital role in avoiding irreversible situations that would prevent the Court from properly examining the application and, where appropriate, securing to the applicant the practical and effective benefit of the Convention rights asserted. [A] failure by a respondent State to comply with interim measures will undermine the effectiveness of the right of individual application . . . and the State's formal undertaking in Article 1 to protect the rights and freedoms set forth in the Convention.[107]

[104] Although rare, Rule 39 orders can be directed at applicants. See *Ilaşcu v. Moldova and Russia* (GC, 8 July 2004), para. 11, wherein the Court ordered an applicant to cease his hunger strike.

[105] Rule 36 Commission Rules of Procedures.

[106] *Cruz Varas and Others v. Sweden* (Plenary, 20 March 1991), para. 98.

[107] *Mamatkulov and Askarov v. Turkey* (GC, 4 February 2005), paras. 124–5.

Although Rule 39 is worded broadly,[108] the Court applies a high threshold: an "imminent risk of irreparable harm" standard.[109]

Since 2012, the Court has agreed to issue interim measures in only about 600 cases, from some 7,000 requests.[110] In 2015, the Court granted 161 injunctions from a total of 1,458 requests.[111] The Rule brings the regime to bear on the exercise of core sovereign powers, the vast majority of interim measures relate to expulsion or extradition in the context of absolute rights guaranteed under Articles 2 and 3 ECHR (respectively, the right to life, and the right to be free of torture and degrading treatment). A state may not expel foreign nationals to a non-European country, the Court has declared, where they risk having these rights violated. In a typical decision from 2009, the Court prohibited Sweden from deporting an Iraqi Christian, and a former member of the Republican Guard, but later lifted the measure upon determining that the expulsion would not lead to an Article 2 violation.[112]

States routinely comply with interim measures, but there are some high-profile exceptions. In *Trabelsi v. Belgium* (2015), the Belgian government defied a Rule 39 order, extraditing the applicant to the United States, where he was wanted for terrorism and risked being sentenced to an irreducible life sentence. In its scathing judgment, the Court observed that:

> [T]he respondent State deliberately and irreversibly lowered the level of protection of the rights set out in Article 3 . . . which the applicant had endeavoured to uphold by lodging his application with the Court. The extradition has . . . rendered any finding of a violation

[108] Rule 39 entered into force in 2005, and was amended slightly in 2012 and 2013.

[109] Interim Measures Factsheet: 2 (last updated September 2016). Available at: http://www.echr.coe.int/Documents/FS_Interim_measures_ENG.pdf.

[110] ECHR: Statistics on Rule 39 (updated through 2016). Available at: http://www.echr.coe.int/Documents/Stats_art_39_01_ENG.pdf.

[111] Interim Measures Factsheet: 2.

[112] *F.H. v. Sweden* (5 June 2009), paras. 39–46.

> of the Convention otiose, as the applicant has been removed to a country which is not a Party to that instrument, where he alleged that he would be exposed to treatment contrary to the Convention. The Court considers that none of the arguments put forward by the Belgian Government justified its non-compliance with the interim measure. [I]t was not for the Belgian State . . . to substitute its own appraisal for the Court's assessment of these assurances and the merits of the application and decide to override the interim measure indicated by the Court.[113]

We discuss the importance of Rule 39, for the rendering of justice to non-Europeans, in chapter 6.

COMPLIANCE AND IMPLEMENTATION

We have argued that the effectiveness of the Court ultimately depends on its success in inducing positive changes at the domestic level, especially within states that have weak capacity or political will to meet their Convention obligations. The extent to which its rulings help to organize domestic reforms that close gaps in rights protection is a relatively direct measure of effectiveness. It is indisputable that the regime has induced significant reform in every member state, across virtually every important domain of law and policy. Over the past decade, a series of collaborative, comparative research projects have charted the growing impact of the ECHR on national legal orders, including within those that have generated the most applications and violations.[114] The institutions of the Council of Europe have also taken

[113] *Trabelsi v. Belgium* (16 February 2015), paras. 150–1.

[114] Following Keller and Stone Sweet, eds. (2008): Buyse and Hamilton, eds. (2011); Hammer and Emmert, eds. (2011); Anagnostou, ed. (2013); Motoc and Ziemele, eds. (2016).

pains to document important and successful reforms as a result of the Court's rulings.[115]

The Committee of Ministers (comprised of representatives from all forty-seven member states) supervises "the execution" of the Court's rulings, and it "closes" cases by certifying compliance. In the 2000s, the Committee abandoned deference postures, "becom[ing] more proactive, transparent, and [intrusive in its scrutiny] of state actions."[116] Supported by the Court's own Department for the Execution of Judgments, the Committee conducts consultations with state officials and other stakeholders on ways to overcome difficulties in implementation; the negotiations result in "action plans" that are evaluated in subsequent "action reports." Rulings raising compliance issues are classified according to the importance of the violation, and the extent of domestic reform required for closing the case and certifying compliance. In recent years, about 20% of all execution cases receive an "enhanced supervision" classification; these are called "leading cases." The designation covers rulings that have revealed a structural deficiency that will need significant reform in legislation or

[115] A recent study on impact commissioned by the Parliamentary Assembly concluded that: "[T]he effects of the Convention extend to all areas of human life, benefiting individuals, associations, political parties, companies, and persons belonging to particularly vulnerable groups such as minors, victims of violence, elderly persons, refugees and asylum seekers, defendants in judicial proceedings, persons with (mental) health problems, and those belonging to national, ethnic, religious, sexual or other minorities. The areas where the Convention and its case law have brought about change include, but are not limited to, individuals' access to justice, the prohibition of discrimination, property rights, family law issues such as custody rights, the prevention and punishment of acts of torture, the protection of the victims of domestic violence, the privacy of individuals in their correspondence and sexual relations, and the protection of religious freedoms and freedoms of expression and association." Parliamentary Assembly (2016: 2). Available at: https://www.coe.int/hy/web/execution/-/the-impact-of-the-european-convention-on-human-rights. The Committee of Ministers, in its most recent annual report, also contains a long list of significant domestic reforms undertaken to satisfy requirements laid down for the execution of the Court's judgments; Council of Europe, Committee of Ministers (2017: 26–40). Available at: https://rm.coe.int/prems-021117-gbr-2001-10e-rapport-annuel-2016-web-16x24/168072800b.

[116] Anagnostou and Mungiu-Pippidi (2014: 212).

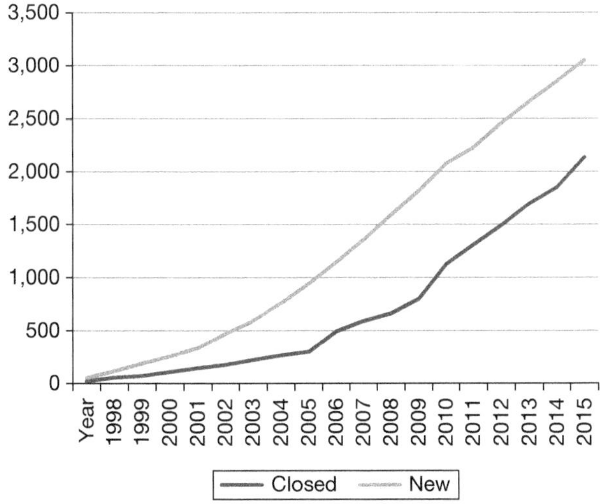

Figure 4.1. Cumulative Annual Number of Leading Cases Closed, and New Cases Opened

Source: Committee of Ministers, Council of Europe: Supervision of the Execution of Judgments and Decisions of the European Court of Human Rights, Annual Reports.

case law to rectify, or those requiring "urgent" individual measures. The Committee gives the rest (about 80% in recent years) a "standard supervision" classification, meaning that states can usually secure compliance through more routine individual measures (paying of compensation to the applicant, for example, or reopening of judicial proceedings). At the end of 2016, there were 9,941 pending execution cases, including 1,493 leading cases.[117]

Figure 4.1 charts the cumulative number of leading cases per annum: (i) opened (new cases) and (ii) closed (certified). From 1998 to 2016, the Committee disposed of 2,133 leading cases, while registering 3,049 new cases. In 2016 alone, it added 206 leading cases and closed 282. At the end of 2016, while every member but Monaco had at least one enhanced supervision case pending, just ten states

[117] The source of the statistics presented in this section is Council of Europe, Committee of Ministers (2017).

accounted for 80% of pending cases: Russia (17%); Ukraine (16%); Turkey (11%); Bulgaria (7%); Moldova (7%); Italy (6%); Romania (5%); Azerbaijan (4%); Greece (3%); and Hungary (3%).

Although political scientists[118] have begun to explore the complex law and politics of implementation, our understanding of the process is patchwork, at best. What makes systematic, comparative research so difficult is that, for any specific case, the factors that matter will combine in multi-dimensional, kaleidoscopic ways. These variables—which include the nature of the party and electoral system, the structure of government, lawmaking procedures (the number of veto points), the capacity of courts to induce legislative and administrative change, the organization of public and private interests, and budgetary constraints—largely determine capacity to secure compliance in a timely manner. Of course, in the states that are most intensively supervised, it is precisely the lack of such capacity that generated problems in the first place. Not surprisingly, leading cases can take a very long time to clear; indeed, some may remain open indefinitely. At the end of 2016, of the 1,493 leading cases pending, 720 (48%) have been on the books for more than five years.

Taken together, these numbers tell us some very important things about the regime's priorities and impact. First, even overloaded, the Court has remained faithful to its mission as constitutional trustee: to help domestic officials enhance the effectiveness of their own systems of constitutional justice. Second, the Committee of Minister's supervisory activities help to organize the regime's incremental progress. Closing a leading case registers meaningful domestic reform, the robustness of which will be tested by future developments in the domestic courts.

Readers should consider this (now dense) empirical record of impact alongside the relevant counterfactual: how effective would domestic rights protection be in the absence of (i) Protocol no. 11,

[118] For an introduction to this literature, see the exchange between Anagnostou and Mungiu-Pippidi (2014: 212) and Voeten (2014).

(ii) domestic incorporation of the Convention, and (iii) the Court's commitment to helping national officials resolve structural problems in their own systems of justice? In our view, domestic legal orders would be unrecognizable, configured in ways that would routinely hinder the effectiveness of both the ECHR and their own charters of rights. Closing gaps in protection would have been much slower and, in many cases, blocked altogether. Even if one accepts these points, however, the regime confronts massive compliance problems that will continue to dominate resource allocation decisions far into the future.

CONCLUSION

This chapter has focused on responses to the failures in domestic rights protection exposed by the success of the individual petition under Protocol no. 11. The Court and the member states have worked together to design new rules and procedures, in order to manage a chronically overloaded docket, and to enhance the effectiveness of the Convention within national orders. The result has been a steady reinforcement of the Court's powers of trusteeship: to manage the flow of applications; to give its important rulings precedential effect; to issue injunctions; and to identify and supervise the reforms necessary to close gaps in domestic systems of constitutional justice. Despite the fact that the Court does not possess the authority to invalidate national law and acts as incompatible with the Convention, the regime features a relatively strong form of structural judicial supremacy.[119]

The legitimacy of these developments rests on a relatively secure footing. Kant himself emphasized that progress toward achieving Right at the international level would partly depend on the efficacy of domestic systems of justice. Pushing further, we have argued that constitutional trusteeship is a crucial component of systemic effectiveness

[119] Chapter 2.

at any level of governance. States fully participated in the construction of the CLO. They enhanced the Court's status as the regime's trustee through Protocols nos. 11 and 14, and strongly supported the development of pilot rulings. In the guise of the Committee of Ministers, states also forged a collective identity, a continuous presence devoted to ensuring the execution of judgments. The individual complaint has propelled the regime forward, revealing a massive social demand for justice that the regime is under a duty to supply. Last, the regime has made progress, and every step forward, big or small, deserves to be credited when it comes to assessing the regime's legitimacy. In the next two chapters, we assess the regime's success in raising standards of rights protection in finer detail.

5

Beyond Rights Minimalism

INTRODUCTION

In the last chapter, we focused on the enhancement of the Strasbourg Court's capacity to fulfill its responsibilities as the constitutional trustee of the regime. Supported by the member states at critical moments, the Court has steadily developed its powers to supervise the functioning of domestic systems of justice, to provoke structural reform, and to provide jurisprudential guidance when it comes to adjudicating Convention rights. These developments ought to weigh heavily in the assessment of the value-added of constructing a transnational level of rights protection. From a Kantian perspective, what matters most is the extent to which the system enforces rights—as positive requirements of legality—while intensifying the legal obligation of state officials to justify their rights-regarding decisions with strong enough reasons (chapter 2). In fact, the Court has routinely expanded the coverage of existing rights, raising standards in ways that have placed even powerful states, with well-functioning systems of constitutional justice, out of compliance with the Convention.

This outcome weighs in the regime's favor. Most of the original state signatories of the ECHR, after all, had assumed that they had enshrined a form of "rights minimalism," giving states substantial latitude to balance values and interests as they saw fit.[1] Minimalism would be assured to the extent that Convention officials would intervene in domestic legal affairs only to counter serious threats to the viability of constitutional democracy. There are further reasons for wonderment. One might suppose that transnational judges, knowing that they possess relatively weaker political legitimacy than their national counterparts, would adopt a posture of deference when adjudicating the qualified rights. After all, the Convention itself explicitly permits states to limit rights for important public purposes. While domestic judges are natives of the legal system in which rights conflicts take place, the authority of transnational judges is easily challenged as alien and less expert on local conditions. Moreover, the philosophical discourse on human rights remains dominated by minimalist logics and conclusions that ought to apply in Europe.[2] The puzzle, then, is this: how has the regime transcended rights minimalism?

We argue here that the answer lies in how decentralized sovereignty works (chapter 3). Three factors deserve emphasis up-front. The first is the development of a highly structured interface between the transnational and domestic legal systems, through the combined effects of three processes already discussed: (i) the institutionalization of the Court's authority as the regime's trustee, (ii) the incorporation of the Convention as directly enforceable in domestic orders, and (iii) the diffusion of proportionality analysis (PA) as a common approach to rights adjudication. Second, the Court expends enormous resources in the attempt to understand the richness and particularity of the disputes it adjudicates, as well as variation in the relevant national law across the regime. In its rulings, the Court carefully traces the process through which individuals exhausted domestic remedies, and it dwells on the arguments briefed by the defendant state and others filing as *amici*.[3] Findings of violation may not convince the respondent state, but it is not plausible to argue that the Court has

[1] Nichol (2005). [2] Introduction to the book.

[3] Which the Court refers to as "third-party interventions."

ignored domestic law or its comparative context. The Court could not provide appropriate guidance to states, especially when the source of a violation is a statute or other general norm, without relatively deep engagement with national law and practice (chapter 4). Third, as discussed below, the mix of incentives facing domestic apex courts have gradually tipped in favor of respect for the Court's progressive case law; indeed, domestic judges now assert the authority to raise standards on their own.

We begin by examining the Strasbourg Court's use of PA. In previous chapters, we have stressed the centrality of proportionality to the enforcement of qualified rights in a Kantian system of constitutional justice, and to the construction of a stable interface between the domestic and transnational levels in the European Convention on Human Rights (ECHR) regime. For present purposes, what is important is that the Court's enforcement of the proportionality principle—in particular, through "consensus analysis" within the necessity phase—grounds its dynamic approach to the progressive development of Convention rights. We then turn to the response of national apex courts: how, and to what extent, have they been led to assume their duties, as "faithful trustees"[4] of the regime? To help address this question, we compiled information on every ruling of a Grand Chamber of the European Court, pursuant to a pleading of a qualified right (Arts. 8–11 and Protocol no. 1), rendered between November 1, 1998 (the entry into force of Protocol no. 11), and December 31, 2015: n = 165.[5] After presenting the aggregate data, we trace outcomes, over time, in case studies on the adjudication of rights related to (i) privacy, gender and sexuality, and reproductive rights (Art. 8); (ii) religious practices (Art. 9); and (iii) freedom of speech and the press (Art. 10).

[4] Bjorge (2015); chapters 2–4.

[5] We counted multiple proceedings that involved virtually identical facts and pleadings as one case, thus removing from the count thirteen similar cases from Turkish applicants, and two from French.

PROPORTIONALITY, CONSENSUS, AND THE MARGIN OF APPRECIATION

In domestic charters of rights adopted in Europe since 1950, most rights are "qualified" by limitation clauses. In the *Travaux préparatoires* on the Convention, Rapporteur Teitgen emphasized that such clauses would codify a "fundamental principle," in terms that echo our discussion of Kantian theory (chapter 2):

> It is legitimate and necessary to limit, sometimes even to restrain, individual freedoms, to allow everyone the peaceful exercise of their freedom and to ensure the maintenance of morality, of the general well-being, of the common good and of the public good. When the State defines, organises, regulates and limits freedom for such reasons, . . . it is only fulfilling its duty. . . . The restriction [the State imposes on an individual right] is a legitimate one precisely by reason of the fact that this is the goal which is aimed at: it sets a limit upon freedom in the general interest, in the interest of the freedom of all.[6]

Under the Convention, states may limit rights covered by Articles 8–11. While the terms of these clauses vary slightly, states are permitted to "interfere with," or "restrict" the "exercise" of, these rights, but only insofar as such interferences are "prescribed by law" (or in "accordance with law"), and only when such limitations are, in the formulation of Article 8: "necessary in a democratic society in the interests of national security or public safety for the prevention of disorder or crime, for the protection of health or morals, or for the protection of the rights and freedoms of others."

Box 5 contains the texts of these provisions, as well as excerpts from the case law discussed in this chapter.

[6] Council of Europe, *Preparatory Work on Article 18 of the European Convention on Human Rights*, CDH (75) 11 (1975: 3–9).

Box 5 Qualified Rights, Proportionality, and the Margin of Appreciation

The Qualified Rights

ART. 8: RIGHT TO RESPECT FOR PRIVATE AND FAMILY LIFE

1. Everyone has the right to respect for his private and family life, his home and his correspondence.
2. There shall be no interference by a public authority with the exercise of this right except such as is in accordance with the law and is necessary in a democratic society in the interests of national security, public safety or the economic well-being of the country, for the prevention of disorder or crime, for the protection of health or morals, or for the protection of the rights and freedoms of others.

ART. 9: FREEDOM OF THOUGHT, CONSCIENCE AND RELIGION

1. Everyone has the right to freedom of thought, conscience and religion; this right includes freedom to change his religion or belief and freedom, either alone or in community with others and in public or private, to manifest his religion or belief, in worship, teaching, practice and observance.
2. Freedom to manifest one's religion or beliefs shall be subject only to such limitations as are prescribed by law and are necessary in a democratic society in the interests of public safety, for the protection of public order, health or morals, or for the protection of the rights and freedoms of others.

ART. 10: FREEDOM OF EXPRESSION

1. Everyone has the right to freedom of expression. This right shall include freedom to hold opinions and to receive and impart information and ideas without interference by public authority and regardless of frontiers. This Article shall not prevent States from requiring the licensing of broadcasting, television or cinema enterprises.
2. The exercise of these freedoms, since it carries with it duties and responsibilities, may be subject to such formalities, conditions, restrictions or penalties as are prescribed by law and are necessary in a democratic society, in the interests of national security, territorial integrity or public safety, for the prevention of disorder or crime, for the protection of health or morals, for the protection of the reputation or rights of others, for preventing the disclosure of information received in confidence, or for maintaining the authority and impartiality of the judiciary.

ART. 11: FREEDOM OF ASSEMBLY AND ASSOCIATION

1. Everyone has the right to freedom of peaceful assembly and to freedom of association with others, including the right to form and to join trade unions for the protection of his interests.

2. No restrictions shall be placed on the exercise of these rights other than such as are prescribed by law and are necessary in a democratic society in the interests of national security or public safety, for the prevention of disorder or crime, for the protection of health or morals or for the protection of the rights and freedoms of others. This Article shall not prevent the imposition of lawful restrictions on the exercise of these rights by members of the armed forces, of the police or of the administration of the State.

Case Law of the European Court: Necessity, Consensus, and Margin of Appreciation

"Where a particularly important facet of an individual's existence or identity is at stake, the margin of appreciation allowed to the State will normally be restricted. Where, however, there is no consensus within the member States of the Council of Europe, either as to the relative importance of the interest at stake or as to the best means of protecting it, particularly where the case raises sensitive moral or ethical issues, the margin will be wider. [B]y reason of their direct and continuous contact with the vital forces of their countries, the State authorities are, in principle, in a better position than the international judge to give an opinion, not only on the 'exact content of the requirements of morals' in their country, but also on the necessity of a restriction intended to meet them." *A, B & C v. Ireland* (GC, 16 December 2010), para. 232.

"The national authorities have direct democratic legitimation and are . . . in principle better placed than an international court to evaluate local needs and conditions. In matters of general policy, on which opinions within a democratic society may reasonably differ widely, the role of the domestic policy-maker should be given special weight. This is the case, in particular, where questions concerning the relationship between State and religions are at stake. [T]he State should in principle, be afforded a wide margin of appreciation in deciding whether and to what extent a limitation of the right to manifest one's religion or beliefs is 'necessary.' [I]n delimiting the extent of the margin of appreciation in a given case, the Court [may] also, if appropriate, have regard to any consensus and common values emerging from the practices of the States Parties to the Convention." *S.A.S. v. France* (GC, 1 July 2014), para. 129.

"The Court recognises that it is for the national authorities to make the initial assessment of necessity, though the final evaluation as to whether the reasons cited for the interference are relevant and sufficient is one for this Court. A margin of appreciation is left to Contracting States in the context of this assessment, which varies according to the nature of the activities restricted and of the aims pursued by the restrictions. Accordingly, when the relevant restrictions concern 'a most intimate part of an individual's private life,' there must exist 'particularly serious reasons' before such interferences can satisfy the requirements of Article 8." *Smith & Grady v. the United Kingdom* (27 September 1999), paras. 88, 89.

"[U]under Article 10 of the Convention, the Contracting States have a certain margin of appreciation in assessing whether and to what extent an interference with the freedom of expression protected by this provision is necessary.

However, this margin goes hand in hand with European supervision, embracing both the legislation and the decisions applying it, even those delivered by an independent court. In exercising its supervisory function, the Court's task is not to take the place of the national courts, but rather to review, in the light of the case as a whole, whether the decisions they have taken pursuant to their power of appreciation are compatible with the [Convention]. Where the balancing exercise has been undertaken by the national authorities in conformity with the criteria laid down in the Court's case-law, the Court would require strong reasons to substitute its view for that of the domestic courts." *Von Hannover v. Germany No. 2* (GC, 7 February 2012), paras. 104, 105, 107.

"The existence of a consensus has long played a role in the development and evolution of Convention protections . . . the Convention being considered a 'living instrument' to be interpreted in the light of present-day conditions. Consensus has therefore been invoked to justify a dynamic interpretation of the Convention." *A, B & C v. Ireland* (GC, 16 December 2010), para. 234.

Skilled judges deploy PA to optimize the effectiveness of qualified rights, given the possibility of their limitation for legitimate purposes, where necessary. In Kantian terms, PA gives a fixed, doctrinal structure to the reason-giving requirement, while enabling judges to enforce the Universal Principle of Right (UPR) in a principled and transparent manner. When applied properly, PA ensures that public acts restrict individual freedom no further than is necessary to secure the external freedom of all (chapters 2 and 3).

The Strasbourg Court has developed its own version of PA. In two preliminary phases, the Court (i) ensures that any Convention right pleaded by the applicant has, in fact, been restricted. Since admissibility depends upon a showing of interference by the state, only rulings extending the scope of a right will direct much attention to this question. The Court then (ii) verifies that the interference was "prescribed by law." If the latter is not covered by a specific legal act or decision, then the hindrance is per se arbitrary and unlawful, and the applicant will prevail. While rare—our data set on Grand Chamber rulings contains only three instances[7]—such judgments expose

[7] *Amann v. Switzerland* (GC, 16 February 2000); *Centro Europa 7 v. Italy* (GC, 7 June 2012); and *Maestri v. Italy* (GC, 17 February 2004).

serious "rule of law" failures. This groundwork completed, the judges proceed to PA. They will check to see that the state act under review fulfills a legitimate purpose, covered by one of the policy headings listed in the limitation clause. Our data set contains only two (of 165) Grand Chamber judgments on qualified rights that declare the absence of a legitimate purpose.[8]

Most of the substantive review of state policy occurs at the "necessity" step in the analysis. In the now "canonical" version,[9] the respondent state bears the burden of (i) justifying the interference under a "pressing social need" standard and (ii) showing that the means chosen to achieve the policy objective was "proportionate to the legitimate aim pursued." It is the Court's duty to assess the adequacy of the reasons given for burdening a rights-holder. The limitation clause is not self-judging, and no formal "political question" doctrine exists.

The Strasbourg Court uses a rich variety of analytical techniques to adjudicate necessity. Most important for present purposes, it analyzes the factors considered to be important under the necessity prong of PA to determine the size of states' "margin of appreciation": the zone of regulatory discretion within which domestic officials may lawfully act when they restrict a right under a limitation clause.[10] If the Court finds that a state measure under review is "necessary" to achieve its legitimate goals, the state will maintain its regulatory autonomy within this zone. The Court, as we will see, may also reduce the margin of appreciation to nil, as when it declares that a right imposes a minimal standard of protection that no public policy interest can override. If it

[8] *Thlimmenos v. Greece* (GC, 6 April 2000); *S.A.S. v. France* (GC, 1 July 2014). In many important cases, judges have written opinions arguing that the majority should have found a violation on absence of legitimate purpose grounds; including the concurrence of Judges Tulkens and Zagrebelsky in *Hirst v. United Kingdom* (GC, 6 October 2005) and the dissent of Judge Sajó in *Parrillo v. Italy* (GC, 27 August 2015).

[9] Sadurski (2016).

[10] The relationship between PA, consensus analysis, and the margin of appreciation has been the subject of intensive debate among state officials, judges, and scholars; see Letsas (2013); Legg (2012); Dzehtsiarou (2015).

finds that a general measure, such as a statute, is the source of a violation, then the state will be subject to repetitive petitions, findings of violation, and enhanced supervision until it changes its law (chapter 4).

The Court has developed, within the necessity stage, a comparative method for helping it determine when the content and scope of a Convention right has expanded. It will typically raise the standard of protection once a sufficient number of states have withdrawn public interest justifications for restricting a right. Put differently, the margin of appreciation is likely to shrink as the inter-state commitment to raising protections grows. Whenever the Court raises the minimal obligatory standard, it puts those laggard states out of compliance. Nonetheless, the Court and its supporters can claim that "consensus analysis" provides an objective and transnational perspective on the process of "weighing" the values to be "balanced" in any dispute. The approach is obviously incompatible with minimalism. But the bias toward raising standards over time is defensible in that it is *majoritarian, transnational*, and *rights protective.*

The Court's methods for testing necessity rest on two strong presumptions. First, a state should never be able to restrict a Convention right more than is necessary for it to achieve a significant public policy purpose. The position aligns with Kantian precepts. The second presumption animates "consensus analysis": if most states in the regime can fulfill a pressing social need without restricting the right so much, or at all, then it cannot be a necessity for the outlier-laggards to do so. The presumption is rebuttable, for example, on a showing of extraordinary facts or crisis. The key point is that consensus analysis enables the Court to pursue a strategy of majoritarianism, which is, in turn, a fundamental mechanism for overcoming rights minimalism.

In our view, *majoritarian activism*[11] deserves pride of place in a cosmopolitan legal order. In a Kantian system of justice, rights inhere in one's humanity, not one's nationality; and the Court's role

[11] For a comparative analysis of majoritarian activism in international courts, see Stone Sweet and Brunell (2013).

in a transnational system is to help perfect transnational Right. In the ECHR regime, determining the content and scope of rights, and guaranteeing their effectiveness, is a *collective* duty under the treaty, as well as an obligation under domestic law. No official, of any state, is alone in her rights-regarding decisions. Although states may protest when it comes to implementing controversial judgments, they eventually comply in the vast majority of cases. A state that chooses to defy a ruling is left to defend a lower standard, on grounds that will appear idiosyncratic and parochial. To the extent that a state cares about reputation, then shaming effects too are harnessed by majoritarianism. Of course, a Kantian system of justice must be responsive to the moral obligation to render justice. Consensus analysis is not opposed to moral considerations and reasoning. Rather, the Court explicitly incorporates, as an important factor of analysis, how moral questions involving rights have been resolved within the community of states in which it is embedded.

In Strasbourg, cases are decided at first instance by a seven-member "Section," whose rulings can be appealed to a seventeen-member "Grand Chamber"; a Section may also refer the case directly to the Grand Chamber without ruling on the merits. Because their judgments are both final and capable of authoritatively establishing and overruling precedent, the activities of Grand Chambers deserve particular attention. Table 5.1 reports information of the results of Grand Chamber judgments on the merits, pursuant to applications that pleaded a right contained in Articles 8–11 ECHR, and were registered under Protocol no. 11. Since November 1, 1998, Grand Chambers have issued 144 such rulings on the merits, eighty-three of which (58%) found violations.

In about half of these cases, the crucial moment occurs when Grand Chambers gauge state consensus within the necessity stage of PA (n = 69; 48%). Cases are won or lost, and precedents are reassessed, at this point in the ruling. Petitioners, the defendant state, and third parties (nongovernmental organizations and states filing as *amici*) collect and report evidence of state practice to the Court, and

Table 5.1. Grand Chamber Rulings under Rights Pleaded under Arts. 8–11 ECHR

			Consensus Analysis	
Right Pleaded	Rulings	Violations	Violations	Non-Violations
Art. 8	72*	40*	20	22
Art. 9	12	7	3	4
Art. 10	48	31	8	7
Art. 11	12	5	2	3
Total	144	83	33	36

Note: The table provides information on all Grand Chamber rulings—rendered between January 1, 1999 and December 31, 2016—in cases in which Arts. 8–11 were pleaded by the applicant. "Violations" is the number of judgments in which the Grand Chamber found a violation of at least one of these provisions; the two right-hand columns report the number and outcomes of cases in which the Court deployed consensus analysis.

* We have excluded cases—all violations—that were based on similar facts and decided by the court on similar reasons.

Source: Judgments of the European Court of Human Rights. Data compiled by Alec Stone Sweet, Christine Landfried, Dominik Rennert, Eliška Holubová, and Jolin Chen.

the Court often undertakes its own investigations. This evidence can take the form of: (i) a count of states that restrict, or no longer limit, a right in a particular way; (ii) a survey of relevant national legislation, case law, and administrative practice; (iii) the positions taken by organs of the Council of Europe and the EU; and (iv) relevant treaties to which states are parties. The Court also treats judicial decisions from beyond the regime as pertinent; it has actively engaged the jurisprudence of the Supreme Court of Canada, the South African Constitutional Court, and the Inter-American Court of Human Rights, for example. The Grand Chamber often blends evidence from these various sources to arrive at a conclusion. Sections process the vast bulk of these cases, and they too routinely engage in "consensus analysis" when evaluating the "necessity" of state measures. At the Grand Chamber level, consensus analysis had led to violations in nearly half of the cases in which such analysis occurs (n = 33; 48%).

To illustrate the role of consensus in raising standards of protection, consider the response to discrimination against homosexuals (discussed further below). In the 1980s, the Court found that laws criminalizing homosexual acts violated Article 8, thereby exposing to review all domestic law denying homosexuals Convention rights.[12] The Court has taken an aggressively majoritarian stance ever since. In 1999, a Section held that the UK's prohibition against gays and lesbians serving in the military violated Article 8; the judges rejected the claim that the ban was necessary to preserve morale in the armed forces, underlining that the UK's position was distinctly a minority one.[13] The UK abandoned the policy. In 2008, a Grand Chamber held that France could not withhold authorization from a lesbian woman attempting to adopt a child, although the judges could count only ten states permitting the practice.[14] Since the Grand Chamber found that the French Council of State had partly based its reasoning on the fact of the woman's homosexuality, the ruling could be considered to be an application of settled case law prohibiting discrimination on the basis of sexual orientation. Nonetheless, the oracular nature of the ruling was obvious, and France changed its law. In 2010, a Section found multiple violations in three cases involving the recurrent refusal of Russian authorities to permit "gay pride" parades.[15] Russia claimed a wide "margin of appreciation" when "homosexual behavior" spilled from the private into the public domain, which the Section rejected on the grounds of solid European consensus to the contrary. In response, Russian courts banned such parades for 100 years, and the Russian legislature enacted a statute criminalizing "pro-gay propaganda," measures that have generated new applications.[16]

Majoritarian activism also applies to negative cases. If the Court finds that state consensus on extending the scope of a right has begun to emerge, but has not yet been consolidated, it will balk at extending the scope of a right. In a 2010 case, for example, a Grand Chamber rejected a petition involving same-sex marriage in these terms:

[12] See *Norris v. Ireland* (Plenary, 26 October 1988).
[13] *Smith and Grady v. the United Kingdom* (27 September 1999).
[14] *E.B. v. France* (GC, 22 January 2008).
[15] *Alekseyev v. Russia* (21 October 2010).
[16] See *Bayev and Others v. Russia* (20 June 2017).

> The Court [finds] that there is an emerging European consensus towards legal recognition of same-sex couples. Moreover, this tendency has developed rapidly over the past decade. Nevertheless, there is not yet a majority of States providing for legal recognition of same-sex couples. The area in question must therefore still be regarded as one of evolving rights with no established consensus. [Thus] States . . . enjoy a margin of appreciation in the timing of the introduction of legislative changes.[17]

The ruling stressed that laggard states would not be able to maintain the *status quo* indefinitely. In 2011, a Section rejected an Article 8 challenge to Austria's ban on in vitro fertilization using donated genetic material, declaring that "there is now a clear trend in the legislation of the Contracting States towards allowing gamete donation for the purpose of *in vitro* fertilisation, which reflects an emerging, but not yet consolidated, 'consensus.'"[18] In these and many other rulings, states have survived a challenge, while being put on notice that change will come.

INTER-LEVEL COORDINATION

Margin of appreciation considerations do not flow from a formalized and freestanding deference doctrine (Box 5). Moreover, such a doctrine is precluded in a Kantian system of justice.

As early as 1976 (*Handyside v. the United Kingdom*), the Court declared that it was "for national authorities to make the initial assessment of the reality of the pressing social need implied by the notion of necessity," but that how they do so—in the exercise of its margin of appreciation—"must go hand in hand with . . . European

[17] *Schalk and Kopf v. Austria* (24 June 2010).
[18] *S.H. and Others v. Austria* (GC, 3 November 2011).

supervision."[19] As a doctrinal matter, supervision typically takes place through the enforcement of the proportionality principle. Strategically, one of the advantages of PA is its flexibility.[20] The framework does not dictate how the values and interests in tension are to be weighed; and it offers several useful escape hatches to judges confronting hard cases. The Court, like most powerful constitutional courts in the world, tends to give state officials wide leeway at the legitimate aim stage, channeling serious scrutiny into the means chosen and balancing, rather than the purposes themselves.[21] Under the necessity prong, the Court sometimes finds that an act falls within the margin of appreciation, despite strong evidence of consensus in the other direction. Doing so gives force to criticism that the Court appears to use margin of appreciation, at least in some hard cases, as an unprincipled, ad hoc deference doctrine. The handful of Grand Chamber rulings falling into this category have also engendered the most controversy (discussed below), making the Court vulnerable to charges of abdication. Even when it finds a violation, the Court may slip into a deference posture, as when it leaves it to the state to determine an appropriate response. In Kantian terms, such rulings may be justified when there are multiple, UPR-compliant policies available;[22] the state's duty is to select from among these options. Thus, while the margin of appreciation is not a deference doctrine *de jure*, the Court can build *de facto* deference into the assessment of its scope.

National high courts confront a complex mix of incentives and constraints when it comes to keeping up with the Strasbourg Court's evolving jurisprudence. Simplifying, there are several basic logics at work. The first is an "avoidance of punishment" rationale: enforcing Convention rights will make the state—in practice, the judiciary—less vulnerable to censure in Strasbourg. This logic is especially

[19] *Handyside v. the United Kingdom* (Plenary, 7 December 1976), paras. 22–3.

[20] Stone Sweet and Mathews (2008); Mathews and Stone Sweet (2011).

[21] Balancing can occur either within necessity analysis, or in a subsequent stage; see chapter 2.

[22] Chapter 2.

pronounced in domestic systems that otherwise prohibit the judicial review of statute, or do not have a judicially enforceable domestic charter of rights. At the same time, predicting the Court's rulings, especially when they rest on the outcomes of PA, is not a simple matter either for domestic authorities. A second dynamic is embedded in domestic politics. Individuals and NGOs may seek to leverage the Convention—through strategic litigation[23]—to alter law and policy, and national judges may work to entrench Convention rights in order to enhance their own authority with respect to legislators and executives.[24] Third, the institutionalization of the Court's trustee status[25] has increased the interest that apex courts have in seeking to influence the evolution of Convention rights. Even for a powerful constitutional court that makes strong (centralized) sovereignty claims, constructive engagement is more likely to constrain the Court than the more costly alternatives: defection and open conflict. Asserting authority within the cosmopolitan legal order (CLO), as a full partner of the Strasbourg Court, may also enhance the capacity of constitutional judges to control all other judges in fragmented systems, the German and Spanish courts being important examples.[26] Far from paralyzing the regime, friction—among domestic organs of government, and between domestic judges and the European Court—has been an important catalyst for the regime's progressive development.

Scholars have begun only recently to explore the domestic impact of Protocol no. 11, the Court's burgeoning case law, and incorporation. The book, *A Europe of Rights: The Impact of the ECHR on National Legal Systems*,[27] documents developments in eighteen states, including with respect to the evolution of constitutional rights doctrine, normative hierarchies, separation of powers, conflict among domestic apex courts, the adoption of proportionality, as well as trends

[23] Anagnostou and Psychogiopoulou, eds. (2010). [24] Chapter 4.
[25] Chapter 4. [26] Chapter 3.
[27] Keller and Stone Sweet, eds. (2008).

in teaching and scholarship. The project reports profound changes in structure and practice, even in states that have had the most difficulty meeting the demands of the regime.

A second book, Bjorge's *Domestic Application of the ECHR: Courts as Faithful Trustees*, reports systematic and comparative findings on the impact of the ECHR on national rights protection in three original signatory states: France, Germany, and the UK. The high courts of these states, one would presume, would be among the most likely in the regime to resist being placed under the tutelage of the European Court. Indeed, jealous of their autonomy, constrained by national separation of powers doctrines, and wedded to their own embedded approaches to rights protection, judges on these courts endured painful episodes of adjustment under the Protocol no. 11 regime. But, by 2015, they had all strongly embraced trusteeship roles under the Convention. They treat the ECHR as a "living instrument" and engage in "evolutionary" and "autonomous" interpretation of Convention rights on their own, including in situations in which the European Court has yet to take a clear position.[28] Each understands subsidiarity as (i) enabling the national courts to develop rights progressively, above the floor set by the case law emanating from Strasbourg, while (ii) requiring respect for the minimal standards established by that same jurisprudence. None regards the margin of appreciation doctrine as applying within domestic orders; instead, each has asserted the competence to review the proportionality of rights-regarding decisions of domestic officials, notwithstanding any European Court judgment to the effect that states possess a wide margin of appreciation in the relevant domain of decision-making.[29] As Bjorge shows:

> [T]he national courts have, and this applies to all three systems equally, taken inspiration from the idea of the margin of

[28] Bjorge (2015: 22–5; ch. 4). [29] Bjorge (2015: ch. 6).

appreciation not in order to limit but to expand the scope of their rights review under the Convention.[30]

In each of these states, apex courts use full-fledged PA to determine if the legal act under review falls within (or outside) the zone of proportionality available to domestic lawmakers. These developments have clearly strengthened the positions of these courts in their respective domestic orders, not weakened them.

Dzehtsiarou's *European Consensus and the Legitimacy of the European Court of Human Rights* (2015), also deserves special mention. Based on interviews with judges in Strasbourg, and intensive analysis of every Grand Chamber ruling, the author argues convincingly that consensus analysis is not only a useful tool for judging necessity, but helps to underwrite the Court's legitimacy, given Strasbourg's firm commitment to treating the Convention as a "living instrument," which it interprets progressively to enhance the effectiveness of rights protection (chapter 4). To the extent that consensus analysis is employed relatively consistently, and in good faith, it will contribute to the Court's legitimacy in several inter-related ways.[31] First, it enables the Court to survey how much "implied consent" among states exists to extend the scope of coverage, or to raise standards of protection in other ways. Second, it facilitates ongoing "dialogue" between the Court, national officials, and other stakeholders on such questions. In fact, parties today file their own assessments of indicators of consensus, as do third-party states and NGOs submitting briefs as *amici*. Third, consensus analysis provides a relatively transparent means for states to monitor the extent to which "the Court honours its subsidiary role."[32] Last, it provides a response to the charge that robust rights review is inherently counter-majoritarian. As we argue, the Court has clearly embraced majoritarian activism as a means of overcoming

[30] Bjorge (2015: 201). [31] Dzehtsiarou (2015: 175–6).
[32] Dzehtsiarou (2015: 175–6).

rights minimalism. Dzehtsiarou is critical of the Court's inconsistent application of consensus analysis, as we are. But, he reports, the Court's methodology has become more consistent over time, and its comparative research more dependable.[33] We, too, have found that it is quite rare for the Court to ignore a clear consensus, or to fabricate one where none exists.

While these studies are exemplary, very few intensive systematic, comparative studies on the domestic impact of the ECHR exist.[34] Much remains a mystery. Questions regarding the formal interactions between domestic supreme courts and Grand Chambers are, of course, more tractable. How often do Grand Chambers review rulings of domestic apex courts? How often do Grand Chambers find a violation on the basis of how such courts have adjudicated a qualified right? Our data set provides some first-order responses, if not conclusive ones.

Since the entry into force of Protocol no. 11, Grand Chambers have produced ninety-eight judgments in which they review a final ruling of a domestic apex court concerning one of the qualified rights: Articles 8–11; and Protocol no. 1 (rights to property and education). In fifty-one (52%) of these cases, the European Court censured the national court, finding a violation of rights where the latter did not. In forty-seven judgments (48%), a Grand Chamber agreed with, or at least found no violation stemming from, the ruling by the domestic apex court. These ratios have remained remarkably stable over nearly two decades. Figure 5.1 plots the number of Grand Chamber judgments that review a national apex court decision on these qualified rights, pursuant to an individual petition registered under Protocol no. 11: n = 69.[35] In thirty-seven judgments (54%), the Court declared at least one violation; in three findings of violation, the

[33] Dzehtsiarou (2015: 40–5).

[34] See also Anagnostou and Mungiu-Pippidi, eds. (2014).

[35] That is, we removed the cases filed with the Commission under the pre-Protocol no. 11 regime.

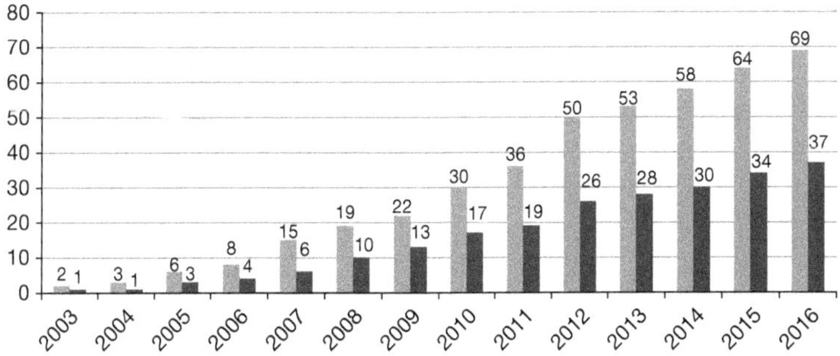

Figure 5.1. Cumulative Number of Domestic Apex Court Rulings Reviewed by a Grand Chamber, and Findings of Violation Found (Pursuant to an Individual Petition under Protocol no. 11)

Source: Judgments of the European Court of Human Rights. Data compiled by Alec Stone Sweet, Christine Landfried, Dominik Rennert, Eliška Holubová, and Jolin Chen.

Court sided with national judges, strongly criticizing executives and legislatures for failing to abide by rulings of apex courts.[36] Thus, in the Protocol no. 11 system, Grand Chambers have declared violations issuing from rulings by national constitutional and supreme courts in thirty-four of sixty-nine cases (49%).[37]

Although we cannot explore the point fully here, these results provide support for certain well-known theories of adjudication, including Priest-Klein,[38] which predicts a "tendency toward 50 percent plaintiff victories among litigated cases" under conditions of uncertainty, given prior opportunities for withdrawal and settlement. Balancing

[36] *Centro Europa 7 v. Italy* (GC, 7 June 2012); *Kurić v. Slovenia* (GC, 26 June 2012); *Ališić v. Bosnia* (GC, 16 July 2014). The data set contains three more judgments in this category, on applications registered prior to November 1998, but decided after that date: *Hasan and Chaush v. Bulgaria* (GC, 26 October 2000); *Broniowski v. Poland* (GC, 22 June 2004); *Hutten-Czapska v. Poland* (GC, 19 June 2006).

[37] In six cases, apex courts had rejected an appeal, or dismissed the case without ruling on the point of law to be criticized by the Court, resulting in a violation in Strasbourg: *Perdigao v. Portugal* (GC, 16 November 2010); *D.H. v. Czech Republic* (GC, 13 November 2007); *Evans v. United Kingdom* (GC, 10 April 2007); *Sahin v. Germany* (GC, 8 July 2003); *Souza Ribiero v. France* (GC, 13 December 2012); *Sommerfeld v. Germany* (GC, 8 July 2003).

[38] Priest and Klein (1984).

situations are typically rooted in strong conditions of uncertainty. Some cases involve new fact contexts and legal claims, which require a Grand Chamber to consider old precedents and new extensions of rights. Others involve domestic failures to properly adjudicate qualified rights, including national resistance to the European Court's case law. Most of the important cases are referred to a Grand Chamber by state officials anxious to defend national approaches to the qualified rights in question. By the time a Grand Chamber reviews a decision of a national high court, judges and other state officials have had multiple opportunities to assess and adapt state law in a bid to remove the case from consideration beyond the domestic arena. The upshot is that these Grand Chamber cases always involve questions of making new law and the multi-level coordination of rights protection.

We now examine in more fine-grained detail how, and the extent to which, the regime has transcended rights minimalism.

RAISING THE FLOOR

When the Court raises the minimal standard, it forecloses margin of appreciation considerations going forward, at least for the specific permutation of the right in question. The minimal standard takes on rule-like characteristics: maintaining the floor is obligatory. In Kantian terms, such rulings stipulate that there is no UPR-compliant reason for a state to maintain weaker protections. The Court typically takes a two-step approach, combining (i) the progressive exposition of the principles underlying the right in question, which it presents as a synthetic exposition of its case law; and (ii) consensus analysis, through which it assesses, comparatively, societal and legal trends in the regime as a whole, and sometimes beyond Europe and in international law.

The Court has been most successful at raising the floor in cases involving discrimination. These rulings exhibit an unambiguous Kantian gloss, in that they extend protections to groups that had been denied equal juridical status under national law. The Convention was designed to secure individual rights; but activated by strategic litigation and an assertion of its own clear policy preferences, the Court has come "to embrace a multifaceted set of rights" claimed by marginalized groups.[39] The Roma, for instance, have long suffered exclusionary treatment in many parts of Europe. In a series of cases brought by the European Roma Rights Centre,[40] the Court has responded by requiring states not only to prohibit such discrimination, but to take into consideration more proactively the "special needs" of this ostracized group.[41] Strategic litigating and similar considerations have also organized the Court's approach to sexual orientation and gender identity,[42] our focus here.

A nascent mode of majoritarian activism appeared in the Court's ruling in *Dudgeon v. the United Kingdom* (1981), which involved a Northern Ireland statute that criminalized homosexual sex. In its judgment, the Court took pains to contrast the law under review with the far less harsh laws of England, Wales, and Scotland. Reflecting on the situation in the rest of Europe, it noted that:

> As compared with the era when that legislation was enacted, there is now a better understanding, and in consequence an increased tolerance, of homosexual behaviour to the extent that in the great majority of the member States of the Council of Europe it is no longer considered to be necessary or appropriate to treat

[39] Anagnostou and Psychogiopoulou, eds. (2010: 4).

[40] The Centre's website is located at http://www.errc.org/strategic-litigation-european-court-of-human-rights.

[41] The leading Grand Chamber case is *D.H. v. the Czech Republic* (GC, 13 November 2007), holding that the state had violated the Convention by funneling Roma children into separate schools, and laying out guidelines for identifying and combatting discrimination.

[42] See the "strategic litigation" section of the International Lesbian, Gay, Bisexual, Trans and Intersex Association—Europe website: http://www.ilga-europe.org/what-we-do/our-advocacy-work/strategic-litigation.

> homosexual practices . . . as in themselves a matter to which the sanctions of the criminal law should be applied.[43]

The Court acknowledged that there were, in Northern Ireland, "profound differences of attitude and public opinion . . . in relation to questions of morality." But it refused to legitimize its outlier status,[44] while signaling to other states that it would look upon public reasons for excluding homosexuals with suspicion.

In *Smith and Grady* (1999), the Court required the UK to permit service members who were openly gay and lesbian to serve in the military. The ruling contributed to the dismantling of separation of power doctrines (i.e., Wednesbury deference) that had prevented the courts from engaging in testing the proportionality of the prohibition (chapter 3). It also highlights Strasbourg's active role in identifying and filling gaps in protection in partnership with national judges. In the domestic rulings, which date prior to the entry into force of the Human Rights Act (1998), UK judges admitted that the military's policy violated the fundamental rights of the petitioners, but confessed to being unable to provide a remedy (due to the constraining presence of Wednesbury unreasonableness and the absence of the Human Rights Act). As the Master of the Rolls of the UK High Court observed:

> [T]he UK's obligation, binding in international law, to respect and ensure compliance with [Art. 8 ECHR] is not one that is enforceable by domestic courts. The relevance of the Convention in the present context is as background to the complaint of irrationality. The fact that a decision-maker failed to take account of Convention obligations when exercising an administrative discretion is not of itself a ground for impugning the exercise of that discretion.[45]

[43] *Dudgeon v. the United Kingdom* (Plenary, 22 October 1981), para. 60.
[44] *Dudgeon*, para. 56.
[45] *Smith and Grady v. the United Kingdom* (27 September 1999), para. 38.

Nevertheless, judges detailed their disagreements with the policy, tracing the route it expected the European Court to follow, and urging the plaintiffs to apply to Strasbourg.[46]

The Section began by invoking *Dudgeon*: since "the relevant restrictions concern 'a most intimate part of an individual's private life,' there must exist 'particularly serious reasons' before such interferences can satisfy" Convention requirements.[47] It then dismissed the reasons given by the government to exclude homosexuals from service, including the risk that to do otherwise would negatively affect fighting moral, and put gays and lesbians themselves at risk of harm from homophobic peers.[48] The Court gave consensus analysis pride of place:

> The Government . . . [has] argued that no worthwhile lessons could be gleaned from the relatively recent legal changes in those foreign armed forces which now admitted homosexuals. The Court disagrees. It notes the evidence before the domestic courts to the effect that the European countries operating a blanket legal ban on homosexuals in their armed forces are now in a small minority. It considers that, even if relatively recent, the Court cannot overlook the widespread and consistently developing views and associated legal changes to the domestic laws of Contracting States on this issue.
>
> Accordingly, the Court concludes that convincing and weighty reasons have not been offered by the Government to justify the policy against homosexuals in the armed forces or, therefore, the consequent discharge of the applicants from those forces.[49]

The UK lifted the ban in 2000, after a government commission determined that there would be no significant negative effects of integrating

[46] *Smith and Grady*, para. 38.
[47] *Smith and Grady*, para. 88.
[48] *Smith and Grady*, paras. 95–102.
[49] *Smith and Grady*, paras. 104–5.

homosexuals into the armed forces. The UK began actively recruiting gays and lesbians into the military shortly thereafter.[50]

After incorporation through the Human Rights Act, the UK courts have a relatively strong record of compliance with the European Court's case law.[51] Indeed, with respect to discrimination, they have applied principles of inclusion in ways that go beyond strict compliance with the Court's judgments. Under the Act, the UK courts may not set aside statutes judged to be incompatible with the Convention; but they are under an obligation to interpret national law in compatibility with the Convention, while taking account of the Strasbourg Court's jurisprudence.[52] In *Ghaidan v. Godin-Mendoza* (2004), for example, UK judges read into statutes governing inheritance and survivorship protections for same-sex couples, notwithstanding clear language to the contrary. As the House of Lords (now the UK Supreme Court) put it:

> There are certain grounds of factual difference which by common accord are not acceptable, without more, as a basis for different legal treatment. Differences of race or sex or religion are obvious examples. Sexual orientation is another. This has been clearly recognised by the European Court of Human Rights.[53]

These types of outcomes reflect the overlapping obligations and interests of two trustee courts, domestic and transnational, in raising standards of protection.

There are not always clear trends in European law and practice, particularly around emerging social or scientific issues. Yet, even in cases in which states are able to demonstrate a "pressing social need," the Court is usually careful to require consideration of rights in

[50] Goldberg (2011). [51] Bjorge (2015: chs. 3, 4, 7).
[52] Besson (2008: 40–3).
[53] *Ghaidan v. Godin-Mendoza* (21 June 2004) [UKHL], para. 9 (Lord Nicholls of Birkenhead).

policy debates going forward. Adjudicating important disputes under Article 8 are rarely one-shot affairs. Rather, they are episodes in a cumulative process of building the principles that will constrain future policymaking.

In *Fretté v. France* (2002), pursuant to another application admitted prior to Protocol no. 11, the Section held that refusing to allow a gay man to adopt a child fell within France's margin of appreciation.[54] Invoking the absence of European consensus "on social issues on which opinions within a democratic society may reasonably differ widely,"[55] it accepted France's claim that the ban was necessary to protect children.[56] Six years later, in *E.B. v. France* (2008),[57] the Grand Chamber reversed, while noting that only ten of the forty-seven member states allowed homosexuals to adopt.

The case was brought by a lesbian who, although involved in a long-term, stable relationship, had been denied authorization to adopt a child by French authorities. The psychologist assigned to evaluate E.B.'s suitability, described her as "enthusiastic and warm-hearted," "very protective of others," and having "very positive . . . ideas about child-rearing," but nonetheless had decided that a lesbian couple would be unlikely to provide "a stable and reliable paternal referent," which children need in order "to forge their identity."[58] State officials turned down the adoption request, in part, because E.B. could not give the "adopted child a sufficiently structured family framework in which to flourish."[59] The case ultimately reached the Council of State, which upheld the decision, noting "the absence of [male] identification markers due to the lack of a paternal role model or referent," as well as E.B.'s homosexual "lifestyle."

[54] *Fretté v. France* (26 February 2002), para. 41.

[55] *Fretté*, para. 41.

[56] The Court paid special attention to the fact that the Council of State, France's supreme administrative court, had also considered the lack of scientific agreement on key issues, *Fretté*, para. 42.

[57] *E.B. v. France* (GC, 22 January 2008).

[58] *E.B.*, para. 11.

[59] *E.B.*, para. 17.

The Grand Chamber began by giving an expansive interpretation to the scope of Article 8:

> [T]he notion of "private life" within the meaning of Art. 8 . . . is a broad concept which encompasses the right to establish and develop relationships with other human beings, the right to "personal development" [and] the right to self-determination. It encompasses elements such as names, gender identification, sexual orientation and sexual life, which fall within the personal sphere protected by Art. 8, and the right to respect for both the decisions to have and not to have a child.[60]

After a detailed review of the decision-making of French officials, it ruled that the state had violated E.B.'s rights, given that "the applicant's homosexuality was a determining factor."[61] The Court's case law on direct discrimination, although built on majoritarian foundations, had become more categorical and protective.[62]

Her position reinforced, E.B. sued again. In November 2009, twenty-two months after winning in Strasbourg and more than eleven years after requesting permission to adopt a child, a French court ordered officials to authorize the adoption. In 2013, the French Parliament legalized same-sex marriage and adoption; and the French supreme civil and administrative courts now treat these statutory rights as overlapping with Article 8, and aggressively enforce the non-discrimination norms in tandem.

The importance of inclusion extends to issues of gender identity. In a stream of cases decided before the entry into force of Protocol no. 11, the Court refused to require legal recognition of a change in gender, given that only a handful of progressive states had moved in

[60] *E.B.*, para. 43.

[61] *E.B.*, para. 84. The Court also emphasized that the psychological report recommended to reject E.B.'s request was based in part "on [E.B.'s] 'unusual attitude' to men in [which] men are rejected"; para. 85.

[62] *E.B.*, para. 96.

that direction.[63] In the last of these, the Court put states on notice that change was coming: "there is an increased social acceptance of transsexualism and an increased recognition of the problems which post-operative transsexuals encounter."[64] Though it found no violation, the Court indicated that states should be reviewing their positions. In *Christine Goodwin v. the United Kingdom* (2002), it finally moved, a Grand Chamber holding that the refusal to recognize sex changes had fallen outside the scope of the UK's margin of appreciation, and was counter to European trends.[65] In a now famous pronouncement, the Court made it clear that consensus analysis involved more than a rote counting of states:[66]

> In accordance with the principle of subsidiarity, it is indeed primarily for the Contracting States to decide on the measures necessary to [resolve] within their domestic legal systems the practical problems created by the legal recognition of post-operative gender status, the Contracting States must enjoy a wide margin of appreciation. The Court . . . attaches less importance to the lack of evidence of a common European approach to the resolution of the legal and practical problems posed, than to the clear and uncontested evidence of a continuing . . . trend . . . of increased social acceptance of transsexuals [and] of legal recognition of the new sexual identity of post-operative transsexuals.[67]

Within the Council of Europe, state officials reacted by constructing a common European approach, gradually codifying rules and

[63] *Rees v. the United Kingdom* (Plenary, 17 October 1986), para. 42; *Cossey v. the United Kingdom* (Plenary, 27 September 1990), para. 40; *Sheffield and Horsham v. the United Kingdom* (GC, 30 July 1998).

[64] *Sheffield and Horsham*, para. 60.

[65] *Christine Goodwin v. the United Kingdom* (GC, 11 July 2002), para. 85.

[66] Dzehtsiarou (2015: 66) calls the international trend claim "far fetched," noting how rare it is for the Court to take such an expansive position in order to narrow the margin of appreciation. Letsas (2013: 116), by contrast, sees *Christine Goodwin* as a turning point in the Court's approach to consensus.

[67] *Christine Goodwin*, para. 85.

principles in order to give "full legal recognition in all areas of life" to transgender persons.[68]

Majoritarian activism has also underwritten the establishment of positive obligations under Article 8. In *Vallianatos v. Greece* (2013), the Grand Chamber announced that the state must extend its civil union law to cover same-sex couples.[69] If states choose to create benefits for heterosexual couples, then the European Court will "require particularly serious reasons by way of justification" for denying homosexuals access to them.[70] By 2013, according to briefs filed by NGOs as *amici*, Greece was alone in excluding same-sex couples from such unions.[71] It is important to recall that the Court treats consensus analysis as a means of helping it weigh the values to be balanced, not as dispositive in itself. The Grand Chamber noted:

> The fact that, at the end of a gradual evolution, a country finds itself in an isolated position . . . does not necessarily imply . . . conflicts with the Convention . . . Nevertheless, . . . the Court considers that the Government have not offered convincing and weighty reasons capable of justifying the exclusion of same-sex couples from the scope of [the law].[72]

The *Vallianatos* ruling did not require states to provide civil unions, but it did place them under an obligation to respect the non-discrimination principle when doing so.[73]

Less than two years later, in *Oliari v. Italy* (2015),[74] the Court implied that protections for stable same-sex couples were obligatory. The case reflected the fact that Italian lawmakers, after decades of inaction,

[68] Council of Europe: *Protecting Human Rights of Transgender Persons* (November 2015). Available at: https://rm.coe.int/1680492119.

[69] *Vallianatos v. Greece* (GC, 7 November 2013).

[70] *Christine Goodwin*, para. 97.

[71] *Vallianatos*, para. 69.

[72] *Vallianatos*, para. 92.

[73] *Vallianatos*, para. 92.

[74] *Oliari v. Italy* (21 July 2015).

had failed to comply with a 2010 ruling of the Italian Constitutional Court (ICC) ordering Parliament to give effect to the fundamental right of such couples to legal recognition. When Parliament defaulted yet again, the President of the ICC lamented that:

> Dialogue is sometimes . . . difficult with [our] natural interlocutor. This is particularly so in cases where [the ICC] solicits the legislature to modify a legal norm which it considered to be [contrary to] the Constitution. Such requests are not to be underestimated.[75]

The Strasbourg Court sided with the ICC. Invoking *Vallianatos*, a Section declared that the right in question was associated with the very core of Article 8. Relying on polls showing general support for homosexuality among Italians, it accused officials of hiding behind an outdated vision of its own society:[76]

> While the Government is usually better placed to assess community interests, in the present case the Italian legislature seems not to have attached particular importance to the indications set out by [its own] national community, including the general Italian population and the highest judicial authorities in Italy.[77]

Greece and Ireland both adopted legislation recognizing same-sex unions shortly thereafter.

In these policy domains, and many others, majoritarian activism has contributed to the Court's success in overcoming forces favoring minimalism. In a 2014 study on the implementation of LGBT rights in Council of Europe countries, Helfer and Voeten found that from 1991 to 1998 no member state adopted anti-discrimination policies to protect LGBT people; after the entry into force of Protocol no. 11, at

[75] *Oliari*, para. 43. [76] *Oliari*, paras. 176, 181. [77] *Oliari*, para. 179.

least sixteen countries enhanced protection, some changing their laws relatively comprehensively.[78] They concluded that:

> [The Court's rulings have] the greatest marginal effect in countries where public acceptance of homosexuals [was] low. This finding is contrary to a prevailing critique of human rights treaties and of international laws and institutions more generally—that they matter most where they are needed least . . . [But it is] consistent with the idea that the [Court] follows a strategy of "majoritarian activism," using the laws and policies of most member countries as a benchmark for developing international standards.[79]

Judgments that find a violation in a state that is relatively receptive to upgrading rights protection tend to bolster efforts to do the same in more reticent countries.[80]

THE LIMITS OF CONSENSUS ANALYSIS

The Court routinely assesses European trends when it adjudicates qualified rights. But there are types of cases in which: (i) it has made little productive use of consensus analysis—including with respect to religious expression; and (ii) it has upheld a national approach that starkly contrasts with the dominant positions of European states on the same question—including abortion. These cases have also generated what are, arguably, the Court's most controversial rulings.

Disputes involving church-state relations are the most prominent examples of rulings falling under the first category. Nonetheless, the Court has established relatively stable principles under Article 9, which it underscores in every important new decision. In Kantian terms, the thrust of these principles is to help states secure the

[78] Helfer and Voeten (2014: 17). [79] Helfer and Voeten (2014: 4).
[80] See also chapter 4 on the *erga omnes* effects of the European Court's case law.

"external freedom of all" (the UPR), given the diversity of belief systems in Europe. In the Court's own words:

> In a democratic society, in which several religions or branches of the same religion coexist within one and the same population, it may be necessary to place restrictions on [Art. 9 freedoms] in order to reconcile the interests of the various groups and ensure that everyone's beliefs are respected. However, in exercising its regulatory power . . . in its relations with the various religions, denominations and beliefs, the State has a duty to remain neutral and impartial. What is at stake here is the preservation of pluralism and the proper functioning of democracy.[81]

The Court has, accordingly, placed states under obligations: to create the conditions for religious pluralism to thrive; to recognize the existence and autonomy of faith-based communities; to refrain from interfering with their "normal functions"; to protect them from incitement to "hatred and hostility"; and to ensure that individuals are not punished in educational institutions and the workplace on the basis of their beliefs.[82]

Consensus analysis has done little work, in part, because church-state relations display wide cross-national variance, and partly because of a relative small caseload (Table 5.1). Applications received rarely concern the same issues. Rulings under Article 9 typically address idiosyncratic domestic decisions or traditions, giving the Court fewer opportunities to track consensus, to build precedent, and to sustain inter-judicial dialogue. It is also worth noting that, since the Treaty of Westphalia (1648), the settlement of religious conflict and the construction of modern notions of state sovereignty have gone

[81] Research Division of the ECHR, *Overview of the Court's Case Law on Freedom of Religion* (2013: 7). Available at: http://www.echr.coe.int/Documents/Research_report_religion_ENG.pdf.

[82] *Overview of the Court's Case Law on Freedom of Religion* (2013: 12–22).

hand in hand, and the Court may well be reticent to disrupt these arrangements.

Although it might be prudent for the Court to abstain from dictating rigid responses to highly sensitive questions, we see no room for a Kantian trustee to abdicate its fiduciary obligations (chapter 2). The most important of these is to determine whether the state measures under review restrict freedoms in a manner that is consistent with the UPR. Variation among states too might justify giving them a wider margin of appreciation, but it does not absolve the Court of its independent duty to conduct serious inquiry into the "pressing social need" for limiting religious practices, and into the proportionality of the means employed. We now turn to three rulings in which deference to states has exposed the Court to charges of abdication.

In *Lautsi v. Italy* (2011), a Grand Chamber reviewed the Italian practice of hanging crucifixes on the walls of public school classrooms, as permitted by regulations dating from the nineteenth century, and reasserted by fascist governments in the inter-war period.[83] Ms. Lautsi complained that crucifixes displayed in her children's school contravened the right to a secular education (also guaranteed by the Italian Constitution and the ICC's case law), and a breach of the neutrality principle.[84] In its handling of the case, the Italian supreme administrative court (*Consiglio di Stato*) had upheld the practice on the grounds of national heritage:

> [I]n Italy the crucifix is capable of expressing, symbolically of course, but appropriately, the religious origin of those values—tolerance, mutual respect, valorisation of the person, affirmation of one's rights, consideration for one's freedom, the autonomy of one's moral conscience vis-à-vis authority, human solidarity and the refusal of any form of discrimination—which characterise Italian civilisation.

[83] *Lautsi and Others v. Italy* (GC, 18 March 2011).

[84] *Lautsi*, para. 41.

> Those values . . . form the basis for and spring from the fundamental norms of our [Constitution] [that] delimit the form of secularism appropriate to the Italian State.[85]

In related cases, the Italian Supreme Court (*Cassazione*) "took a contrary view," and the ICC had avoided the crucifix-in-schools question altogether, on jurisdictional grounds.[86] The ICC's position left Italians with no way to resolve the constitutional question through domestic adjudication, redirecting it to Strasbourg.

In a first ruling, a Section unanimously found for the applicant, stressing that the "presence of the crucifix may easily be interpreted by pupils of all ages as a religious sign, and they will feel that they have been brought up in a school environment marked by a particular religion."[87] The judgment produced a massive outcry. The Lautsi family found itself threatened and verbally abused, and political and religious leaders across Europe roundly condemned the Section's ruling.[88] Once the case was taken up by the Grand Chamber, a flood of *amicus* briefs beset the Court. The governments of Armenia, Bulgaria, Cyprus, the Russian Federation, Greece, Lithuania, Malta, and the Republic of San Marino argued that the Grand Chamber should overrule the Section, and resist an "American-style" standardization of issues of church and state.[89] Romania and Monaco, thirty-three members of the European Parliament, and a number of NGOs also pressed the Grand Chamber to overrule. On the other side, a long list of NGOs supported the Section's view, including the International Commission of Jurists, Eurojuris, and Human Rights Watch.

The Grand Chamber reversed, relying heavily on margin of appreciation considerations. The majority stressed that (i) "States have responsibility for ensuring, neutrally and impartially, the exercise of various religions, faiths and beliefs," (ii) that "the crucifix is above

[85] *Lautsi*, para. 16. [86] *Lautsi*, para. 24. [87] *Lautsi*, para. 55.
[88] Itzcovich (2013: 289). [89] *Lautsi*, para. 47.

all a religious symbol," and that (iii) Ms. Lautsi's grievance was "understandable."[90] One might have expected the Court to delve more deeply into the merits of the complaint, in light of its own jurisprudential principles. After all, as the Court has stated many times, it is through necessity testing that the size of the margin of appreciation is to be determined. The comparative law materials, however, could not give much guidance. The majority of states did not regulate the issue at all, and only four states expressly allowed religious symbols to be displayed in schools, if under various constraints laid down by constitutional courts.[91] Noting that "there is no European consensus on the question of the presence of religious symbols in State schools,"[92] it retreated into deference mode. The ruling provides little indication of serious deliberation on necessity. Repudiating the Section's view, the Grand Chamber repeated Italy's argument to the effect that the crucifix constituted only a "passive symbol" of religion, and noted that the applicant had provided no evidence of actual harm.[93]

In two more cases, the European Court upheld state measures suppressing religious expression in ways that, arguably, contradicted its own asserted principles. After Turkey barred women from wearing headscarves in public universities, the Court, in *Leyla Sahin* (2005), concluded that the measure fell within the State's margin of appreciation. Emphasizing that context and national history were of special significance when it came to religious disputes,[94] and confirming the position of the Turkish Constitutional Court, the Grand Chamber accepted Turkey's claim that the ban was necessary "to preserve the secular nature" of the university.[95] On the facts, it is difficult to see how secularism was under threat, given that the only disturbance created by Ms. Sahin's wearing of the scarf was to attract disciplinary action.[96]

[90] *Lautsi*, paras. 60, 66. [91] *Lautsi*, paras. 26–7. [92] *Lautsi*, para. 70.
[93] *Lautsi*, paras. 66, 72.
[94] *Leyla Sahin v. Turkey* (GC, 10 November 2005), para. 109.
[95] *Leyla Sahin*, para. 116.
[96] Dissent of Judge Tulkens, *Leyla Sahin*, para. 9.

In *S.A.S. v. France* (2014), the Court upheld a 2010 French law banning full-face burqas in public spaces, including the street. In an unusually searching review of "legitimate aim," the Grand Chamber rejected a number of rationales proffered by France, including to ensure equality (on the presumption that women wearing such a veil would be marked as inferior);[97] but it agreed that the ban could proportionately serve the interests of public safety, but "only in a context of a general threat."[98] In the most spectacular part of the decision, the Grand Chamber accepted a novel justification for limiting religious expression—which France labeled the "respect for the minimum requirements of life in society" or "living together"—insofar as it could be linked to the proper purpose of protecting "the rights and freedoms of others":[99]

> The Court takes into account . . . that the face plays an important role in social interaction. [Individuals in public] places . . . may not wish to see [the development of] practices or attitudes [that would] fundamentally call into question the possibility of [creating] open interpersonal relationships, which, by virtue of an established consensus, forms an indispensable element of community life . . . The Court is therefore able to accept that the barrier raised against others by a veil concealing the face is perceived . . . as breaching the right of others to live in [spaces capable of creating social relationships]. That being said, in view of the flexibility of the notion of "living together" and the resulting risk of abuse, the Court must engage in a careful examination of the necessity of the impugned limitation.[100]

It then admitted that for the women concerned, the ban might "have the effect of" (i) "isolating them and restricting their autonomy," (ii) "impairing the exercise of their freedom to manifest their beliefs

[97] *S.A.S. v. France* (GC, 1 July 2014), paras. 118, 119.
[98] *S.A.S.*, paras. 115, 139.
[99] *S.A.S.*, paras. 25, 121.
[100] *S.A.S.*, para. 122.

and their right to respect for their private life," and (iii) threatening their very "identity." It nonetheless ruled that the ban passed the proportionality test, in that it was "not expressly based on the religious connotation of the clothing in question but solely on the fact that it conceals the face."[101]

A second set of cases, much smaller, is comprised of rulings in which the Court upholds state measures that interfere with rights despite a strong state consensus to the contrary.[102] In the most important case, *A, B & C v. Ireland* (2010), three women challenged statutory and constitutional provisions prohibiting abortions except to save the mother's life. Fearing punishment (including "penal servitude for life") in their native Ireland, all three traveled to the UK for abortions.[103] One of the applicants, an impoverished mother of four, was obliged to rush back to Ireland the day after her abortion, and started "bleeding profusely" on the train.[104] Another—referred to as "C"—suffered from a rare form of cancer and could only be treated by chemotherapy, which would likely have killed her fetus. In principle, C had the right to an abortion under Irish law, in order to save her life, but her doctors refused, fearing legal consequences—the so-called "chilling effect."[105] All three claimed that Ireland's law violated their right to privacy (Art. 8), subjected them to degrading treatment (Art. 3), and denied them an effective remedy in domestic law (Art. 13).

The development of Irish abortion law has been particularly fraught. In 1983, Irish citizens adopted through referendum a constitutional amendment to include explicit protection for the right to life of the

[101] *S.A.S.*, paras. 141, 146, 151.

[102] Cases discussed in Dzehtsiarou (2015: 30–6).

[103] *A, B & C v. Ireland* (GC, 16 December 2010). At the time, between 4,000 and 7,000 women traveled annually from Ireland to the UK for abortions, para. 183. Today, the number has dropped closer to 3,000. See UK Department of Health Abortion Statistics (2016): 77. Available at: https://www.gov.uk/government/statistics/report-on-abortion-statistics-in-england-and-wales-for-2016.

[104] *A, B & C*, para. 16.

[105] *A, B & C*, paras. 23, 24.

unborn, "with due regard to the equal right to life of the mother."[106] The Irish Supreme Court interpreted these new provisions restrictively, to permit abortion only where "there is a real and substantial risk to the life, as distinct from the health, of the mother," which also covered the risk of suicide.[107] The judgment catalyzed override efforts to restrict access to abortion even further but, in 1992 and 2002, constitutional referenda to eliminate the self-harm exception failed.[108] Meanwhile, the ECHR and EU courts began condemning Ireland's prohibitions on women traveling overseas for abortions, and on the dissemination of information related to abortion services provided in other EU countries.[109] Referenda incorporating these judgments into Irish constitutional law were successful, producing Art. 40.3.3 of the Constitution in its current form.[110] But the Parliament implemented these changes imperfectly at best. It failed, for example, to define the term, "unborn"; it did not lay down clear procedures for accessing the medical interventions that would be necessary to protect the life of pregnant women; and it did not establish clear time limits for accessing a "lawful abortion."[111] Irish women thus possessed a narrowly constrained right to terminate a pregnancy, but could expect to be thwarted if they actually sought to exercise it.

The Court, guided in part by numerous *amici*, determined that at least thirty member states permitted abortion in cases where the mother's life was not at risk—a clear European trend toward liberalization—and that C could have obtained an abortion in at

[106] *A, B & C*, paras. 35–6.
[107] *A, B & C*, para. 42.
[108] *A, B & C*, paras. 47, 54.
[109] *A, B & C*, para. 38.
[110] *A, B & C*, paras. 47–9. Art. 40.3.3 of the Constitution of Ireland: "The State acknowledges the right to life of the unborn and, with due regard to the equal right to life of the mother, guarantees in its laws to respect, and, as far as practicable, by its laws to defend and vindicate that right. This subsection shall not limit freedom to travel between the State and another state. This subsection shall not limit freedom to obtain or make available, in the State, subject to such conditions as may be laid down by law, information relating to services lawfully available in another state."
[111] *A, B & C*, para. 64.

least forty member states.[112] Facing this dominant consensus against its position, the Irish government made a plea for autonomy: "The rights guaranteed by the Convention [are] not dependent upon the assessment of the popular will at any given time and, indeed, sometimes rights [such as the right to life of the fetus] might have to be protected against the popular will.[113]" The European Court staged a retreat:

> There can be no doubt as to the acute sensitivity of the moral and ethical issues . . . or as to the importance of the public interest at stake. A broad margin of appreciation is, therefore, in principle to be accorded to the Irish State in determining the question whether a fair balance was struck between the protection of . . . the right to life of the unborn, and the conflicting rights [of the applicants] to respect for their private lives. [T]he question remains whether this wide margin of appreciation is narrowed by the existence of a relevant consensus. . . .
>
> [T]he Court considers that there is indeed a consensus amongst a substantial majority of the Contracting States of the Council of Europe towards allowing abortion on broader grounds than accorded under Irish law. . . . However, the Court does not consider that this consensus decisively narrows the broad margin of appreciation . . .
>
> [E]ven if it appears from the national laws referred to that most Contracting Parties may in their legislation have resolved those conflicting rights and interests in favour of greater legal access to abortion, this consensus cannot be a decisive factor in the Court's examination of whether the impugned prohibition on abortion in Ireland for health and well-being reasons struck a fair balance between the conflicting rights and interests, notwithstanding an evolutive interpretation of the Convention. . . .

[112] *A, B & C*, para. 112. [113] *A, B & C*, para. 187.

> [Accordingly] the Court does not consider that the prohibition in Ireland of abortion for health and well-being reasons, based as it is on the profound moral views of the Irish people as to the nature of life . . . exceeds the margin of appreciation accorded in that respect to the Irish State.[114]

Despite the truncated quality of the reasoning, the Court did take pains to premise its position on the fact that Irish women could (i) travel abroad to obtain an abortion, and (ii) obtain medical information on abortion services,[115] rights that had been inscribed in Article 40.3.3 of the Irish Constitution following findings of violation of treaty law by the two European courts.

The *A, B & C* judgment has been widely criticized, not least, for appearing to deploy margin of appreciation considerations in ways that imply a stand-alone deference doctrine. In doing so, judges in dissent noted, the Court had betrayed its own most basic commitments:

> [I]n situations where the Court finds that a consensus exists among European States on a matter touching upon a human right, it usually concludes that [this] consensus decisively narrows the margin of appreciation which might otherwise exist if no such consensus were demonstrated. This approach is commensurate with the "harmonising" role of the Convention's case-law. Indeed, one of the paramount functions of the case-law is to gradually create a harmonious application of human rights protection, cutting across the national boundaries of the Contracting States and allowing the individuals within their jurisdiction to enjoy, without discrimination, equal protection regardless of their place of residence.[116]

[114] *A, B & C*, paras. 233–41. [115] *A, B & C*, paras. 239–41.

[116] *A, B & C*, Dissenting opinion of Judges Rozakis, Tulkens, Fura, Hirvelä, Malinverni, and Poalelungi, para. 5.

We agree with this criticism. At the same time, deference did not extend to the evaluation of deficiencies in Irish law as it stood. Most important, the Court condemned the absence of a legislative framework capable of rendering effective a woman's right to seek an abortion when her own life was in danger. It then ordered Ireland to produce such legislation, and laid down guidelines for doing so.[117]

In requiring reform, the Court initiated a dialogue with, and within, Ireland. The judgment led the Irish Parliament to convene extensive hearings,[118] which resulted in the Protection of Life During Pregnancy Act (2013), a statute designed to secure the rights of women to a life-saving termination.[119] And, in 2017, the newly elected Prime Minister promised to organize a referendum on the question of broader access to abortion by the end of 2018.[120] Almost simultaneously, however, the UN Human Rights Committee found that Ireland's abortion law for constituted "cruel, inhuman, and degrading treatment,"[121] accepting pleadings from an applicant that the European Court had rejected in *A, B & C*.[122] A vote to repeal Article 40.3.3 of the Irish Constitution is scheduled for May 2018.

In Strasbourg, the Court has used *A, B & C*[123] as a platform for enhancing protections for women in other states with restrictive abortion laws. In *P. and S. v. Poland* (2012), a fourteen-year-old girl, who had become pregnant after having been raped, endured a

[117] *A, B & C*, paras. 264–6.

[118] The hearings included testimony by religious leaders, civil society representatives, medical professionals, politicians, and lawyers, and set out not only the possible methods for complying with the procedural requirements of the Strasbourg judgment, but also the underlying values animating Irish abortion law. See Joint Committee on Health and Children Report on Protecting of Life During Pregnancy Bill (2013). Available at: https://www.oireachtas.ie/parliament/media/committees/healthandchildren/Volume1.pdf.

[119] Protection of Life During Pregnancy Act of 2013: chapter 2.

[120] https://inews.co.uk/essentials/news/world/irelands-new-leader-announces-abortion-referendum-despite-popes-visit/.

[121] United Nations Human Rights Committee, communication no. 2425/2014. 12 June 2017.

[122] Under Art. 3. *A, B & C*, paras. 164–5.

[123] See also, *Tysiąc v. Poland* (20 March 2007).

tortuous path to termination.[124] When P. sought an abortion under a derogation permitting the procedure for pregnancies resulting from rape, local doctors invoked the "conscience clause," which allowed them to refuse to perform it on the basis of their beliefs.[125] A court then placed P. in a juvenile shelter, for her own good, given that her mother had supported her decisions to seek termination.[126] Ultimately, P. was able to obtain an abortion, albeit nearly 500 kilometers from her home.[127]

The Court, relying heavily on *A, B & C*,[128] focused its critical attention on the "striking discordance between the theoretical right to abortion" and the "reality of its practical implementation"[129] in Polish law:

> [O]nce the State, acting within its limits of appreciation, adopts statutory regulations allowing abortion in some situations, it must [not limit] possibilities to obtain [it]. [The] State is under a positive obligation to create a procedural framework enabling a pregnant woman to effectively exercise her right of access to lawful abortion.[130]

The Court found a violation of Article 8 and, again, set out detailed guidelines for reform. Among other things, it stipulated that "states [must] organise their health service system [so] as to ensure that the effective exercise of freedom of conscience by health professionals . . . does not prevent patients from obtaining access to services to which they are entitled."[131] It then indicated to officials how they must balance:

> [Polish law] includes elements [that would allow] the right to conscientious objection to be reconciled with the patient's

124 *P. and S. v. Poland* (30 October 2012), para. 6.
125 *P. and S.*, paras. 10, 21, 92.
126 *P. and S.*, para. 30.
127 *P. and S.*, paras. 40–1.
128 *P. and S.*, paras. 55–6.
129 *P. and S.*, para. 70.
130 *P. and S.*, para. 99.
131 *P. and S.*, para. 106.

> interests, by making it mandatory for such refusals to be made in writing and included in the patient's medical record and, above all, by imposing on the doctor an obligation to refer the patient to another physician competent to carry out the same service. However, it has not been shown that these procedural requirements were complied with in the present case or that the applicable laws governing the exercise of medical professions were duly respected. [132]

The Court thus interpreted existing Polish law in light of Convention requirements, which seemingly mandated a specific set of protections.

The abortion cases show the Court "reading procedural safeguards" into Convention rights. As Gerards has argued, it tends to do so in "dilemma cases," including those that involve complex moral questions like abortion, euthanasia, and religion.[133] From a Kantian perspective we might think of this as a second-best alternative. The Court may well decline to raise the floor in order to avoid direct confrontation with a member state, even when consensus analysis would support enhancing protection. But it has not shirked away from insisting that rights on paper are rendered effective in practice.

CONFLICTS BETWEEN RIGHTS

Thus far, we have examined cases in which the key issue concerns whether to raise the minimal standard of rights protection. Such decisions issue from the scrutiny of the justifications marshaled by the respondent state for limiting a qualified right—under the "pressing social need" standard—reasons that the Court typically considers in light of the positions taken by other states. Some important cases,

[132] *P. and S.*, para. 107. [133] Gerards (2017: ch. 6, 147).

however, involve conflicts between two rights claims that domestic courts have resolved in ways that send the loser to Strasbourg.

In our view, the Court is in its weakest position, as an oracular trustee, when: (i) the case involves two claims linked to one or more qualified rights; (ii) it acknowledges that a national trustee court had tested the proportionality of the state measure in good faith; but (iii) disagreeing with the substantive outcome, it rebalances. Such rulings are zero-sum in structure: the value added of a new round of substantive balancing, which will merely shift burdens from one claimant to another, is zero. They also raise critical questions about Strasbourg's subsidiary role. To the extent that the Court rebalances to produce a new rule or standard, it will repudiate any discordant national jurisprudence on the same question.

In *Evans v. the United Kingdom* (2007), the Grand Chamber confronted a situation in which any decision on the merits entailed enhancing one person's rights while diminishing another's. A cancer survivor, whose only chance of having a genetic child rested on fertilized embryos that she and her ex-husband [J.] had stored when married, challenged a UK law that gave her ex-husband the right to withhold consent. The conflict pitted the Article 8 rights of both: "if the applicant is permitted to use the embryos, J. will be forced to become a father, whereas if J's refusal . . . is upheld, the applicant will be denied the opportunity of becoming a genetic parent."[134] After characterizing the UK law as "the culmination of an exceptionally detailed examination of the social, ethical and legal implications of developments in the field of human fertilisation and embryology,"[135] the Grand Chamber ruled that Parliament had struck an appropriate balance. In *Evans* and many other cases, the Court performs a subsidiary role, as the authoritative monitor of the procedural integrity of the domestic balancing process.

[134] *Evans v. the United Kingdom* (GC, 10 April 2007), para. 73.
[135] *Evans*, para. 86.

This supervisory function intersects with a core fiduciary obligation of the Court, as the regime's trustee. But the Strasbourg Court is not always so circumspect, as demonstrated by a series of rulings challenging how domestic judges had balanced privacy concerns (Art. 8) and press freedoms (Art. 10).[136] In the most high-profile of these—*Von Hannover v. Germany I* (2004)—the Court picked a fight with one of its most powerful and influential interlocutors: the German Federal Constitutional Court (GFCC).[137] The case raised the question of whether Princess Caroline of Monaco could prevent German newspapers from publishing photographs taken of her, in private moments, while on vacation in France. French law tilted toward allowing her to do so; but German law put greater weight on freedom of the press. Paparazzi therefore harassed Princess Caroline in France, with the intention of selling the photos to German tabloids.[138] The German Supreme (Civil) Court rejected her request to block publication: as a public figure "*par excellence*," Princess Caroline was not entitled to the same privacy protections as an ordinary citizen.[139] Under German constitutional doctrine, in cases where two fundamental rights conflict, PA is truncated: judges are expected to move directly to balancing. Upon appeal, the GFCC certified that the Supreme Court had adopted an appropriate approach to balancing, and dismissed Princess Caroline's complaint.[140]

The German part of this saga illustrates domestic pluralism in action. Indeed, the outcome produced is rooted in a peace settlement

[136] Including: *Heinisch v. Germany* (21 July 2011; failure to strike a fair balance between freedom of expression and reputation); *Ileana Constantinescu v. Romania* (11 December 2012; disproportionate criminal defamation conviction); *Axel Springer v. Germany* (GC, 7 February 2012; disproportionate restrictions on a publisher); *Smolorz v. Poland* (16 October 2012; improper consideration of factors in a defamation conviction); *Ageyevy v. Russia* (18 April 2013; failure to protect reputation in defamation proceedings against the press); *Cârstea v. Romania* (28 October 2014; failure to properly balance reputation against freedom of the press).

[137] *Von Hannover v. Germany* (24 June 2004).

[138] *Von Hannover*, para. 44.

[139] *Von Hannover*, para. 23.

[140] *Von Hannover*, para. 25.

negotiated between the Constitutional Court and the Supreme Court. In the landmark *Lüth* judgment of 1958, the GFCC had announced that judges were under a duty to take account of constitutional rights when relevant to private law disputes, and that they were to do so through balancing. The move would radically expand the scope of constitutional rights, while placing the adjudication of civil disputes under the supervision of the GFCC, when rights concerns warranted. The move would also lead to recurrent skirmishes with the German Supreme Court (an older and, at that time, a more prestigious institution than the GFCC), which saw itself as the master of its own domains. Over several decades of adjudicating conflicts pitting privacy rights against media prerogatives, the courts had gradually arrived at a delicately poised equilibrium, one that mixed agreement on basic principles with respect for one another's relative autonomy.[141]

In *Von Hannover I*, the European Court rebalanced, ruling that "the criteria on which the domestic courts [had] based their decisions were not sufficient to protect the applicant's private life effectively."[142] Just as provocatively, it also generated a binding interpretation of the German statute in question. The par excellence language of the law must "be interpreted narrowly," the Court insisted, in order "to ensure that the State complies with its positive obligation under the Convention to protect private life and the right to control the use of one's image."[143] It then generated a checklist of factors—adding new criteria as guidelines for balancing—that the German courts would henceforth have to consider when privacy interests and press freedoms collide.

The ruling provoked intense hostility in Germany, not least, because it threated to disturb the inter-judicial compromise that had been struck by the Supreme Court and the Constitutional Court, while placing both under Strasbourg's pedagogical authority. Nevertheless,

[141] For an overview, see Quint (1989).

[142] *Von Hannover*, para. 74.

[143] *Von Hannover*, para. 72.

when Princess Caroline again sued the tabloids, the GFCC chose to avoid direct confrontation,[144] considering the dispute under its own framework as well as that of the European Court.[145] In a long and complex judgment, the GFCC stressed that it was primarily for the civil courts to strike the balance in such cases, but that:

> [T]here would be a violation of the Constitution if the protective scope or extent of a fundamental right had been wrongly determined, and the balancing exercise [was] accordingly flawed, or if the requirements under constitutional law or the Convention had not been duly taken into account.[146]

Ultimately, the GFCC concluded that press interests outweighed Princess Caroline's privacy rights, demonstrating that it could generate the same result under both Convention and German doctrine.[147] The Princess returned to Strasbourg.

In *Von Hannover v. Germany II* (2012), the Grand Chamber responded in kind, embracing inter-judicial comity and commending the German courts:

> Where the balancing exercise has been undertaken by the national authorities in conformity with the criteria laid down in the Court's case-law, the Court would require strong reasons to substitute its view for that of the domestic courts.[148]

> Whilst the Supreme Court [has] changed its approach following the *Von Hannover* judgment, the GFCC [has] not only confirmed that approach, but also undertaken a detailed analysis of the Court's case-law in response to the applicants' complaints that the

[144] Bjorge (2015: 37).
[145] *Von Hannover v. Germany No. 2* (GC, 7 February 2012), paras. 42–53.
[146] *Von Hannover No. 2*, para. 45.
[147] *Von Hannover No. 2*, para. 53.
[148] *Von Hannover No. 2*, para. 107.

> [Supreme Court] had disregarded the Convention and the Court's case-law.[149]

On the basis of these considerations, the Grand Chamber held unanimously that there had been no violation.

The structure of this exchange, ironically enough, is reminiscent of the GFCC's own dialogic engagement with the German Supreme Court on these same questions. It may be that the GFCC recognized that partnership with the Strasbourg Court would enhance its capacity to control the Supreme Court. As in other landmark rulings, the GFCC requires the civil courts—as a matter of domestic constitutional law—to "take into account" the Convention and the Court's case law.[150] But the impact of *Von Hannover I* has been registered beyond a surface commitment to a balancing checklist. There is evidence that the ruling has led "the German courts [to attach] much less weight to the freedom of the press than before," congruent with the European Court's position.[151]

The *Von Hannover* cases might have initiated a prolonged and destructive confrontation between the two most powerful trustee courts in the regime. Instead, a delicate constitutional dialogue ensued. The GFCC ordered the German courts to base their judgments more explicitly on Convention rights and doctrine, and the European Court formally announced that it would be far more cautious when it comes to (re)balancing behind the back of a domestic trustee. While these are positive outcomes, we doubt that German courts now protect the rights in question more effectively than they did before *Von Hannover I*. Put in Kantian terms, there were multiple ways to resolve this case in UPR-compliant ways, and thus no domestic gap in rights protection for Strasbourg to fill. In our view, the Court has nothing to gain and much to lose in undermining a national apex court that has balanced in good faith to resolve a conflict between two rights claims.

149 *Von Hannover No. 2*, para. 125.

150 See chapter 3 for the discussion of *Görgülü* and the preventive detention cases.

151 *Von Hannover No. 2*, para. 90.

CONCLUSION

This chapter has focused on the adjudication of the qualified rights. Facilitated by the progressive development of (i) general principles, (ii) iterative dialogues with domestic apex courts, and (iii) consensus analysis, the Court has engaged in majoritarian activism, a strategy that has enabled it to overcome forces favoring inertia and rights minimalism. The impact of the Court's rulings is registered, most tellingly, when national officials change national law to comply with the Court's judgments, and when they make new policy and adjudicate future cases in light of the Court's evolving case law. Enhancing the effectiveness of rights protection in Europe is a joint project, involving officials at all levels of governance. From a Kantian perspective, real progress toward achieving a Rightful condition has been made. Under the tutelage of the Court, the regime has worked to secure the equal juridical status of formerly marginalized or excluded groups, not least, through the consolidation of positive state duties of recognition and protection. The Court has also taught national judges how to use the doctrinal techniques that are appropriate to a Kantian system of constitutional justice, which the latter may well adapt to their own purposes. Even when the Court has declined to upgrade the minimal standard, it has ordered laggard states to render effective the protections that are in place. Underwriting these outcomes is a learning process.[152] Most important, the trustee courts of Europe now share a common approach to assessing the validity of state measures that would limit a qualified right, requiring officials to justify restrictions under a pressing social need standard, and to ensure their proportionality.

[152] On the importance of learning to Kant's conception of history and moral development, see Kleingeld (1999).

6

Beyond Borders

INTRODUCTION

In a cosmopolitan legal order (CLO), justiciable rights are held by individuals by virtue of their humanity; state officials hold fiduciary duties to protect and respect the rights of all that come under their authority; and trustee courts, at both the domestic and transnational levels supervise how officials do so.[1] By definition, such a system exists if certain jurisdictional issues are settled in a particular way. In Kantian terms, the code of rights—the cosmopolitan constitution—must apply wherever the officials of the member states exercise authority over persons. The determining factor is the exercise of authority of the state's agents. That is, the binding nature of rights, and judicial review of state acts, is not blocked by considerations of (i) territory—where the acts attributable to member states took place, or (ii) nationality—the citizenship of rights claimants, or (iii) the legal source (a statute, or a UN Security Council Resolution) that authorized state action.

This chapter traces the process through which the European Court has gradually embraced these precepts as central components of its mission as the regime's trustee. We begin with an overview of how Grand Chambers have constructed the right to life (Art. 2),

[1] Chapters 1–3.

the prohibition of torture and inhuman treatment (Art. 3), and the right to a court and judicial remedy (Arts. 6 and 13). This case law, combined with an expansive approach to jurisdiction (Art. 1), undergirds the Court's cosmopolitan jurisprudence. We describe and assess three strains of this jurisprudence. The first operationalizes the Kantian principle of hospitality, covering expulsion, extradition, and the treatment of refugees. The second extends protections to persons whose rights have been violated by states who are not parties to the Convention, or by state parties exercising jurisdiction outside of Convention territory. The third instantiates dialogues with other treaty-based regimes when it comes to overlapping obligations to protect rights. These dialogues suggest that constitutional pluralism is an emergent property of the structure of international law beyond Europe.

Box 6 contains excerpts of the Convention and the UN Charter in this chapter.

Box 6 **Selected Provisions of the ECHR and the UN Charter**

ECHR: Rights and Obligations

ART. 1: OBLIGATION TO RESPECT HUMAN RIGHTS
The High Contracting Parties shall secure to everyone within their jurisdiction the rights and freedoms defined in Section I of this Convention.

ART. 2: RIGHT TO LIFE

1. Everyone's right to life shall be protected by law. No one shall be deprived of his life intentionally save in the execution of a sentence of a court following his conviction of a crime for which this penalty is provided by law. [Note: the death penalty is today prohibited by Protocol no. 6.]
2. Deprivation of life shall not be regarded as inflicted in contravention of this Article when it results from the use of force which is no more than absolutely necessary:
   (a) in defence of any person from unlawful violence;
   (b) in order to effect a lawful arrest or to prevent the escape of a person lawfully detained;
   (c) in action lawfully taken for the purpose of quelling a riot or insurrection.

ART. 3: PROHIBITION OF TORTURE

No one shall be subjected to torture or to inhuman or degrading treatment or punishment.

ART. 5: RIGHT TO LIBERTY AND SECURITY

1. Everyone has the right to liberty and security of person. No one shall be deprived of his liberty save in the following cases and in accordance with a procedure prescribed by law:
   (a) the lawful detention of a person after conviction by a competent court; . . .
2. Everyone who is arrested shall be informed promptly, in a language which he understands, of the reasons for his arrest and of any charge against him . . . .
4. Everyone who is deprived of his liberty by arrest or detention shall be entitled to take proceedings by which the lawfulness of his detention shall be decided speedily by a court and his release ordered if the detention is not lawful . . . .

ART. 6: RIGHT TO A FAIR TRIAL

1. In the determination of his civil rights and obligations or of any criminal charge against him, everyone is entitled to a fair and public hearing within a reasonable time by an independent and impartial tribunal established by law . . . .

ART. 13: RIGHT TO AN EFFECTIVE REMEDY

Everyone whose rights and freedoms as set forth in this Convention are violated shall have an effective remedy before a national authority notwithstanding that the violation has been committed by persons acting in an official capacity.

ART. 15: DEROGATION IN TIME OF EMERGENCY

1. In time of war or other public emergency threatening the life of the nation any High Contracting Party may take measures derogating from its obligations under this Convention to the extent strictly required by the exigencies of the situation, provided that such measures are not inconsistent with its other obligations under international law.
2. No derogation from Article 2, except in respect of deaths resulting from lawful acts of war, or from Articles 3, 4 § 1 and 7 shall be made under this provision.

Charter of the United Nations:

PREAMBLE

We the peoples of the United Nations, determined to reaffirm faith in fundamental human rights, in the dignity and worth of the human person, in the equal rights of men and women and of nations large and small . . .

ART. 1
"The Purposes of the United Nations are . . .

3. To achieve international co-operation in solving international problems of an economic, social, cultural, or humanitarian character, and in promoting and encouraging respect for human rights and for fundamental freedoms for all without distinction as to race, sex, language, or religion . . .

ART. 24

1. In order to ensure prompt and effective action by the United Nations, its members confer on the Security Council primary responsibility for the maintenance of international peace and security, and agree that in carrying out its duties under this responsibility the Security Council acts on their behalf.
2. In discharging these duties the Security Council shall act in accordance with the Purposes and Principles of the United Nations. The specific powers granted to the Security Council for the discharge of these duties are laid down in Chapters VI, VII, VIII, and XII.

ART. 25
The Members of the United Nations agree to accept and carry out the decisions of the Security Council in accordance with the present Charter.

ART. 103
In the event of a conflict between the obligations of the Members of the United Nations under the present Charter and their obligations under any other international agreement, their obligations under the present Charter shall prevail.

THE "ABSOLUTE" RIGHTS AND STATE DUTIES

In Kantian terms, a right is "absolute" in any context in which no Universal Principle of Right (UPR)-compliant reasons are available to justify its restriction.[2] As a textual matter, Articles 2 and 3 are presumptively non-derogable, neither including a limitation clause. Moreover, while Article 15 permits states to claim exemptions from Convention obligations "in times of emergency," Articles 2 and 3 are insulated from such requests. For its part, the Court has declared, in *Makaratzis v. Greece* (2004), that:

> Art. 2, which safeguards the right to life and sets out the circumstances when deprivation of life may be justified, ranks as

[2] Chapter 2.

> one of the most fundamental provisions in the Convention, from which no derogation is permitted . . . Together with Article 3 [which prohibits torture and inhuman and degrading treatment or punishment], it also enshrines one of the basic values of the democratic societies making up the Council of Europe.[3]

One might think that a human rights court would have good prudential reasons for interpreting the scope an absolute right narrowly, not least, to maintain flexibility in hard cases at the margins. In contrast, judges run little risk in giving wide scope to qualified rights, since they are empowered to assess the reasons state officials give to limit them within the proportionality framework.[4] Yet the European Court has steadily expanded the application of Articles 2 and 3, closing gaps in rights protection.

Figure 6.1 plots outcomes in all Grand Chamber judgments on the merits pursuant to pleadings of Articles 2 and 3 under Protocol no. 11; n = 47. In thirty-four of these cases (72%), the Court found at least one violation.[5] The result sharply contrasts with outcomes produced on Articles 8–11—the qualified rights—in which applicants and states have virtually an equal chance of prevailing.[6] Grand Chambers are also far more united when they interpret and apply Articles 2 and 3. Of the 34 findings of violation, Grand Chambers were unanimous in nineteen (56%), and registered two or fewer dissenting votes in twenty-five (74%).

In adjudicating Articles 2 and 3, the Court does not normally engage in consensus analysis to determine the size of a state's "margin

[3] *Makaratzis v. Greece* (GC, 20 December 2004), para. 56.

[4] Chapters 2 and 5.

[5] This count includes five cases in which the Court declared that expulsion of a person from Europe would violate, or would have violated, Art. 2 or Art. 3, if it were to be effected. *Saadi v Italy* (GC, 28 February 2008); *Tarakhel v. Switzerland* (GC, 4 November 2014); *F.G. v. Sweden* (GC, 23 March 2016); *J.K. and Others v. Sweden* (GC, 23 August 2016); *Paposhvili v. Belgium* (GC, 13 December 2016).

[6] Chapter 5 and Figure 5.1. Counting all such cases decided since the entry into force of Protocol no. 11 (n = 64), Grand Chambers found at least one violation of Art. 2 and/or Art. 3 in forty-four (69%).

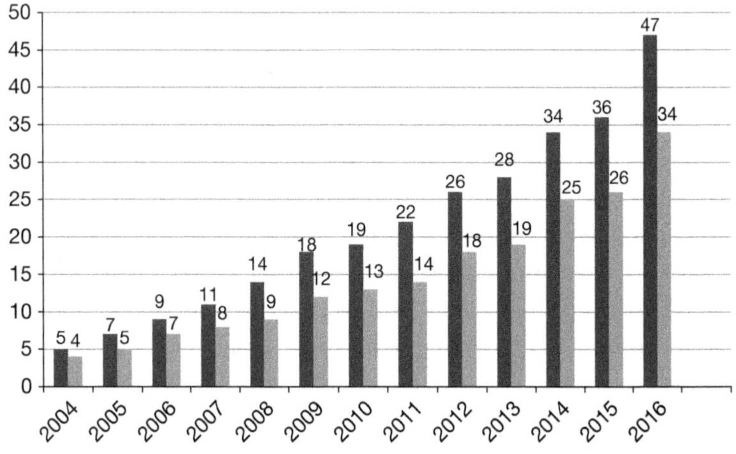

Figure 6.1. Arts. 2 and 3 ECHR: Cumulative Number of Grand Chamber Rulings, and GC Rulings Finding Violations (Pursuant to an Individual Petition under Protocol no. 11)

Source: Judgments of the European Court of Human Rights. Data compiled by Alec Stone Sweet, Christine Landfried, Dominik Rennert, Eliška Holubová, and Jolin Chen.

of appreciation."[7] Article 2 permits states to use lethal force,[8] but no more than is "absolutely necessary" to protect others from "unlawful violence," to "[quell] an insurrection or riot," and to effect arrests or prevent the escape of a prisoner. The standard, the Court stresses, is "a

[7] There are, nonetheless, important exceptions. In the abortion cases, balancing and the margin of appreciation are in play because the question involves both Art. 2 and Art. 8 (chapter 5). In *Lambert v. France* (GC, 5 June 2015), the Court rejected an Art. 2 application challenging the French Council of State's ruling that allowed termination of medical care to a comatose patient with no chances of surviving without assistance, a decision supported by some members of immediate family, but not the applicants. The Court based its decision on the lack of European consensus on the underlying issues, while praising the Council of State's "meticulous" process of developing an effective framework for dealing with them, which "exceed[ed] the requirements laid down by the law"; *Lambert*, para. 168. In a series of Art. 3 rulings, involving challenges to sentences of life imprisonment, the Court expressly recognized the states' margin of appreciation when it comes to sentencing, while insisting that Art. 3 requires states to develop mechanisms for the periodic review of life sentences in view of possible release; *Vinter and Others v. the United Kingdom* (GC, 9 July 2013); *Kaytan v. Turkey* (15 September 2015).

[8] For the Court's own synopsis of its case law, see ECHR: *Factsheet- Right to Life* (June 2013). Available at: http://www.echr.coe.int/Documents/FS_Life_ENG.pdf.

stricter and more compelling test of necessity . . . than that normally applicable when determining [under the qualified rights] whether State action is 'necessary in a democratic society.' "[9] With respect to the Convention's prohibition of "torture," and of "inhuman or degrading treatment or punishment," Strasbourg emphasizes the absence of a limitation clause to support its firmness: neither derogation nor balancing against other interests is permitted under Article 3.

Moreover, the hard substantive obligations that inhere in the "absolute" rights have steadily generated positive obligations, including state duties to develop protections, procedures for processing claims, and effective remedies.[10] Under Article 2, for instance, states are expected to initiate and maintain training programs for police and soldiers, so that the latter can properly "assess whether or not there is an absolute necessity to use firearms . . . with due regard to the pre-eminence of respect for human life as a fundamental value."[11] The Court also requires states to investigate wrongful death claims, prosecute violators, and compensate victims.

Most major Article 3 rulings concern the conditions of incarcerating prisoners, including overcrowding, poor hygiene, and lack of medical treatment. Although these cases are heavily fact-dependent, the Court has used them to construct general standards and principles, and to compile a register of domestic practices that fail to fulfill them.[12] The Court has read the right to human dignity into Articles 2 and 3, reinforcing the latter's non-derogable characteristics. States must "respect,"[13] and not "diminish,"[14] the dignity of a detainee or prisoner, for

[9] *McCann and Others v. the United Kingdom* (GC, 9 September 1995), para. 149. *McCann* is the first case on the use of lethal force decided by the Court.

[10] A similar process has taken place with respect to qualified rights (chapter 5).

[11] *Nachova and Others v. Bulgaria* (GC, 6 July 2005); *Wasilewska and Kalucka v. Poland* (23 February 2010).

[12] ECHR *Factsheet—Detention Conditions and Treatment of Prisoners* (2016). Available at: http://www.echr.coe.int/Documents/FS_Detention_conditions_ENG.pdf.

[13] *Florea v. Romania* (14 September 2010).

[14] *Peers v. Greece* (9 April 2001); *Valašinas v. Lithuania* (24 July 2001).

example. The Court also treats as absolute many of the positive duties that flow from these provisions, thereby placing national officials under continuous pressure to reform, or risk falling out of compliance. This results from the fact that the Court treats as quasi-absolute procedural obligations derived from Article 5 (requiring judicial involvement when a person's liberty is at stake) and Article 13 (to provide an effective remedy for violation of Convention rights).[15]

Positive duties do not dissipate at Europe's edge. Domestic authorities, for example, must not be even indirectly complicit in torture beyond European Convention on Human Rights (ECHR) territory. In *Saadi v. Italy* (2008),[16] the Court reaffirmed that Article 3 barred states from extraditing individuals to a non-ECHR country when "substantial grounds have been shown for believing that the person concerned, if deported, [would face] a real risk of being subjected to treatment contrary to Art. 3."[17] Exercising authority to grant interim measures under its Rules of Procedure,[18] the Grand Chamber ordered Italy to stay a decision to deport Mr. Saadi, a Tunisian national, to Tunisia. Italy complied. The Court went on to hold that his deportation would violate Article 3, citing to reports by Human Rights Watch, Amnesty International, and the US State Department showing that torture was routine in Tunisian prisons.

[15] *Assanidze v. Georgia* (GC, 8 April 2004), paras. 169–71; *Khlaifia v. Italy* (GC, 15 December 2016), para. 268. In *McKay v. the United Kingdom* (GC, 3 October 2006), para. 30, the Court declared that "Article 5 of the Convention is, together with Articles 2, 3 and 4, in the first rank of the fundamental rights that protect the physical security of an individual . . . and as such its importance is paramount. Its key purpose is to prevent arbitrary or unjustified deprivations of liberty . . . ".

[16] *Saadi v. Italy* (GC, 28 February 2008).

[17] *Saadi*, para. 125, cited as a settled principle of the Court's case law.

[18] Recall that the Court is the author of its own procedures; see chapter 4. In a "Practice Direction" of September 2016, the Court clarified its authority under Rule 39 of the Rules of Court, stating that it would rely on interim measures "only . . . in exceptional cases when, having reviewed all the relevant information, it considers that the applicant faces a real risk of serious, irreversible harm if the measure is not applied." In such situations, the Court attempts to intervene directly within the national legal order in order to stop a violation from occurring in the first place. Available at: http://www.echr.coe.int/Documents/PD_interim_measures_ENG.pdf.

In *Saadi*, the Court also pointedly rejected arguments made by Italy and the UK (as *amicus*) suggesting that states did not bear the same Article 3 obligations when the ill-treatment "is inflicted by the authorities of another State."[19] The UK had requested the Court to revisit its earlier precedent, challenging the principle that "the absolute nature of the prohibition of treatment contrary to Art. 3"[20] precluded balancing against security interests:

> [B]ecause of its rigidity that principle had caused many difficulties for the Contracting States by preventing them in practice from enforcing expulsion measures. The [UK] observed in that connection that it was unlikely that any State other than the one of which the applicant was a national would be prepared to receive into its territory a person suspected of terrorist activities. In addition, the possibility of having recourse to criminal sanctions against the suspect did not provide sufficient protection for the community.[21]

Further, insofar as its Article 3 commitments threatened to weaken Article 2 protections, a move to balancing would be justified:

> Terrorism seriously endanger[s] the right to life, which [is] the necessary precondition for enjoyment of all other fundamental rights. . . . It [is] true that the protection against torture and inhuman or degrading treatment or punishment provided by Article 3 of the Convention [is] absolute. However, in the event of expulsion, the treatment in question would be inflicted not by the signatory State but by the authorities of another State. The signatory State [is] then bound by a positive obligation of protection against torture implicitly derived from Article 3. Yet, in the field of implied positive obligations, the Court [usually accepts the view] that the

[19] *Saadi*, para. 138. [20] *Saadi*, para. 117. [21] *Saadi*, para. 117.

> applicant's rights must be weighed against the interests of the community as a whole.[22]

Although the Grand Chamber acknowledged that "States face immense difficulties in modern times in protecting their communities from terrorist violence," it insisted that such problems do not "call into question the absolute nature of Article 3."[23] Indeed:

> Since protection against the treatment prohibited by Article 3 is absolute, that provision imposes an obligation not to extradite or expel any person who, in the receiving country, would run the real risk of being subjected to such treatment. [T]here can be no derogation from that rule. It must therefore reaffirm the principle stated in the *Chahal* judgment that it is not possible to weigh the risk of ill-treatment against the reasons put forward for the expulsion in order to determine whether the responsibility of a State is engaged under Article 3, even where such treatment is inflicted by another State.[24]

Italy complied with the judgment.

"WITHIN THEIR JURISDICTION . . ."

The primary role of the European Court is to ensure that states meet their obligations under Article 1 ECHR:

> The High Contracting Parties shall secure to everyone within their jurisdiction the rights and freedoms defined in . . . this Convention.

[22] *Saadi*, paras. 119–20. [23] *Saadi*, para. 137. [24] *Saadi*, para. 138.

In most cases, the weight of the Court's reasoning rests on the content of the enumerated rights, but here we are interested the state's "jurisdiction," a threshold inquiry that has had constitutive effects. There exists a heated debate concerning the correct meaning and import of the term—"jurisdiction"—in human rights treaties.[25] The Court has taken a piecemeal approach, extending jurisdiction on a case-by-case basis, precisely where significant gaps in protections have emerged. The evolution of extraterritorial application of the Convention has been bumpy, and the leading rulings have generated controversy. Nonetheless, the Court has succeeded in extending the Convention's coverage to contexts never imagined by the regime's founders, from the high seas to the war zones of Iraq, and even to secret orders of White House officials.

In early drafts of Article 1, the founders referred to member states' obligations to "all persons residing within their territories."[26] In removing the reference to "residence," the framers gave Article 1 a cosmopolitan complexion: every person who comes within the *jurisdiction* of a member state is a rights-holder. The *travaux préparatoires*, however, had little to say about how the contours of state jurisdiction should be delineated.[27] In the pre-Protocol no. 11 regime, the Commission floated the principle that Convention duties would travel with the agents of member states wherever they operated in the world.[28] Thus, in 1975, when the wife of a former Nazi, the last man held for war crimes at Spandau prison in Berlin, claimed that the UK violated her rights by holding her husband in sustained solitary confinement, the Commission concluded that "there is in principle . . . no

[25] Besson (2012); Heijer (2011: 32); Jackson (2016: 818); Dannenbaum (2012: 731).

[26] *Banković v. Belgium* (GC, 12 December 2001), para. 19.

[27] Besson (2012: 863).

[28] "Under the first approach, which is most evidently present in the case law of the former European Commission . . . human rights obligations serve as a code of conduct for all activity of a state, regardless of territorial considerations, in which the condition of jurisdiction is satisfied if an act or omission of a state affects a person to such an extent that he or she can be considered a victim of a human rights violation," Heijer (2011: 60).

reason why acts of the British authorities in Berlin should not entail the liability of the UK."[29] But the Commission had very few occasions to elaborate the point further.

The issue became more pressing as European states engaged in joint peacekeeping efforts, counter-terrorism alliances, collaborative migration control, and other efforts that would take place outside *l'espace juridique Européenne*.[30] As streams of context-specific cases, in different spheres of action, flowed into Strasbourg, the Court gradually developed stronger, more coherent doctrines.

EXPULSION AND EXTRADITION

In 1985, a nineteen-year-old German named Jens Soering was arrested in England for check fraud.[31] At that time, Mr. Soering was wanted for the brutal murder of his girlfriend's parents in the State of Virginia, where the prosecutor promised to seek the death penalty.[32] The petitioner raised a novel argument: that to endure years on death row, while being subjected to the dangers of violence and sexual assault, would amount to treatment contrary to Article 3.[33] The Plenary Court agreed.[34]

The United States, of course, was not bound by the ECHR. Mr. Soering, however, was in the custody of UK authorities, who had sought Strasbourg's assistance in resisting US extradition demands.[35] The Court held that Article 3 required the state to investigate conditions in the extradition-requesting state, before proceeding to extradition.[36] The judgment went further, laying out the well-documented failings

[29] *Hess v. the United Kingdom* (Plenary, 28 May 1975). The case was declared inadmissible because the UK only jointly controlled the prison along with the other allied forces.

[30] De Schutter (2006: 201).

[31] *Soering v. the United Kingdom* (Plenary, 7 July 1989), para. 12.

[32] *Soering*, para. 13.

[33] *Soering*, paras. 25, 76, 101.

[34] *Soering*, para. 99.

[35] *Soering*, para. 111.

[36] *Soering*, para. 91.

of the American criminal justice system, and the conditions on death row in Virginia.[37] On this evidence, the Court found, extradition would expose Mr. Soering to a known risk that a core Convention right could be violated. Strasbourg's recourse to extra-record sources, in order to condemn conditions outside of the Council of Europe, would become a powerful tool in its arsenal, as the *Saadi* case illustrates.

In *Soering v. UK* (1989), the Court articulated a position—derived from Europe's "common heritage of political traditions, ideals, freedom and the rule of law"—on which it would heavily rely in the future:

> It would hardly be compatible with the underlying values of the Convention . . . were a Contracting State knowingly to surrender a fugitive to another State where there were substantial grounds for believing that he would be in danger of being subjected to torture, however heinous the crime allegedly committed. Extradition in such circumstances, while not explicitly referred to in . . . Article 3, would plainly be contrary to the spirit and intendment of the Article.[38]

States must not only refrain from killing and torturing people, they are also under a positive obligation to protect individuals, under Articles 2 and 3, from prohibited acts of third-party state officials.[39]

Post-Protocol no. 11 cases concerning the scope of a proactive duty of care are now common. In *F.G. v. Sweden* (2016), a Grand Chamber reviewed an Iranian asylum seeker's claim that he faced torture, inhuman and degrading treatment, or death in Iran due to his conversion from Islam to Christianity.[40] After Sweden refused to grant asylum, the applicant sought redress at the Strasbourg Court, which ruled that:

[37] *Soering*, para. 107. [38] *Soering*, para. 88. [39] Heijer (2011: 54).
[40] *F.G. v. Sweden* (GC, 23 March 2016).

> It is for the Court to consider in an expulsion case whether, in all the circumstances of the case before it, substantial grounds have been shown for believing that the person concerned, if returned, would face a real risk of being subjected to treatment contrary to Article 3 of the Convention.[41]

In such cases, the Court will normally conduct its own review of the evidence of the risks entailed by expulsion, while demanding that domestic officials do the same.[42]

As initiated in *Soering*, interim measures have been a vital tool in halting deportations pending a ruling on the merits.[43] A favorable judgment from Strasbourg would provide cold comfort to a person already turned away to face torture or death. Under Article 34, states have a duty to ensure an effective right of petition, which the Court has interpreted to mean that they cannot expel individuals who have requested an injunction pursuant to Rule 39, pending a ruling on that request.[44] Further, the Court has held that the *only* way for states to comply with their obligations under Article 13 (the right to an effective remedy) would be to suspend a deportation order subject to judicial review.[45] States have not always complied with the Court's order against expulsion or extradition, but these are the rare exceptions.[46] It is of enormous importance that most domestic systems have now

[41] *F.G.*, para. 116.

[42] The Court's expectation that member states will actively investigate conditions in the receiving country extends to expulsions between member states. *M.S.S. v. Belgium and Greece* (GC, 21 January 2011).

[43] *Soering*, para. 4. The Court's power to issue such injunctions is discussed in chapter 4.

[44] After the Court ruled in *Gebremedhin v. France* (26 April 2007) that Art. 13 required that asylum appeals have automatic suspensive effect, France revised its asylum law to guarantee the suspensive effect of an appeal to the appellate asylum body. See http://www.asylumineurope.org/reports/country/france/asylum-procedure/general/short-overview-asylum-procedure.

[45] See *Čonka v. Belgium* (5 February 2002).

[46] Chapter 4.

implemented procedures to give automatic suspensive effect to deportation orders pending appeals within national courts.[47]

States remain responsible under the Convention, even after deporting an individual, in situations in which harms were foreseeable. In a 2017 ruling, a Section held that Switzerland had violated Article 3 when it sent a Tamil asylum seeker back to Sri Lanka without sufficiently reviewing the evidence on state torture, in view of his participation in the operations of an insurgency group, the Tamil Tigers. Although Switzerland subsequently granted the petitioner asylum, and even helped his family return to the country, the Court awarded compensation for the initial breach.[48]

HOSPITALITY AND NON-REFOULEMENT

Under customary international law and the Convention Relating to the Status of Refugees (1951, 1967), states may not return asylum seekers to a country where they risk persecution based on "race, religion, nationality, membership of a particular social group or political opinion."[49] This prohibition is called the *non-refoulement* principle, of which the post-*Soering* line of cases is an expression.

It is also a concrete instantiation of the Kantian principle of hospitality. In its most narrow formulation, Kant defined Cosmopolitan Right in the following terms:

> [W]e are concerned here with Right, not with philanthropy, and in this context *hospitality* means the right of a stranger not to be treated in a hostile manner by another upon his arrival on the other's territory. If it can be done without causing his death,

[47] *De Souza Ribeiro v. France* (GC, 13 December 2012).
[48] *X. v. Switzerland* (26 January 2017). [49] Art. 33(1).

> the stranger can be turned away, yet as long as he behaves peacefully . . . his host may not treat him with hostility.[50]

While scholars have intensively debated the scope to be given to the "universal principle of hospitality,"[51] few would deny the deep connections it has with that of *non-refoulement*.[52] As Kleingeld puts it:

> [Hospitality] has significant implications. When refusing a person is impossible without leading to a person's death, admission is obligatory, at least until circumstances have improved. And one cannot legally expel a person to a country where she or he will die or be killed as a result of being expelled. Kant here . . . anticipates many of the refugee rights, including the principle of *non-refoulement*, that were established in the twentieth century.[53]

Indeed, in an early draft of *Perpetual Peace*, Kant had proposed that "a ship seeking port in a storm, or a stranded group of sailors cannot be chased away from the beach or the oasis . . . and sent back to imminent danger."[54]

Since 2010, Europe has experienced an explosive number of asylum claims caused by a severe refugee crisis that shows no signs of abating. The so-called "Arab Spring" left much of North Africa in political and economic chaos, revived ethnic conflict, and provoked a mass exodus.[55] The Syrian civil war, and the ongoing armed conflict with the so-called Islamic State in Iraq and surrounding territories, added at least 15 million more displaced people. In 2015 alone, more than

[50] *Toward Perpetual Peace among States* (8: 357–8). See chapter 1.

[51] For a review of this literature, see Brown (2009: 59–66).

[52] See Benhabib (2004: ch. 1); Criddle and Fox-Decent (2016: ch. 7); Kleingeld (2011: ch. 3).

[53] Kleingeld (2011: 77).

[54] Kleingeld (2011: 78).

[55] Moreno-Lax (2012: 577).

1.2 million refugees demanded asylum in Europe, overwhelming the capacity to process claims properly.[56]

From Africa, thousands have died making the dangerous passage across the Mediterranean to Europe. In an effort to stem the tide, countries began intercepting migrants' ships on the high seas, and returning the passengers to North African ports. The Court had long held that the principle of *non-refoulement*[57] required member states to assess asylum claims with diligence. But it confronted a novel situation in *Hirsi Jamaa v. Italy* (2012). The Italian coast guard had intercepted the applicants' rickety boat, and then forced the passengers onto an Italian ship, which returned them to Tripoli without being given the opportunity to demand asylum.[58] The case bundled together the claims of twenty-four petitioners from Somalia and Eritrea, who claimed that they were owed the same protections applicable to asylum seekers on Italian soil.[59]

The Court agreed. Because the migrants were under the effective control of Italian flagships,[60] the *non-refoulement* principle prohibited the petitioners' return to Libya, a country where they risked treatment contrary to Article 3.[61] In support, the Grand Chamber referenced reports of human rights organs and NGOs:

> [D]uring the period in question no rule governing the protection of refugees was complied with by Libya. Any person entering the country by illegal means was deemed to be clandestine and no distinction was made between irregular migrants and asylum-seekers. Consequently, those persons were systematically arrested and detained in conditions that outside visitors, such as

[56] Eurostat: Asylum Statistics (2016). Available at: http://ec.europa.eu/eurostat/statistics-explained/index.php/Asylum_statistics.

[57] For an overview of the Court's application of the *non-refoulement* principle, see de Weck (2016).

[58] *Hirsi Jamaa v. Italy* (GC, 23 February 2012), paras. 9–11.

[59] *Hirsi Jamaa.*

[60] *Hirsi Jamaa*, para. 74.

[61] *Hirsi Jamaa*, para. 113.

> delegations from the UNHCR, Human Rights Watch and Amnesty International, could only describe as inhuman. Many cases of torture, poor hygiene conditions and lack of appropriate medical care were denounced by all the observers. Clandestine migrants were at risk of being returned to their countries of origin at any time and, if they managed to regain their freedom, were subjected to particularly precarious living conditions as a result of their irregular situation. Irregular immigrants, such as the applicants, were destined to occupy a marginal and isolated position in Libyan society, rendering them extremely vulnerable to xenophobic and racist acts.[62]

Strasbourg presents its ruling in *Hirsi Jamaa* as an obvious and necessary extension of *Soering*, *Saadi*, and the *non-refoulement* principle to an emergent context, which the Convention, as a "living instrument,"[63] is meant to cover. Yet prior to *Hirsi*, domestic courts in the regime had routinely excluded migrants from rights protection until they had reached solid ground, the stance of US courts as well.[64] Had the Court permitted consensus analysis to control, the judgment would have been presumptively precluded. Instead, the Court forcefully took a cosmopolitan position.

AMERICA'S "WAR ON TERROR" AND "EXTRAORDINARY RENDITION"

Following the September 11, 2001 terrorist attacks on the World Trade Center and other targets, the US began an aggressive global campaign to apprehend and interrogate suspected terrorists. American authorities sought assistance from its European allies, and many

[62] *Hirsi Jamaa*, para. 125.
[63] *Hirsi Jamaa*, paras. 70, 114, 175.
[64] The US Supreme Court has ruled, in the context of Haitian refugees in *Sale v. Haitian Centers Council*, that interception and push-back policies on the high seas do not violate the United States' legal obligations; 509 U.S. 155 (1993).

complied. As the *Al Nashiri v. Poland* (2014) case revealed, the Polish government accorded covert American planes access to a remote airport and a nearby intelligence services building.[65] This airport would become just one stop on the so-called "Guantanamo Express," a global network of logistical support stretching from Afghanistan to Thailand, across Europe, and from Morocco to Cuba. It is through these routes and facilities that the Central Intelligence Agency (CIA) transported "high value" suspects, subjecting them to what the Bush Administration referred to as "enhanced interrogation techniques," which Europeans consider to be "torture."[66] The CIA "rendered" some detainees, including the applicant, Mr. Al Nashiri (the purported mastermind of the 2000 bombing of the USS Cole, off the Yemen coast) through Poland. CIA operatives interrogated their subjects in the intelligence building for weeks, including through the use of waterboarding.[67] After subjecting Mr. Al Nashiri to such treatment over four years in secret detention centers—"black sites"—in five different countries, the CIA shipped him to prison in Guantanamo in 2006, where he endured more torture.

Meanwhile, near Skopje, the capital of the Former Yugoslav Republic of Macedonia (FYROM), a German citizen of Lebanese origin, Khaled El-Masri, was stopped in a border check.[68] At the request of the US, FYROM officials kept Mr. El-Masri prisoner in a Skopje hotel for several weeks, refusing to give reasons for his detention or allowing any contact with the outside world.[69] After nearly a month of confinement, CIA agents arrived to interrogate him, which they did in a language he did not speak (English). The ordeal culminated in a brutal beating, rape with a sharp object, forced tranquilization, and

[65] *Al Nashiri v. Poland* (24 July 2014), paras. 95–6, 297.

[66] *Al Nashiri*, paras. 48–68 (going into extreme detail on the CIA's rendition and enhanced interrogation practices post-9/11).

[67] *Al Nashiri*, paras. 48–68.

[68] *El-Masri v. the Former Yugoslav Republic of Macedonia* (GC, 13 December 2012), para. 17.

[69] *El-Masri*, paras. 18–19.

rendition. Placed in an adult diaper, he was then led to a private airplane,[70] which rendered him to the "Salt Pit" in Afghanistan, the most notorious of the "black sites."[71] There, operatives repeatedly tortured Mr. El-Masri, who protested his innocence in two hunger strikes, which resulted in force-feeding.[72] After four months in the Salt Pit, the CIA concluded that they had abducted the wrong man and that, in fact, Mr. El-Masri had no discernible ties to terrorism.[73] The CIA then flew him, blindfolded again, to an unknown location, where he was left alone on a hilltop, and told to start walking. Fearing that he would be shot if he turned around, Mr. El-Masri walked until he reached a town, at which point he discovered that he was in Albania.[74] Mr. El-Masri then returned to Germany, having lost forty pounds and his home; his family, assuming the worst, had gone to Lebanon.

These cases began in the US court system, American officials being directly responsible for the abductions and torture. As of 2017, Mr. Al Nashiri's suit languishes in federal court, suspended while the competence of military tribunals to judge Guantanamo detainees remains in legal limbo.[75] With the support of the American Civil Liberties Union, Mr. El-Masri brought an action against multiple defendants: the director of the CIA; private airline companies used in the operation; and unnamed CIA agents for violation of the US Constitution (prohibition against arbitrary detention and cruel and unusual punishment) and international law (the prohibition of state-sponsored torture). In 2006, a Federal District Court dismissed his case, invoking the "state secrets doctrine."[76] Once a case is placed under that doctrine, pleadings are blocked altogether. In fact, there were no secrets to be kept. Mr. El-Masri had already given open testimony before numerous national

[70] *El-Masri*, paras. 21–2.
[71] *El-Masri*, para. 24.
[72] *El-Masri*, paras. 26–7.
[73] *El-Masri*, para. 128. ("[T]the US Secretary of State Condoleezza Rice had admitted to [Angela Merkel], in a private discussion, that the US had mistakenly abducted and detained the applicant.")
[74] *El-Masri*, para. 32.
[75] *In re Al-Nashiri*, 835 F.3d 110 (D.C. Cir. 2016).
[76] *El-Masri v. Tenet*, 437 F.Supp. 2d 530 (E.D.Va. 2006).

and international bodies, and news outlets had reported the same facts asserted in his filings in Federal Court. In 2007, the Court of Appeals for the 4th Circuit upheld the dismissal, and the US Supreme Court declined to hear the case.[77]

The American state secrets doctrine is a product of judge-made, federal common law. From the point of view of rights protection, the doctrine requires judges to abdicate their responsibilities as protectors of rights, creating a glaring gap. As invoked in Mr. El-Masri's case, it made the executive—in effect, the American security apparatus—the sole branch of government with authority to speak to cases involving rendition and torture, which the executive has exercised by remaining silent. Global interests are also implicated. As the US Department of State has long recognized, the right of every human being to be free from torture constitutes a *jus cogens* norm, one of a handful of the most fundamental human rights recognized by all civilized nations. Once American courts had shunned Mr. El-Masri, European judicial officials acted. In admitting these applications, the European Court was fully aware that it was, in effect, donning the mantle of a transnational court of first instance.

The Court now encountered a serious procedural and evidentiary problem. The governments of Poland and the FYROM denied any knowledge of the CIA's activities, refused to respond to the pleadings, and rejected Strasbourg's requests for evidence. They, too, invoked a "states secrets" doctrine, which the Court brushed aside:

> In cases where the Government have advanced confidentiality or security considerations as the reason for their failure to produce the material requested, the Court has had to satisfy itself that there were reasonable and solid grounds for treating the documents in question as secret or confidential.[78]

[77] *El-Masri v. the United States*, 552 U.S. 947 (memorandum denying certiorari).

[78] *Al Nashiri*, para. 365. See also, paras. 399–400, 411. ("No trace of the applicant can, or will, be found in any official records in Poland because his presence on the

"The concept of 'State secrets,'" the Court bluntly noted, "has often been invoked to obstruct the search for the truth."[79]

The Court decided to produce, on its own, a robust factual record of what had taken place.[80] It had taken on a delicate task, to tread where powerful domestic courts had long refused to go. Without the cooperation of the respondent states, the Court would need to amass an irrefutable factual case if it were to ground any finding of violation. To do so, it relied on the Council of Europe's investigation into European partnerships with the CIA, which culminated in the Marty Report of 2006;[81] and it compiled available evidence from Wikileaks cables, news coverage, government hearings and reports, to which the judgments devoted hundreds of pages.[82]

The Court's findings—that the treatment of Al Nashiri and El-Masri violated Article 3 and Article 5 (unlawful detention)—are unremarkable; of that there is no question. Striking are the holdings of state liability, given that the applicants had spent so little time in Europe.[83] With the world watching closely, the Court aggressively moved to fill a significant human rights vacuum, created by the US, but in which European states were complicit. Although FYROM denied any knowledge of the events El-Masri described and refused to produce any evidence other than "official" records, the Court nonetheless found that FYROM officials were aware of the torture, detention, and rendition of El-Masri.[84] In *Al Nashiri*, the Court determined that the Polish government also must have known what was happening on its

plane and on Polish territory was, by the very nature of the rendition operations, purposefully not to be recorded.")

[79] *El-Masri*, para. 191.

[80] *Al Nashiri*, paras. 10, 131, 281.

[81] *Al Nashiri*, para. 46.

[82] *Al Nashiri*, paras. 151, 155, 191.

[83] *Al Nashiri*, para. 329. ("At no point is it found or alleged in the Marty Inquiry or in any of the findings of my investigations that Poland instigated or orchestrated the detention, interrogation and ill-treatment of the detainees on its territory.")

[84] *El-Masri*, para. 75 (Testimony of Marty Report investigator: "I have been struck by the attention to detail I have learned about on the part of the Macedonian authorities, as they sought to cover up or interfere with almost every avenue of independent investigation into the truth of what happened."); paras. 40–1, 239, 206.

territory, and the likely torture and inhuman treatment of those being transported on the CIA's secret planes.[85] Liability is triggered by this knowledge alone, even in circumstances where no Polish official directly interacts with a detainee. Once a prisoner lands on European soil, the Court indicated, he was subject to the same protections enjoyed by men like Jens Soering.[86] The Court ordered the FYROM and Poland to compensate the victims; and Poland was ordered to work to prevent the US from seeking the death penalty in Mr. Al Nashiri's case.[87]

As important, these judgments served to organize domestic reforms, injecting the Convention into decision-making that would otherwise be dominated by security concerns. Some of the US's most important allies, including the UK, have incorporated state responsibility for collaborating on rendition cases into domestic law. In *Belhaj v. Straw* (2017), the UK Supreme Court heard an appeal from a Libyan dissident, who was abducted along with his pregnant wife in 2004 in a joint operation of US and UK intelligence forces, and rendered to Libya. There, he was imprisoned and tortured. Overturning the High Court, and rejecting the claims of immunity for third party acts of state, the UK Supreme Court held that Belhaj had standing to sue the UK intelligence branches and the former Secretary of State for their complicity in his ill treatment.[88]

DUTIES IN WAR ZONES—TERRITORY AND PEOPLE

European states have waged remarkably few wars during the lifetime of the Convention. Until recently, the case law concerning state duties on the field of battle, or as an occupying force, was relatively thin.

[85] *Al Nashiri*, para. 428.
[86] *Al Nashiri*, paras. 448–9, 490, 453, 518.
[87] *Al Nashiri*, para. 589.
[88] *Belhaj & Rhamatulla v. Straw & Others* [2017] UKSC 3.

In the early 2000s, the Court issued a series of judgments involving military occupations by European states within territory under the ongoing protection of the Convention.[89]

In *Cyprus v. Turkey* (2001), the Court confronted a case concerning the effects of Turkish operations in Northern Cyprus from 1974 to 1996 (the date of the Cyprus petition). During this period, Turkey installed and supported a surrogate government in the North, denied Greek Cypriots access to their property, persecuted those that remained, and tried civilians in military courts. The Court rejected Turkey's claims that local officials (not Turkey) bore responsibility for any alleged violation, addressing Article 1 in these terms:

> Having effective overall control over northern Cyprus, [Turkey's] responsibility cannot be confined to the acts of its own soldiers or officials in northern Cyprus but must also be engaged by virtue of the acts of the local administration which survives by virtue of Turkish military and other support. It follows that, in terms of Article 1 of the Convention, Turkey's "jurisdiction" must be considered to extend to securing the entire range of substantive rights set out in the Convention . . . and that violations of those rights are imputable to Turkey. [A]ny other finding would result in a regrettable vacuum in the system of human-rights protection in the territory in question. . . .[90]

The Grand Chamber found violations of nine different provisions of the Convention and Protocol no. 1. Three years later, in *Ilaşcu v. Russia and Moldova* (2004), the Court announced a forward-looking principle:

[89] See Heijer (2011: 54). *Ilaşcu v. Russia and Moldova* (GC, 8 July 2004); *Cyprus v. Turkey* (GC, 10 May 2001); *Loizidou v. Turkey* (preliminary objections) (GC, 23 March 1995).

[90] *Cyprus v. Turkey*, paras. 77–8.

> Where a Contracting State exercises overall control over an area outside its national territory, its responsibility is not confined to the acts of its soldiers or officials in that area but also extends to acts of the local administration which survives there by virtue of its military and other support.[91]

States had been put on notice.

While the very purpose of this branch of case law is to ensure coverage of the Convention in situations in which a *de jure* sovereign no longer governed, the doctrine of "overall control" could also lead to a vacuum in protection. In *Banković v. Belgium* (2001), the Grand Chamber rejected an application brought by the families of victims of a NATO attack on a radio station in Belgrade,[92] then outside the territory of the Council of Europe.[93] The Court declared that aerial bombings were insufficient to establish that NATO members exercised "effective control."[94] The ruling has been heavily contested, not least, because it concerned the right to life. Because NATO could not ensure all Convention rights in Belgrade, the Court had indicated, no NATO state could be held responsible for acts whose effects *were* within NATO's control. The judgment stood "for the proposition that [European] states . . . may commit human rights violations abroad that they may not commit at home."[95] As important, being a ruling on admissibility, the Court had denied applicants a full judgment on the merits.

Banković has since been overruled in all but name. In 2011, the Court issued two major rulings, virtually unanimously on the important points of law.[96] *Al-Skeini v. UK*,[97] concerned the fate of six Iraqi civilians killed during the UK's participation in the Coalition

[91] *Ilaşcu*, para. 316.
[92] *Banković v. Belgium* (GC, 19 December 2001), para. 8.
[93] *Banković*, para. 80.
[94] *Banković*, paras. 54, 71, 75.
[95] Jackson (2016: 827).
[96] The second case is *Al-Jedda v. the United Kingdom*, described below.
[97] *Al-Skeini v. the United Kingdom* (GC, 7 July 2011).

Provisional Authority, which governed Iraq in 2003–4. During this period, increasing violence, coupled with a lack of adequate resources to maintain peace, turned the Basra region into a chaotic and dangerous place for Iraqis and the forces in occupation.[98] UK soldiers killed and detained a large number of Iraqi civilians in events ranging from shoot-outs at checkpoints to arrests instigated by local rivals bent on misleading military police.[99] In one brutal incident, British soldiers beat a fifteen-year old boy suspected of looting, and threw him into a river, where he drowned.[100] In another, a hotel receptionist died after three days in custody; his father, having been asked to identify the body, found his "son's body and face . . . covered in blood and bruises; his nose was broken and part of the skin of his face had been torn away."[101] The UK military investigated these events, but with limited rigor and weak results.[102]

The families of these and four other victims brought suit in the UK courts, after authorities had denied requests for further inquiry and consideration of liability and compensation. The Secretary of State contended that the Human Rights Act had no extraterritorial application;[103] and a divisional court held that, with the exception of the victim who had died in a British military prison, the relatives of the victims did not have a cognizable claim.[104] In a final ruling, the House of Lords decided that the Human Rights Act had the same extraterritorial application as Article 1, but that under the *Banković* test, the UK had not exercised effective control over the Basra region, thereby escaping liability.[105] The applicants then went to Strasbourg, pleading the failure of the UK to fulfill its procedural obligations under Article 2 (to mount an effective investigation into the circumstances of the deaths, and to provide an effective judicial remedy).[106]

[98] *Al-Skeini*, para. 22.
[99] *Al-Skeini*, paras. 34–5, 40, 44, 48–9, 64.
[100] *Al-Skeini*, para. 56.
[101] *Al-Skeini*, para. 64.
[102] *Al-Skeini*, para. 30.
[103] *Al-Skeini*, para. 78.
[104] *Al-Skeini*, paras. 74–5.
[105] *Al-Skeini*, para. 87.
[106] *Al-Skeini*, para. 87.

The Grand Chamber found for the applicants based on reasoning that is manifestly incompatible with its holding in *Banković*:

> It is clear that, whenever the State, through its agents, exercises control and authority over an individual, and thus jurisdiction, the State is under an obligation under Article 1 to secure to that individual the rights and freedoms under . . . the Convention that are relevant to the situation of that individual.[107]

The Grand Chamber underscored the fact that the British army could not be expected to secure the same level of rights protection in Iraq as in the UK. Nonetheless, in assuming control over security in Basra, it had also assumed a duty to conduct investigations into civilian deaths and provide effective remedies for victims in the domestic courts.[108] The Court had thus shifted focus from control over territory, to control over individuals. Although executive officials protested,[109] the UK courts responded positively, allowing a long list of similar cases brought by Iraqis against the armed forces to proceed in domestic courts.[110]

Jaloud v. the Netherlands (2014) put the final nail in the coffin for *Banković*.[111] Dutch troops serving in a UN peacekeeping force had shot and killed the applicant's son in an incident at a checkpoint. Criminal proceedings against the soldiers were blocked when a prosecutor decided that Article 2 "did not bind Netherlands troops [since they] had not exercised effective authority in Iraq."[112] Strasbourg

[107] *Al-Skeini*, para. 137. [108] *Al-Skeini*, paras. 149, 171–2, 174–7.

[109] In October of 2016, the UK government issued a press release stating that it planned to derogate from the ECHR in all cases involving overseas military operations, however, no such derogation has yet occurred. See UK Government: *Government to Protect Armed Forces from Persistent Legal Claims in Future Overseas Operations* (4 October 2016).

[110] *Al-Saadoon and Others v. Secretary of State for Defense* [2016] EWCA Civ 811.

[111] *Jaloud v. the Netherlands* (GC, 20 November 2014).

[112] *Jaloud*, para. 45.

rejected that view, and further findings of a Dutch appellate court, on Article 1 grounds:

> The Court is satisfied that [the Netherlands] exercised its "jurisdiction" . . . for the purpose of asserting authority and control over persons passing through the checkpoint. [T]he death of Mr Azhar Sabah Jaloud occurred within the "jurisdiction" of the Netherlands, as that expression is to be construed within the meaning of Art. 1 . . .[113]

As *Al-Skeini* and *Jaloud* demonstrate, the Court has moved close to the early Commission approach to jurisdiction and responsibility.[114]

This line of case law suggests that wherever a state's agents exercise authority, they owe duties of care to any person that comes under their control.[115] The implication is that any act attributable to a member state's agent—taking place anywhere, in any legal context—is within the purview of the Court's authority as the regime's trustee.

RIGHTS PROTECTION AND INTER-JUDICIAL DIALOGUE

As discussed in chapter 3, the consolidation of constitutional pluralism in Europe has left some basic questions of hierarchy, as

[113] *Jaloud*, para. 152. [114] See Miller (2010: 1229).

[115] Outside the context of military occupation, the Court has found that when a state's agents exercise "full and exclusive control" over the applicant, this triggers Art. 1 jurisdiction. When Turkish officials apprehended the leader of the PKK in a Kenyan airport, the Court determined that "the applicant was effectively under Turkish authority and therefore within the 'jurisdiction' of that State for the purposes of Article 1 of the Convention, even though in this instance Turkey exercised its authority outside its territory"; *Öcalan v. Turkey* (GC, 12 May 2005), para. 17. The Court also held that sailors on a Cambodian ship, which was boarded on the high seas by a French flagship searching for drug smugglers, were under Convention protection since French agents exercised "full and exclusive control" over the crew; *Medvedyev v. France* (GC, 29 March 2010), para. 67.

between domestic apex courts and the European courts, unresolved. The EU and the ECHR have evolved on the basis of terms of engagement that have been negotiated by courts within a pluralistic frame. In the ECHR, inter-judicial dialogues have established a relatively stable discursive "interface,"[116] allowing judges to express disagreement, to propose cooperative solutions, and to negotiate settlements. In earlier chapters, we tracked two momentous outcomes of these developments: (i) the steady upgrading of standards of European rights protection, and (ii) the growing embeddedness of transnational law within domestic legal orders. Underwriting these developments is a reciprocity norm, which entails the mutual recognition of the autonomy and authority of the European courts by domestic apex courts, and *vice-versa*. The exchange of reciprocity notices has taken place through a set of formal exchanges, which we will call *Solange* dialogues.

These dialogues have famously produced an equilibrium outcome, one that institutionalizes reciprocity.[117] On the one hand, domestic trustee courts proclaim the power of the "final word" when it comes to the enforcement of rights provisions within the national order. National constitutional courts, for example, have asserted the authority to declare as *ultra vires* an interpretation of a European court that would, if implemented in the domestic order, conflict with core values of its own constitution.[118] This power has rarely, if ever, actually been exercised. On the other hand, domestic trustee courts recognize the authority of the European courts, and seek to ensure that the latter's jurisprudence can be pleaded before, and enforced by, all other national judges. In the archetypal case, the constitutional court adopts a posture of presumptive deference to the courts of the EU or the ECHR, when the latter act within the scope of their authority under

[116] Krisch (2010: 186–94).
[117] Krisch (2010: 186–94). See also Sabel and Gerstenberg (2010).
[118] Sadurski (2008).

treaty law, while proclaiming a duty to defend the fundamentals of the domestic constitution when under threat.

In *Bosphorus v. Ireland* (2005),[119] the Strasbourg Court deployed the *Solange* mechanism of coordination with respect to the CJEU's interpretation of an EU Regulation, itself implementing a 1993 UN Security Council Resolution. The resolution imposed sanctions on Serbia and Montenegro in the face of mounting evidence of state-sponsored mass killings and genocide in neighboring territories of the ex-Yugoslavia. The applicant, a Turkish airline that had leased airplanes from Serbia, saw its planes impounded by Irish authorities after stopping in Ireland for repairs,[120] a clear hindrance to its right to property (Art. 1 of Protocol no. 1). Ireland defended the seizure on the basis of its duty, under the UN Charter, to enforce the sanctions. Chapter 7 of the Charter grants to the Security Council wide powers to initiate sanctions, while Article 103 requires that member states implement them. The upshot is that, in the UN system, states have only a "subordinate, non-discretionary" role to play when it comes to the enforcement of Chapter 7 resolutions; indeed, they are under a duty to act as faithful agents of the Security Council.

In its judgment, the Grand Chamber stressed the important purpose of the EU Regulation, and its connection to UN sanctions:

> [T]he general interest pursued by the impugned measure was compliance with legal obligations flowing from the Irish State's membership [in the EU]. It is, moreover, a legitimate interest of considerable weight. . . . The Court has also long recognised the growing importance of international cooperation and of the consequent need to secure the proper functioning of international organisations.[121]

[119] *Bosphorus Hava Yollari Turizm Ve Ticaret Anonim Sirketl v. Ireland* (GC, 30 June 2005).

[120] *Bosphorus*, para. 23.

[121] *Bosphorus*, para. 150.

Although enforcing the sanctions would mean limiting the Turkish company's property rights, the Strasbourg Court saw no reason to second-guess the CJEU:

> State action taken in compliance with such legal obligations is justified *as long as* the relevant organisation is considered to protect fundamental rights, as regards both the substantive guarantees offered and the mechanisms controlling their observance, in a manner which can be considered *at least equivalent to that for which the Convention provides.*[122] [Emphases added.]

This doctrine of "equivalent protection" echoes the German Federal Constitutional Court's (GFCC) holding in *Solange II*, justifying a posture of presumptive deference.

The original *Solange* saga (1974–87; chapter 3), induced the CJEU to incorporate into the EU treaties a corpus of judicially enforceable rights under the rubric of general principles of EU law. Until 2009, when the EU promulgated its own Charter of Rights, the CJEU treated the European Court's case law as a source of inspiration for its own rights-based jurisprudence. Thus, the *Bosphorous* ruling, which is dependent upon the settlement between the GFCC and the CJEU, lays the foundation for a reciprocity agreement between the two European regimes.

While intra-judicial dialogue may result in upgrading inter-judicial cooperation, that outcome is by no means assured. The mechanism, after all, is rooted in a first-order threat: the court of system X will withhold recognition from a court of system Y, if Y does not adequately protect rights. Once Y demonstrates that it protects rights effectively, X will withdraw its objection, and recognize Y as a peer of equal status. X earns Y's recognition, and thus presumptive deference,

[122] *Bosphorus*, para. 155.

through commitment to practices that X holds as basic to its mission as a rights-protecting trustee.

TOWARD CONSTITUTIONAL PLURALISM IN THE INTERNATIONAL SYSTEM

The development of constitutional pluralism in Europe—the construction of a *polyarchy of courts*, in Sabel and Gerstenberg's terms[123]—is predicated on a joint commitment to rights that has been forged through *Solange* dialogues. But what happens when European officials are required to enforce law generated by a treaty system—such as that of the UN—in which no judicial review of rights claims exists? Can a *Solange* style exchange serve any useful purpose? And what would such an exchange signify about the underlying structure of authority in the international system?

In chapter 3, we contrasted (i) classic theories of "centralized sovereignty," which privilege top-down hierarchy and systemic unity, with (ii) a model of "decentralized sovereignty," in which a system of otherwise autonomous courts jointly enforces a multi-level, rights-based constitution that grounds the legitimacy of all law. From the perspective of centralized sovereignty, international law possesses constitutional features to the extent that states are obligated to enforce international norms.[124] There is, further, a long tradition of conceptualizing the UN Charter as the world's constitution, not least, because of the nature of the obligation to enforce Security Council Resolutions:

[123] Sabel and Gerstenberg (2010).

[124] As applied to the cases discussed in this section, see De Búrca (2010) and Krisch (2010). For analysis on the UN Charter as a constitution, more generally, see Crawford (1997); Macdonald (1999); Doyle (2011).

> Art. 25: The Members of the United Nations agree to accept and carry out the decisions of the Security Council in accordance with the present Charter.
>
> Art. 103: In the event of a conflict between the obligations of the Members of the United Nations under the present Charter and their obligations under any other international agreement, their obligations under the present Charter shall prevail.

Al-Jedda and *Bosphorous* involved cases in which the domestic courts had refused to enforce Convention rights, on the grounds that they had no authority to review the lawfulness of Security Council Resolutions, given the latter's primacy. Under a decentralized model, however, the Security Council (and the UN Charter system as a whole) is subject to a higher law—human rights—that all judges must enforce.

The cases to which we now turn provide "intimations"[125] of the development of constitutional pluralism at the international level.[126] To get to the notion of "constitutional pluralism" one must specify what is simultaneously "constitutional" and "pluralistic" about the structure of a legal system. When considering the interface between international regimes, scholars variously identify, as the basic scaffolding of a constitution: *jus cogens* norms; the substantive provisions of charters of rights; and standards of procedural due process, and access to justice, which exist as autonomous, judicially enforceable, general principles of law. These norms, which find expression in a host of multi-lateral and regional treaties, are firmly supported by *opinio juris*, and overlap rights provisions inscribed in the vast majority of national constitutions that have entered into force and survived since 1950.[127] The feature that makes the international system "constitutional"—whether considered as a distinct unit of legal analysis, or in Kantian terms—is an overarching normative structure: (i) the code of

[125] Walker (2015a).

[126] Kumm (2009); Maduro (2009); Stone Sweet (2009a, 2013); Walker (2002).

[127] Chapters 1–3. See also, Gardbaum (2008).

rights that all state officials are under a legal duty to enforce; and (ii) a set of shared techniques—the most important of which being proportionality analysis—used to adjudicate rights claims. At the same time, the distribution of authority within this presupposed constitution is pluralistic: the system is comprised of discrete hierarchies, national and treaty-based, each of which may have a strong claim to autonomy and legitimacy. Sovereignty—the authority to enforce fundamental rights—is "decentralized," to the extent that no "ultimate conflict rule" or "final authority" to resolve conflicts between any two legal norms or jurisdictions exists.[128]

In principle, constitutional pluralism is an empirically verifiable property of a composite legal order: rights (the higher law, constitutional norms) are enforced by a polyarchy of courts and other organs. We also know that it is largely an inter-judicial construction, one possible outcome of iterated *Solange* dialogues. The well-known *Kadi* cases, processed by the EU courts, made these issues salient, and gave them empirical content. We dwell on these rulings here because they have heavily structured the Strasbourg Court's approach to similar cases.

Beginning in 1999, the UN Security Council adopted a series of Chapter 7 resolutions imposing sanctions on named individuals suspected of aiding and abetting terrorist activities. These persons were publicly "listed" as targets of mandatory punitive measures, including travel bans, and the freezing and confiscation of assets. It deserves emphasis in advance that the UN Charter proclaims that its organs, including the Security Council, are "required to perform its tasks while fully respecting and promoting human rights."[129] Indeed, the various UN human rights committees strongly criticized the Security Council for establishing sanctions while failing to provide

[128] The resulting situation contrasts with centralized sovereignty, or a constitutional order characterized by a final word on such conflicts; chapter 3 and Stone Sweet (2013).

[129] *Al-Dulimi v. Switzerland* (GC, 21 June 2016), para. 148.

individuals with any means of challenging them, or for their "delisting." Instead, affected persons sued in national courts and, after the 2001 attacks on the World Trade Center, the list grew longer and litigation multiplied.

On EU territory, Regulation 881/2002 made sanctions directly effective in all domestic orders. Mr. Kadi, who without any warning found that his bank accounts had been frozen, challenged the Regulation's lawfulness before both national and EU courts, pleading violations of the right to property, due process, and his right of access to a judge. The rulings of these courts raise many complex issues, and they have been the source of extensive commentary.[130] Ultimately, in *Kadi v. the Council of the EU* (2008), the CJEU subjected the EU's implementation of the sanctions to searching review under EU fundamental rights, stressing that:

> [T]he review by the Court of the validity of any [EC] measure in the light of fundamental rights must be considered to be the expression, *in a community based on the rule of law*, of a *constitutional guarantee stemming from the EC Treaty as an autonomous legal system* which is not to be prejudiced by an international agreement.[131] [Emphases added.]

Notwithstanding Article 103 of the Charter, the CJEU annulled Regulation 881/2002 on the grounds raised by the plaintiffs. While the legislative organs were under a duty to implement Security Council measures, the CJEU declared, they were not thereby authorized to derogate "from the EU's core constitutional principles, which include the principles of liberty, democracy and respect for human rights and fundamental freedoms."[132]

[130] De Búrca (2010); Krisch (2010: ch. 5); Sabel and Gerstenberg (2010).

[131] *Kadi v. the Council of the EU*, Joined Cases C-402/05 P and C-415/05 P (3 September 2008), para. 316.

[132] *Kadi*, para. 303.

The ruling can, and has been, analyzed as a first move in a *Solange* dialogue:[133] so long as the UN Charter system does not provide for effective judicial protection of fundamental rights, the CJEU will review challenges to Security Council resolutions, if only indirectly, once transposed as EU law. In the UN system, however, there exists no trustee court with which to negotiate a reciprocity settlement. Nonetheless, in response to the CJEU, the UN Security Council adopted Resolution 1904/2009, which created an Ombudsperson to review individual petitions, and to make formal recommendations to a special committee of the Security Council established to oversee a delisting process.[134]

Meanwhile, the EU Commission refused to delist Mr. Kadi, whose assets remained frozen, prompting follow-up litigation in the General Court of the EU (GCEU), the court of first instance for annulment proceedings. In *Kadi v. the Commission* (2010), the GCEU announced that it would engage in "full review" of the implementation, within the EU, of the sanctions regime, "at the very least" and "so long as" the de-listing "procedure . . . clearly fails to offer guarantees of effective judicial protection." The GCEU then annulled the regulation at issue while rejecting, as insufficient, the reforms provoked by *Kadi I*. The system established by SC 1904/2009, it declared, neither provided "effective judicial procedure for review of decisions of the Sanctions Committee," nor for a "mechanism to ensure that sufficient information be made available to the person concerned in order to allow him to defend himself effectively." [135] In 2013, the Grand Chamber of the CJEU confirmed the General Court's ruling, declaring that the courts must ensure that those who challenge the sanctions are given the full

[133] Sabel and Gerstenberg (2010); Stone Sweet (2013).

[134] The first Ombudsperson would later state that: "the decision of the CJEU, coming at the culmination of ongoing criticism—academic, political, and otherwise—as to the lack of a fair and transparent process, led directly to the . . . establishment of the Office of the Ombudsperson"; Scheinen (2011).

[135] CGEU: *Kadi v. EU Commission*, Case T-85/09 (30 September 2010), paras. 126–8.

panoply of due process protections, including reviewable reasons for a challenged listing.[136]

The Security Council responded by codifying procedures for information exchange and "dialogue" with listed individuals, and by bolstering the influence of the Ombudsperson's recommendation to delist. The UN Special Rapporteur on Human Rights and Counter Terrorism, Martin Scheinin, weighed in within two weeks of these changes. While acknowledging that the Security Council "has proven responsive to criticisms" and had strengthened due process, Scheinin nonetheless concluded that the new procedures still did not "meet international human rights standards concerning due process or fair trial." Scheinin explicitly endorsed a *Solange* strategy: "as long as proper due process is not guaranteed at the United Nations level . . . national [or regional] courts will need to exercise judicial review over the . . . measures implementing the sanctions."[137]

In October 2012, the Security Council delisted Mr. Kadi.[138] This process is slow going,[139] but it has generated a rights-based, interactive structure.

The *Kadi* rulings directly influenced the Strasbourg Court's approach to Security Council resolutions. In *Al-Jedda v. UK* (2011), a judgment rendered within months of *Al-Skeini*, the Grand Chamber censured the UK for having imprisoned the applicant in Iraq for more than three years without bringing charges, contrary to Article 5 ECHR. In its defense, the UK claimed that Mr. Al-Jeddah had "conspired" to commit acts of terrorism, that his incarceration was necessary for "imperative reasons of security," and that the UK was acting as

[136] CJEU: *Kadi III*, Cases C-584/10 P, C-593/10 P, and C-595/10 P (18 July 2013).

[137] Stone Sweet (2013: 499). Scheinen (2009: 637) has also stated that, since "the Kadi [ruling] is compatible with international human rights law, as expressed in UN human rights treaties," it "has much support in institutional UN law."

[138] SC 10785, October 5, 2012. Online at: http://www.un.org/News/Press/docs/2012/sc10785.doc.htm.

[139] As of January 2017, the Ombudsperson had received seventy-eight petitions and submitted sixty-eight reports to the Security Council; so far, the Security Council has agreed to delist in forty-nine cases, while rejecting thirteen petitions.

a lawful agent of the UN.[140] The House of Lords dismissed the case, holding that state obligations under Security Council resolutions overrode the ECHR. The Strasbourg Court found for the applicant, after a broad discussion of the *Kadi* cases,[141] while positioning itself to be a potential check on the Security Council:

> In interpreting its resolutions, there must be a presumption that the Security Council does not intend to impose any obligation on Member States to breach fundamental principles of human rights. In the event of any ambiguity . . . the Court must choose the interpretation which is most in harmony with the requirements of the Convention and which avoids any conflict of obligations. In light of the United Nations' important role in promoting and encouraging respect for human rights, it is to be expected that clear and explicit language would be used were the Security Council to intend States to take particular measures which would conflict with their obligations under international human rights law.

The holding displays a surface commitment of deference to the UN Charter system, while imposing obligations with bite on the Convention's members.

The most recent episode in this ongoing saga is a Grand Chamber's judgment in *Al-Dulimi v. Switzerland* (2016), which involved the same sanctions regime that had ensnared Mr. Kadi.[142] The applicant, whose bank assets had been confiscated, complained that the Federal Court of Switzerland had denied him judicial protection of due process required under Article 6.[143] If the sanctions regime could

[140] *Al-Jedda v. UK* (GC, 7 July 2011), paras. 88, 98.

[141] *Al-Jedda*, paras. 51, 104, 109.

[142] Switzerland—which, as a non-EU member, was not bound by the *Kadi* decisions—pleaded the non-discretionary obligation to implement sanctions, although the Federal Court took pains to provide Mr. Al-Dulimi with the resources and time to pursue his claims; *Al-Dulimi*, paras. 31–2, 109.

[143] *Al-Dulimi*, para. 95.

not meet the criterion of equivalent protection (*Bosphorus*), could it somehow be interpreted to be in conformity with the Convention (*Al-Jeddah*)? In 2013, a Section of the Court ruled that the de-listing system violated Article 6,[144] while criticizing the Swiss Federal Court for having "refused to [fully] examine the merits of the impugned measures" under the proportionality principle.[145]

The Grand Chamber, too, found a violation, but balked at applying either the *Bosphorus* criterion or a full-fledged proportionality test:

> [W]here a [Security Council Resolution] does not contain any clear or explicit wording excluding the possibility of judicial supervision of the measures taken for its implementation, it must always be understood as authorising the courts of the respondent State to exercise sufficient scrutiny so that any arbitrariness can be avoided. By limiting that scrutiny to arbitrariness, the Court takes account of the nature and purpose of the measures provided for by the Resolution in question, in order to strike a fair balance between the necessity of ensuring respect for human rights and the imperatives of the protection of international peace and security.[146]

Controversially, under the guise of harmonious interpretation (*Al-Jeddah*), the Grand Chamber side-stepped the hierarchy issues taken up by the EU courts in the *Kadi* sequence. Instead, it held that, since the Security Council had not addressed the scope of judicial supervision of the implementing measures, the sanctions regime could "not be understood as precluding any judicial scrutiny of the measures taken to implement it."[147] Thus:

> Switzerland [is] not faced in the present case with a real conflict of obligations capable of engaging the primacy rule in Art. 103 of the

[144] The Grand Chamber would characterize the test as "settled case law," *Al-Dulimi*, para. 83.

[145] *Al-Dulimi*, paras. 83–4.

[146] *Al-Dulimi*, para. 140.

[147] *Al-Dulimi*, para. 148.

> UN Charter. This finding makes it unnecessary for the Court to determine the question of the hierarchy between the obligations of the States Parties to the Convention . . . and those arising from the UN Charter . . . [Switzerland] cannot validly confine itself to relying on the binding nature of Security Council resolutions, but should persuade the Court that it has taken—or at least has attempted to take—all possible measures to adapt the sanctions regime to the individual situation of the applicants, at least guaranteeing them adequate protection against arbitrariness.[148]

The ruling thus pushed a conflict avoidance rule—of harmonious interpretation—to its limits, requiring the Court to read implied due process guarantees into the sanctions regime.[149] Put in terms of a *Solange* dialogue, ECHR states would enforce sanctions so long as the courts ensured that the person challenging them had not been targeted in an arbitrary way.

The majority opinion reflects a compromise that must have been difficult to broker. By contrast, two separate opinions filed in *Al-Dulimi* point more directly to the evolution of rights-based constitutionalism at the international level. In Judge Keller's view, in this case, "there [was] no room for [simultaneous] compliance with both the ECHR and the UN Charter":[150]

> [F]or the time being, it is possible to argue that the targeted sanctions regime set up by the UN Security Council shows a structural deficiency capable of rebutting the presumption of equivalent protection. Given that several actors—among them some prominent figures from inside the UN—have convincingly argued that the sanctions regimes do not sufficiently respect human rights guarantees, and that the applicants in the present case have been

[148] *Al-Dulimi*, para. 149.
[149] See Keller, Concurring Opinion, *Al-Dulimi*, para. 7.
[150] Keller, Concurring Opinion, *Al-Dulimi*, para. 8.

> unable to gain access to a court regarding these matters for such a long period of time, the presumption is rebutted in this instance and States must therefore take action.[151]

Judge Keller implies that the Court should have issued a much stronger *Solange* statement.[152]

The concurrence written by Judge Pinto de Albuquerque, and joined by three of his peers, proceeds from a declaration, reminiscent of the CJEU, that the Strasbourg Court is the constitutional court of an autonomous legal order. The opinion also contains an extended, highly critical review of the UN Charter system, focusing on the conditions under which the primacy rule of Article 103 of the Charter might be honored:

> Security Council resolutions [that] flagrantly contradict the aims and principles of the United Nations (Article 24 § 2 of the Charter) do not benefit from the precedence rule. Before applying the Article 103 rule, the internal validity of the resolution [which depends on conformity with rights] must therefore be checked [by domestic and regional courts].[153]

In a fascinating section on constitutional theory, the concurrence develops a picture of the normative structure of the international system, one that broadly conforms to our Kantian account:

> Individuals being the epi-centre of international law, human rights are today the central factor of [its] legitimation . . . [T]he language

[151] Keller, Concurring Opinion, *Al-Dulimi*, para. 22.

[152] Keller, Concurring Opinion, *Al-Dulimi*, para. 23.

[153] Pinto, Concurring Opinion, *Al-Dulimi*, para. 5. Judge Pinto's view of the sanctions regime was equally scathing: "it is hardly compatible with international humanitarian law, international criminal law or international human rights law. . . . The same political body legislates and decides on listing and delisting individuals and entities. Worse still, the accuser may also be the judge, since the State requesting listing may be asked to decide on the listing and delisting," para. 36.

> of international human rights law is individual-centred, not State-centred. The primary role of sovereignty is the responsibility to protect human rights. The relations between a State and its own nationals are no longer viewed, as in the past, as a purely domestic question. The Copernican revolution that international law faced with the birth of the [international bill of rights] and their regional counterparts created a new narrative in international law with constitutional overtones.[154]

The passage sets up an extended analysis of the UN Charter's shortcomings, as an incomplete *constitutional* system, leading to a *Solange*-style refusal of recognition:

> The reasons for the constitutional black hole within the UN are twofold. On the one hand, the International Court of Justice [does not subject] the bodies and officials of the UN, and in particular . . . the Security Council, to an effective constitutional control. On the other hand, the [Charter system lacks] a non-optional, binding, judicial human rights protection system. . . . Until the day a World Human Rights Court comes into existence, with compulsory jurisdiction over both the bodies and officials of the United Nations and its members, or the International Court of Justice gains compulsory jurisdiction in such matters, the UN *will not have a constitutional nature*. As things stand presently, there may be an emerging foundational source of law at the UN, but [the Charter is not a] true global Constitution as yet, in the absence of justiciable, human rights limits on the exercise of public power and use of public force. [Since] the Charter . . . has not yet acquired the nature of a Constitution for the international community . . . there [exists] no hierarchical relationship between Charter obligations

[154] Pinto, Concurring Opinion, *Al-Dulimi*, para. 7.

> and obligations resulting from other international . . . agreements, *most notably human rights treaties.*[155] [Emphases added.]

In consequence, Judge Pinto insisted, Security Council Resolutions "may, in specific instances of conflict, be displaced by international norms with a stronger constitutional claim and whose effect is not offset by the secondary rule of Article 103 of the Charter."[156]

With respect to the application of *Al-Jeddah* to *Al-Dulimi*'s application, the Pinto and Keller opinions are as close to dissents as one is likely to find in a concurring opinion.

The majority, as well as Judges Pinto and Keller, proved to be unwilling to declare that the right to a court (Art. 6) was either absolute or expressed a *jus cogens* norm. Both European courts, however, appear to be committed to the view that access to justice, and therefore the provision of judicial due process, is a non-negotiable component of any future *Solange* settlement.

CONCLUSION

This chapter charts the growing capacity of the European Court to protect the rights of those who are not citizens of member states of the Council of Europe. The Court has institutionalized elements of Kant's principle of hospitality in its case law on *non-refoulement*. It has interpreted state jurisdiction in expansive terms, thereby extending its own basis of authority and the coverage of the Convention. And it has worked diligently to fill gaps in the protection of fundamental rights resulting from the failures of domestic courts to recognize the claims of non-citizens, whether on grounds of nationality, territory, or security. In such situations, it has functioned as the *de facto* court of first instance. As the regime's trustee, it has also steadily evolved

[155] Pinto, Concurring Opinion, *Al-Dulimi*, para. 8.
[156] Pinto, Concurring Opinion, *Al-Dulimi*, para. 39.

new rules, principles, and remedies that national courts are required to respect and incorporate. Finally, from the standpoint of global law, we see that the Court has taken its place in a pluralist, rights-based international order, as one trustee of this global order. The Court is now positioned to help build and enforce an emerging global constitution, of which the Convention is but one component.

Conclusions

We have argued that a European cosmopolitan legal order was instantiated by the combined effects of (i) Protocol no. 11 and (ii) the incorporation of the Convention into national legal orders. At the regime level, states have steadily strengthened the supervisory capacities of its constitutional trustee in Strasbourg. Within domestic orders, national officials, including judges, have gradually abandoned the doctrines of centralized sovereignty, while institutionalizing complex forms of rights pluralism. As a result, virtually no act of any European state official is immune from fundamental rights review.

While other forms of cosmopolitan judicialization are possible, the European experience has established significant normative criteria for evaluating the performance of a cosmopolitan legal order (CLO). The regime has played a major role in helping post-authoritarian states achieve stable constitutional democracy, thereby expanding the "zone" of liberalism on the Continent. It has generated a dense human rights jurisprudence that directly impacts how domestic systems of constitutional justice operate. And it has raised the standards of protection and justification that state officials must meet, wherever they exercise authority over persons.

A CLO does not materialize with the entry into force of a regional treaty expressing the commitment of states to protect rights. Rather, one appears only when the regime has developed such that it meets the criteria that define the CLO as such. The outcome is not preordained. In Europe, the stages through which a CLO emerged were heavily influenced by background conditions, external shocks, critical historical junctures, and momentous political decisions. The latter include: the Second World War and reconstruction; the diffusion of rights-based constitutional democracy; the building of stable, treaty-based institutions; the collapse of the Soviet empire; incorporation and the development of domestic constitutional pluralism; and so on. Recall that the European Convention on Human Rights (ECHR) entered into force (1953) without a Court; and the Court began operations (1959) in the absence of a general right of individual petition. Until the 1990s, most domestic apex courts did not possess the power to enforce a domestic charter of rights against offending statutes (and other acts); and many states denied that they were under an obligation to change laws found by the Strasbourg Court to be the direct source of violations of the Convention. These and many more institutional impediments were eventually overcome by states, which proved willing to invest in the effectiveness of rights protection on an ongoing basis. Thus, while the European experience enables us to contemplate a CLO in action, it offers no simple "recipe" for successful transplantation.

These points made, it is also obvious that the European regime imperfectly protects rights. We have emphasized the deep, structural changes that enabled the CLO to come into being: it matters that, today, individuals may plead rights that domestic apex courts are positioned to enforce. Nonetheless, the European Court and the Committee of Ministers, overloaded and often overwhelmed, is activated by the failings of domestic systems of justice. Where massive failings are chronic, the regime's organs devote enormous resources to helping states initiate and sustain systemic reform. Where the application process identifies significant gaps in national protection, the Court works diligently to persuade state officials to close them. The capacity of national courts to render justice largely determines the Court's role and function. On the positive side, as apex courts gain in effectiveness, they will reduce the Court's burdens while developing capacity to influence the evolution of rights doctrine in dialogues with Strasbourg. In the absence of inter-judicial comity—the mutual recognition of the respective legitimacy claims of trustee courts—and a willingness to engage in meaningful dialogue—the CLO would fail in its mission. As this book documents, progress toward achieving a Rightful condition has been made, but the process will continue to be an arduous one, as Kant had predicted.

While focused on Europe, the theoretical account of constitutional justice we have elaborated applies to all systems of rights protection, not least as a heuristic frame for evaluation and comparison. In enacting a rights-based constitution, the People place their freedom in trust, in the form of a charter of rights. Rights constrain the exercise of public authority, being positive requirements of legality. In a Kantian-congruent system of constitutional justice, all individuals possess an entitlement to judicial review of those acts that would constrain their freedom, as instantiated in the charter. All public officials are placed under a fiduciary duty to respect the Universal Principle of Right (UPR), which permits officials to limit rights, but only in order to secure the reciprocal, external freedom of all. The trustee of the system, a constitutional court: (i) assesses the rights-regarding acts of all other public officials; (ii) issues authoritative interpretations of the content, scope, and application of the charter; (iii) certifies that officials act according to the UPR; and (iv) invalidates acts that violate rights (chapter 2).

A CLO is a composite, multi-level regime in which domestic and transnational systems of constitutional justice evolve symbiotically. To be complete, each level of governance must feature its own charter of rights, justiciable entitlements, fiduciary obligations binding on officials, and a trustee court (chapters 1–3). The transnational trustee, however, does not possess the authority to invalidate domestic law that violates the regime's charter. If it were to obtain such authority, the CLO would (put bluntly) take on the complexion of a state. Instead, the regime's trustee possesses the authority to declare violations, while giving reasons for doing so; and state officials are under a duty to comply with the Court's rulings. This type of system largely conforms to Kant's injunctions, laid down in *Perpetual Peace*, against the creation of a global state.[1] It is important to stress, however, that a CLO is a *juridical* system of governance grounded in the dynamic, integrative qualities of human rights. The European CLO thus appears as a kind of midway point between (i) the type of federation Kant considers in *Perpetual Peace* and (ii) a more hierarchically constituted system of rights protection. The Court governs through an evolving jurisprudence of rights protection, to the extent that domestic officials find it in their interest to comply with this case law, and to invest in efforts to increase the effectiveness of the regime over time. As the book shows, state officials at both the national and regime levels, have steadily enhanced the regime's capacity to address domestic failures; and the most powerful domestic trustee courts have largely supported these efforts (chapters 4–5).

BEYOND EUROPE

There are recurrent outbreaks of cosmopolitan justice in every region of the globe, but only Europe offers an example of a CLO formally inscribed in positive law. Why is this so? Kantian theory provides a compelling, first-order response (chapters 1–3). A CLO will emerge only once a number of states establish systems of constitutional justice at both the domestic and international levels, and jointly commit to bolstering the effectiveness of rights protection. Put differently, each of the definitive articles considered in *Perpetual Peace* must come together in ways that allow a Kantian-congruent, transnational system of justice to emerge and reproduce itself over time. Those who

[1] The fact that Kant had expressed different views on this issue prior to *Perpetual Peace* has been the subject of a great deal of commentary and controversy; see Habermas (1997); Kleingeld (2011); Brown (2009: ch. 3); Corradetti (2016, 2017).

reject this reading of the development of the ECHR will reject the very premises of our book.

Pushing beyond Europe, other creation stories, taking different pathways, are imaginable. Kumm has argued, for example, that a group of powerful domestic judges would be able to forge a cosmopolitan order on the basis of mutual trust, common constitutional principles such as proportionality, and sustained inter-judicial dialogues structured by streams of similar cases.[2] Success, however, would be far more likely under a human rights treaty, a court, and a steady, expansive caseload. Consider the probable trajectory of the ECHR without the Strasbourg complex, and without the right of individual petition. Under this counterfactual, there would have been little pressure for incorporation (without which a CLO could not have emerged).

The Inter-American Convention on Human Rights (IACHR) regime, too, demonstrates the importance of a treaty-based charter of rights and a court. The Inter-American Court has been a positive force for democratization[3] in contexts that have chronically produced authoritarian rule, military *coups d'état*, and civil war. The Commission and the Court regularly confront violations of the core of the most fundamental rights, including the right to be free of state torture, disappearances, and other forms of extra-judicial punishment that state officials have administered, often with impunity.[4] These organs have produced important historical records of systematic abuse, narratives of individual claimants' sufferings, and a dense case law establishing basic principles of rights protection and rule of law. In important rulings finding violations, the Inter-American Court routinely issues orders detailing the structural reforms states must initiate and see to completion. For decades, the effectiveness of that Court's jurisprudence has been relatively ineffective, hindered

[2] Kumm (2009).

[3] As Parish and Peceny (2002) put it, member states use the regime to engage in the "collective defense" of constitutional democracy.

[4] Wright (2014); Skaar, Garcia-Godos, and Collins, eds. (2016).

by the resistance of domestic officials. More recently, however, national judges, leveraging the activities of the IACHR Commission and the Court, have become more assertive in their interactions with legislatures and executives. Indeed, as recent scholarship has shown, many courts now insist on accountability and engage in rights interpretation in synergy with the case law of the Inter-American Court.[5] A few apex courts have begun to incorporate the Inter-American Convention, giving it status at a constitutional rank.[6] And some scholars, and at times judges on the Inter-American Court itself, have invoked Kant's ideas as foundational of the regime.[7] These developments are massively significant. Yet many state officials still actively defy Court orders; and Trinidad and Tobago (1998) and Venezuela (2012) have even denounced the Convention.[8] It merits emphasis that, until recently, most of the member states belonging to the Inter-American system had no meaningful experience with robust judicial protection of rights, slowing the emergence of (i) effective systems of domestic constitutional justice and (ii) stable mechanisms of inter-level coordination.

[5] See Gonzalez-Bertomeu and Gargarella, eds. (2016); González-Ocantos (2016); Skaar, Garcia-Godos, and Collins (2016).

[6] In a 1996 ruling, the Supreme Court of Argentina "unanimously held that the Constitution includes not only the treaties on human rights, but also the case-law of international tribunals"; Ricardo Lorenzetti, President of the Supreme Court of Argentina, Presentation at the International Summit of High Courts, Global Governance: Dialogue Between Courts (November 1–3, 2010). Available at: http://www.summitofhighcourts.com/docs/papers/argentina.pdf. In response to a 2009 judgment issued by the Inter-American Court of Human Rights, the Mexican Supreme Court directed all Mexican judges to ensure that their decisions are compatible with the American Convention on Human Rights (ACHR), as interpreted by the Inter-American Court; judgment of the Supreme Court of Mexico in the Cases 912/2010, 14 July 2011. Available in Spanish at: http://dof.gob.mx/nota_detalle.php?codigo=5212527&fecha=04/10/2011.

[7] See "*Juridical Condition and Human Rights of the Child*," Advisory Opinion Oc-17/2002 of 28 August 2002, concurring opinion of Judge Cançado Trindade, para. 41; see also Cançado Trindade (2010: 233).

[8] In 2017, Venezuela has promised to withdraw from the Organization of American States altogether.

It might also be possible for a court of a trade regime to develop capacities of rights protection, endogenously as it were, which might then facilitate the building of an interface with domestic systems. While the World Trade Organization has famously failed to prioritize rights,[9] the sudden appearance of an activist court for the fifteen-member Economic Community of West African States (ECOWAS) has dramatically altered the legal landscape on that continent.[10] Alter, Helfer, and McAllister have documented how the ECOWAS Court, which began as a guarantor of a set of economic freedoms, converted itself into a general human rights court once it gained compulsory jurisdiction over individual petitions in 2004. In a series of stunning rulings, the ECOWAS Court asserted powers to enforce core elements of the cosmopolitan constitution (chapter 3): the Universal Declaration of Human Rights, the International Covenant on Civil and Political Rights, the International Covenant on Economic, Social and Cultural Rights, and the African Charter on Human and Peoples' Rights.[11] Put in terms of the definitive articles laid out in *Perpetual Peace*, one finds the judges expanding "hospitality"—narrowly conceived as a right to engage in international commerce—to the full panoply of rights in the contemporary sense. ECOWAS is, like the WTO, a mixed regime, being made up of both liberal-democratic and authoritarian states. In mixed regimes, progress toward building an effective system of transnational justice will be relatively difficult, or impossible. In the ECOWAS, "backlash" has in fact ensued, although its Court has so far survived attempts to abolish its human rights jurisdiction.[12]

[9] Joseph (2011). [10] Alter, Helfer, and McAllister (2013).

[11] The pan-African analog to the European and Inter-American Courts is the African Court of Human and Peoples' Rights, which began operating under the auspices of the African Union in 2004. As of 2017, thirty of fifty-four African Union states had ratified the protocol establishing the Court, but only seven (Burkina Faso, Cote d'Ivoire, Ghana, Malawi, Mali, Tanzania, and Rwanda) had ratified the protocol permitting individual petitions. The regime's court issued its first ruling on the merits only in 2009, and has a very small caseload.

[12] Alter, Gathii, and Helfer (2016: 296–300).

CONTESTATION AND STAGES OF DEVELOPMENT

If and how any system of cosmopolitan justice would emerge, Kant argued in *Perpetual Peace* and elsewhere, would depend heavily on a fundamental transformation in how states viewed sovereignty, and the content and scope of law in the transnational realm. Wise leaders, on their own and in tandem, might take initiatives designed to achieve a Rightful condition, at both the domestic and international levels; and such experiments, where successful, might induce other states to follow suit (chapters 1, 3).[13] As we have emphasized throughout the book, Kant also warned that the paths to Public, Cosmopolitan, and International Right would be fraught with obstacles and contestation.

It is a brute fact that some of the most powerful states in the world today reject the model of a rights-based, global constitutional structure. The US has refused to ratify many of the core components of the international bill of rights, and has limited the domestic applicability of treaties it has ratified, through reservations.[14] At the same time, its domestic system of rights protection remains woefully incomplete, and its standards of protection, across a wide range of domains, have fallen well below those in place in Europe and elsewhere.[15] China has recently hardened convictions to the effect that constitutional and international human rights are to be interpreted and applied in light of the priorities of the ruling party, to promote "collective" goods, rather than "individual" justice.[16] The basic features of constitutional justice, as defined in this book, are anathema to the Chinese political system.[17] More broadly, a significant majority of states feature relatively weak or ineffective domestic systems of constitutional justice,[18] and their leaders would reject arrangements akin to those established by Protocol no. 11. Even within the ECHR, leaders of a number of

[13] See Kant's famous statements in *Perpetual Peace* at 8: 355–6 [Box 1].

[14] Hertel and Libal, eds. (2011).

[15] Blau and Moncada (2006).

[16] Ministry of Foreign Affairs of the People's Republic of China (2016).

[17] Jiang (2014); Seymour and Wong (2015).

[18] Law and Versteeg (2013).

states have contested the legitimacy of the Strasbourg Court and elements of its jurisprudence, and have occasionally threatened withdrawal from the regime, including the current president of Russia and the prime minister of the UK. At the same time, the present ruling parties in Hungary and Poland have engaged in assaults on their own apex courts, undermining their capacity to exercise effective trusteeship.[19] These facts effectively constrain the development of a CLO of global scope.

But there are also reasons for optimism. The European CLO is only of recent vintage, and the Inter-American, ECOWAS, and other regimes have developed capacity to influence domestic systems in unexpected and significant ways. In Asia, where no regional court exists, one observes the rapid development of constitutional courts and rights review in South Korea and Taiwan, and tentative moves in the same direction in Malaysia and Indonesia.[20] The apex courts of Hong Kong, Malaysia, South Korea, and Taiwan have all adopted (and adapted) the proportionality principle as their general approach to rights adjudication.[21] They thus join a growing number of courts in the Americas, including those of Colombia and Mexico, and the Constitutional Court of South Africa.

Kant viewed sharp social and political contestation as a type of mechanism for the institutionalization of any significant move toward Right and justice. The philosopher believed that progress would be sustained only insofar as human beings could ascertain the benefits of a Rightful condition, through a socialization process that we would today characterize in terms of *internalization*. But Kant's arguments—which emphasize universal, transcendental moral obligations—tell us little about what might or will happen in any particular time or place. Of course, any contemporary struggle to realize justice will be partly determined by the complex ways in which historical legacies shape actors' perceptions of what is needed or possible, typically in highly

[19] Kelemen (2017); Bugaric and Ginsburg (2016).
[20] Yap (2017).
[21] Stone Sweet and Mathews (2017).

conflictual contexts. On the ground, as Ingram emphasizes, cosmopolitanism can never be divorced from hard "cosmopolitics."[22]

GLOBAL CONSTITUTIONALISM

As defined in this project, a CLO is a multi-level, transnational system of rights protection, capable of rendering constitutional justice in a Kantian sense.[23] It is therefore characterized by certain structural properties. First, the CLO confers on all persons, by virtue of their humanity, an individual entitlement to challenge the rights-regarding decisions of all public officials who exercise authority over them. The entitlement comes as supplementary to protections required by *jus cogens* norms. Second, it is fully judicialized: within it, domestic and international trustee courts possess the authority to enforce rights as positive requirements of legal validity (legitimacy). The CLO does not replace domestic systems of justice, but supplements them with another layer of rights protection. Third, rights adjudication is governed by the Universal Principle of Right: officials who make and apply the law are under a duty to ensure the equal juridical status of all, within a Rightful condition. In the absence of a global state the cosmopolitan constitution is enforced by a decentralized sovereign comprised of those domestic and treaty-based, regional courts that exercise jurisdiction over human rights claims. In the European CLO, decentralized sovereignty manifests itself in forms of constitutional pluralism, strong doses of which one finds at both the domestic and international levels in Europe (chapter 3). Beyond Europe, the absence of a global CLO means that the international bill of rights will be enforced haphazardly.

[22] Ingram (2013). See also Benhabib (2011).

[23] As Koskenniemi (2006: 31) puts it: "Moral politics and legal practice cannot be separated. Law is simply the name for the external institutions that administer what is a moral-political project."

As other neo-Kantians have done,[24] we presuppose the cosmopolitan constitution (chapter 3) and then examine (chapters 4–6) concrete legal developments, "reference points" in Corradetti's terms, which reveal "the regulation of the institutional progression toward a cosmopolitan condition."[25] As chapter 6 documents, some courts have begun to adopt stances that also posit a constitutional structure to global law, and have begun to act upon these beliefs. European courts, for example, have adopted positions that flatly deny the view that the terms of the UN Charter forbid judicial review of acts taken in pursuance of, or required by, UN Security Council Resolutions. Insofar as the Charter system does not provide for the effective enforcement of rights, rights-protecting judges have no good reason to defer to the Security Council's authority. Kantian theory supplies an explanation of the resulting situation, that of a nascent constitutional-pluralist structure. The legitimacy of global law, even when emanating from an organization that makes strong, formal supremacy claims (the UN), depends on the propriety of its purpose and its conformity with rights, as governed by the UPR. Judges have a fiduciary duty, in cases at bar, to refuse to apply implementing measures that fail these requirements (chapters 2, 3). European courts, in effect, treat the Charter system *as if*[26] it were a legitimate constitutional order, and fill gaps accordingly.[27]

From the perspective developed here, the constitutionalization of global law is a historical process that involves the evolution of three juridical features or variables. The first involves the recognition of hierarchy with respect to sources of law. Global constitutionalism entails the institutionalization of human rights as higher law, constitutional norms that ground the legitimacy of all other legal norms. Second, rights, as positive requirements of legality, generate fiduciary

[24] Benhabib (2006, 2009); Brown (2009); Corradetti (2016).
[25] Corradetti (2016: 107). [26] Corradetti (2016: 117).
[27] See Pinto, Concurring Opinion, *Al-Dulimi and Montana Management Inc. v. Switzerland* (GC, 21 June 2016).

duties, which are owed by all officials to every individual that comes under the scope of their authority. Of particular importance are those judicial officials, on constitutional and supreme courts, who have special responsibilities as caretakers of the regime. The third concerns the construction of a cosmopolitan commons: those legal norms, procedures, and dispositions that enable a polyarchy of trustee courts to render justice, in the absence of a global state, on the basis of mutual regard and respect. Where these features are present, the constitutionalization process will register progress in degrees, insofar as these three elements symbiotically develop as inter-locking elements of a new legal system.

References

Aleinikoff, T. Alexander. 1987. "Constitutional Law in the Age of Balancing." *Yale Law Journal*, 96: 943–1005.

Alexy, Robert. 2002. *A Theory of Constitutional Rights*. Oxford: Oxford University Press.

Alter, Karen. 2001. *Establishing the Supremacy of European Law*. Oxford: Oxford University Press.

Alter, Karen, James Gathii, and Laurence Helfer. 2016. "Backlash Against International Courts in West, East and Southern Africa: Causes and Consequences." *European Journal of International Law*, 27(2): 293–328.

Alter, Karen, Laurence Helfer, and Jacqueline McAllister. 2013. "A New International Human Rights Court for West Africa: The ECOWAS Community Court of Justice." *American Journal of International Law*, 107: 737–79.

Anagnostou, Dia, ed. 2013. *The European Court of Human Rights: Implementing Strasbourg's Judgments on Domestic Policy*. Edinburgh: Edinburgh University Press.

Anagnostou, Dia and Alina Mungiu-Pippidi. 2014. "Domestic Implementation of Human Rights Judgments in Europe: Legal Infrastructure and Government Effectiveness Matter." *European Journal of International Law*, 25(1): 205–27.

Anagnostou, Dia and Evangelina Psychogiopoulou, eds. 2010. *The European Court of Human Rights and the Rights of Marginalised Individuals and Minorities in National Context*. Leiden, ND: Martinus Nijhoff Publishers.

Andenæs, Mads and Eirik Bjorge. 2011. "National Implementation of ECHR Rights: Kant's Categorical Imperative and the Convention." University of Oslo Faculty of Law Legal Studies Research Paper Series No. 2011-15: 59.

Anderson-Gold, Sharon. 2001. *Cosmopolitanism and Human Rights*. Chicago: University of Chicago Press.

Anderson-Gold, Sharon. 1988. "War and Resistance: Kant's Implicit Doctrine of Human Rights." *Journal of Social Philosophy*, 19: 37–50.

Banham, Gary. 2007. "Cosmopolitics: Law and Right." In D. Morgan and G. Banham, eds., *Cosmopolitics and the Emergence of a Future*. New York: Palgrave Macmillan: 25–39.

Baodong, Li. 2016. "China is Committed to a Human Rights Development Path with Chinese Characteristics." Ministry of Foreign Affairs, People's Republic of China.

Barak, Aharon. 2012a. *Proportionality: Constitutional Rights and Their Limitations*. Cambridge: Cambridge University Press.

Barak, Aharon. 2012b. "Proportionality." In M. Rosenfeld and A. Sajó, eds., *Handbook of Comparative Constitutional Law*. Oxford: Oxford University Press: ch. 35.

Barak, Aharon. 2010. "Proportionality and Principled Balancing." *Law & Ethics of Human Rights*, 4: 1–16.

Beitz, Charles. 2001. "Human Rights as a Common Concern." *American Political Science Review*, 95: 269–82.

Benhabib, Seyla. 2011. "Cosmopolitanism without Illusions." In S. Benhabib, ed., *Dignity in Adversity: Human Rights in Troubled Times*. Cambridge: Polity Press: 1–19.

Benhabib, Seyla. 2009. "Claiming Rights across Borders: International Human Rights and Democratic Sovereignty." *American Political Science Review*, 103: 691–704.

Benhabib, Seyla. 2006. *Another Cosmopolitanism: Hospitality, Sovereignty, and Democratic Iterations*. Oxford: Oxford University Press.

Benhabib, Seyla. 2004. *The Rights of Others: Aliens, Citizens and Residents*. Cambridge: Cambridge University Press.

Besson, Samantha. 2016. "Subsidiarity in International Human Rights Law—What is Subsidiary about Human Rights?" *American Journal of Jurisprudence*, 61: 69–107.

Besson, Samantha. 2012. "The Extraterritoriality of the European Convention on Human Rights: Why Human Rights Depend on Jurisdiction and What Jurisdiction Amounts to." *Leiden Journal of International Law*, 25: 857–84.

Besson, Samantha. 2011. "The Erga Omnes Effect of Judgments of the European Court of Human Rights." In *La Cour Européenne des droits de l'homme après le Protocole 14—Premier bilan perspectives*. Zurich: Schulthess: 125–75.

Besson, Samantha. 2008. "The Reception Process in Ireland and the UK." In H. Keller and A. Stone Sweet, eds., *A Europe of Rights: The Impact of the ECHR on National Legal Systems*. Oxford: Oxford University Press: 31–106.

Bingham, Thomas. 2010. *Widening Horizons: The Influence of Comparative Law and International Law on Domestic Law*. Cambridge: Cambridge University Press.

Bjorge, Eirik. 2015. *Domestic Application of the ECHR: Courts as Faithful Trustees*. Oxford: Oxford University Press.

Blau, Judith and Alberto Moncada. 2006. *Justice in the United States: Human Rights and the U.S. Constitution*. Lanham, MD: Rowman & Littlefield.

Brems, Eva and Janneke Gerards, eds. 2014. *Shaping Rights in the ECHR: The Role of the European Court of Human Rights in Determining the Scope of Human Rights*. Cambridge: Cambridge University Press.

Brown, Garrett Wallace. 2010. "The Laws of Hospitality, Asylum Seekers and Cosmopolitan Right: A Kantian Response to Jacques Derrida." *European Journal of Political Theory*, 9: 308–27.

Brown, Garrett Wallace. 2009. *Grounding Cosmopolitanism: From Kant to the Idea of a Cosmopolitan Constitution*. Edinburgh: Edinburgh University Press.

Brown, Garrett Wallace. 2006. "Kantian Cosmopolitan Law and the Idea of a Cosmopolitan Constitution." *History of Political Thought*, 27: 661–84.

Brown, Garrett Wallace and David Held, eds. 2010. *The Cosmopolitanism Reader*. Cambridge: Polity Press.

Brown, Michael, Sean M. Lynn-Jones, and Steven Miller, eds. 1996. *Debating the Democratic Peace*. Cambridge, MA: MIT Press.

Bugaric, Bojan and Tom Ginsburg. 2016. "The Assault on Postcommunist Courts." *Journal of Democracy*, 27: 69–82.

Buyse, Antoine and Michael Hamilton, eds. 2011. *Transitional Jurisprudence and the ECHR: Justice, Politics and Rights*. Cambridge: Cambridge University Press.

Cançado Trindade, Antônio Augusto. 2010 (2nd ed.). *International Law for Humankind: Towards a New Jus Gentium*. The Hague: Martinus Nijhoff.

Candela Soriano, Mercedes. 2008. "The Reception Process in Spain and Italy." In H. Keller and A. Stone Sweet, eds., *A Europe of Rights: The Impact of the ECHR on National Legal Systems*. Oxford: Oxford University Press: 393–450.

Cederman, Lars-Erik. 2001. "Back to Kant: Reinterpreting the Democratic Peace as a Macrohistorical Learning Process." *American Political Science Review*, 96: 15–31.

Cohen, Joshua. 2004. "Minimalism About Human Rights: The Most We Can Hope For?" *Journal of Political Philosophy*, 12: 190–213.

Conant, Lisa. 2002. *Justice Contained: Law and Politics in the EU*. Ithaca: Cornell University Press.

Corradetti, Claudio. 2017. "Thinking with Kant 'beyond' Kant: Actualizing Sovereignty and Citizenship in the Transnational Sphere." *Danish Yearbook of Philosophy*, 50(1): 59–82.

Corradetti, Claudio. 2016. "Kant's Legacy and the Idea of a Transitional *Jus Cosmopoliticum*." *Ratio Juris*, 29: 105–21.

Crawford, James. 1997. "The Charter of the United Nations as a Constitution." In H. Fox, ed., *The Changing Constitution of the United Nations*. London: British Institute of International and Comparative Law: ch 1.

Criddle, Evan and Evan Fox-Decent. 2016. *Fiduciaries of Humanity: How International Law Constitutes Authority*. Oxford: Oxford University Press.

Cushman, Fiery, Liane Young, and Marc Hauser. 2006. "The Role of Reasoning and Intuition in Moral Judgments: Testing Three Principles of Harm." *Psychological Science*, 17: 1082–9.

Dannenbaum, Tom. 2012. "Watered-Down Rights on the High Seas: *Hirsi Jamaa and Others v. Italy*." *International and Comparative Law Quarterly*, 61: 728–50.

Davis, Kevin. 1991. "Kantian Publicity and Political Justice." *History of Philosophy Quarterly*, 8(4): 409–21.

De Búrca, Gráinne. 2011. "The Evolution of EU Human Rights Law." In P. Craig and G. de Búrca, eds., *The Evolution of EU Law*. Oxford: Oxford University Press: ch. 16.

De Búrca, Gráinne. 2010. "The European Court of Justice and the International Legal Order After *Kadi*." *Harvard International Law Journal*, 51: 32–49.

Deutsch, Karl, et al. 1957. *Political Community and the North Atlantic Area: International Organization in the Light of Historical Experience*. Princeton: Princeton University Press.

Donald, Alice and Philip Leach. 2016. *Parliaments and the European Court of Human Rights*. Oxford: Oxford University Press.

Doyle, Michael. 2011. "Dialectics of a Global Constitution: The Struggle over the UN Charter." *European Journal of International Relations*, 18(4): 601–24.

Doyle, Michael. 2005. "Three Pillars of the Liberal Peace." *American Political Science Review*, 99: 463–6.

Doyle, Michael. 1986. "Liberalism and World Politics." *American Political Science Review*, 80: 1151–69.

Doyle, Michael. 1983a. "Kant, Liberal Legacies, and Foreign Affairs." *Philosophy and Public Affairs*, 12: 205–35.

Doyle, Michael. 1983b. "Kant, Liberal Legacies, and Foreign Affairs, Part 2." *Philosophy and Public Affairs*, 12: 323–53.

Dunoff, Jeffrey and Joel Trachtman, eds. 2009. *Ruling the World? Constitutionalism, International Law and Global Governance*. Cambridge: Cambridge University Press.

Dyson, Kenneth. 1980. *The State Tradition in Western Europe*. Oxford: Martin Robertson.

Dzehtsiarou, Kanstantsin. 2015. *European Consensus and the Legitimacy of the European Court of Human Rights*. Cambridge: Cambridge University Press.

Epp, Charles. 1998. *The Rights Revolution: Lawyers, Activists, and Supreme Courts in Comparative Perspective*. Chicago: University of Chicago Press.

Fabbrini, Federico. 2008. "Kelsen in Paris: France's Constitutional Reform and the Introduction of *A Posteriori* Constitutional Review of Legislation." *German Law Journal*, 9: 1297–312.

Fabbrini, Federico and Miguel Poiares Maduro. 2017. "Supranational Constitutional Courts." *iCourts Working Paper Series*, No. 98, 2017.

Ferrara, Alessandro. 2003. "Two Notions of Humanity and the Judgment Argument for Human Rights." *Political Theory*, 31: 392–420.

Finnis, John. 1980. *Natural Law and Natural Rights*. Oxford: Oxford University Press.

Flikschuh, Katrin. 2010. "Kant's Sovereignty Dilemma: a Contemporary Analysis." *Journal of Political Philosophy*, 18(4): 469–93.

Flikschuh, Katrin. 2000. *Kant and Modern Political Philosophy*. Oxford: Oxford University Press.

Føllesdal, Andreas. 2016. "Subsidiarity in Global Governance: Subsidiarity in International Human Rights Courts: Respecting Self-Governance or Protecting Human Rights—or Neither?" *Law and Contemporary Problems*, 79: 147–63.

Føllesdal, Andreas and Reidar Maliks. 2015. *Kantian Theory and Human Rights*. New York and Oxford: Routledge.

Føllesdal, Andreas, Birgit Peters, and Geir Ulfstein. 2013. *Constituting Europe: The European Court of Human Rights in a National, European and Global Context*. Cambridge: Cambridge University Press.

Forst, Ranier. 2011. *The Right to Justification: Elements of a Constructivist Theory of Justice*. New York: Columbia University Press.

Friedman, Barry. 1998. "The History of the Countermajoritarian Difficulty, Part One: The Road to Judicial Supremacy." *New York University Law Review*, 73: 333–433.

Gardbaum, Stephen. 2012. *The New Commonwealth Model of Constitutionalism: Theory and Practice*. Oxford: Oxford University Press.

Gardbaum, Stephen. 2008. "Human Rights as International Constitutional Rights." *European Journal of International Law*, 19: 749–68.

Garlicki, Lech. 2007. "Constitutional Courts versus Supreme Courts." *International Journal of Constitutional Law*, 5: 44–68.

Gaubatz, Kurt Taylor. 1996. "Kant, Democracy, and History." *Journal of Democracy*, 7: 136–50.

Gerards, Janneke. 2017. "Procedural Review by the ECtHR: A Typology." In E. Brems and J. Gerards, eds., *Procedural Review in European Fundamental Rights Cases*. Cambridge: Cambridge University Press: 127–60.

Gheciu, Alexandra. 2005. "Security Institutions as Agents of Socialization? NATO and the 'New Europe.'" *International Organization*, 59: 973–1012.

Giannopoulos, Christos. 2015. "Considerations of Protocol N. 16: Can the New Advisory Competence of the European Court of Human Rights Breathe New Life into the European Convention on Human Rights?" *German Law Journal*, 16: 337–50.

Goldberg, Suzanne. 2011. "Open Service and our Allies: A Report on the Inclusion of Openly Gay and Lesbian Servicemembers in US Allies' Armed Forces." *William and Mary Journal of Women and the Law*, 17(3): 547–90.

Gonzales-Bertomeu, Juan and Roberto Gargella, eds. 2016. *The Latin American Case Book: Courts, Constitutions, and Rights*. London and New York: Routledge.

González-Octantos, Ezequiel. 2016. *Shifting Legal Visions: Judicial Change and Human Rights Trials in Latin America*. Cambridge: Cambridge University Press.

Grabbe, Heather. 2006. *The EU's Transformative Power: Europeanization through Conditionality in Central and Eastern Europe*. New York: Palgrave Macmillan.

Greer, Steven and Luzius Wildhaber. 2012. "Revisiting the Debate about 'Constitutionalising' the European Court of Human Rights." *Human Rights Law Review*, 12: 655–87.

Grimm, Dieter. 2007. "Proportionality in Canadian and German Constitutional Jurisprudence." *University of Toronto Law Journal*, 57: 383–97.

Habermas, Jürgen. 1997. "Kant's Idea of Perpetual Peace, with the Benefit of Two Hundred Years' Hindsight." In J. Bohman and

M. Lutz-Bachmann, eds., *Perpetual Peace: Essays on Kant's Cosmopolitan Ideal.* Cambridge, MA: The MIT Press: 113–54.

Haider, Dominik. 2013. *The Pilot Judgment Procedure of the European Court of Human Rights.* Leiden: Martinus Nijhoff Publishers.

Halberstam, Daniel. 2015. "It's the Autonomy, Stupid! A Modest Defense of Opinion 2/13 on EU Accession to the ECHR and the Way Forward." *German Law Journal*, 16: 105–46.

Halberstam, Daniel. 2012. "Local, Global, and Plural Constitutionalism: Europe Meets the World." In G. de Búrca and J. Weiler eds., *The Worlds of European Constitutionalism.* Cambridge: Cambridge University Press: 150–202.

Hammer, Leonard and Frank Emmert, eds. 2011. *The European Convention on the Human Rights and Fundamental Freedoms in Central and Eastern Europe.* The Hague: Eleven.

Han, David. 2014. "The Mechanics of First Amendment Audience Analysis." *William and Mary Law Review*, 55: 1705–17.

Hanisch, Christophe. 2016. "Kant on Democracy." *Kant-Studien*, 107(1): 67–88.

Hart, H. L. A. 1994. *The Concept of Law.* Oxford: Clarendon.

Heijer, Martin den. 2011. *Europe and Extraterritorial Asylum.* Oxford: Hart.

Held, David. 2010. *Cosmopolitanism: Ideas and Realities.* Cambridge: Polity Press.

Helfer, Laurence and Erik Voeten. 2014. "International Courts as Agents of Legal Change: Evidence from LGBT Rights in Europe." *International Organization*, 68: 77–110.

Hertel, Shareen and Kathryn Libal. 2011. *Human Rights in the United States: Beyond Exceptionalism.* Cambridge: Cambridge University Press.

Hiebert, Janet. 2012. "Governing under the Human Rights Act: The Limitations of Wishful Thinking." *Public Law*, 1: 27–44.

Hiebert, Janet. 2011. "Governing Like Judges?" In T. Campbell, K.D. Ewing, and A Tomkins, eds., *The Legal Protection of Human Rights.* Oxford: Oxford University Press: ch. 3.

Hirschl, Ran. 2011. "The Nordic Counternarrative: Democracy, Human Development, and Judicial Review." *International Journal of Constitutional Law*, 9: 449–69.

Hodgson, Louis-Philippe. 2010. "Kant on the Right to Freedom: A Defense." *Ethics*, 120: 791–819.

Hoffmeister, Frank. 2006. "Germany: Status of European Convention on Human Rights in Domestic Law." *International Journal of Constitutional Law*, 4: 722–31.

Hunt, Murray. 2003. "The European Convention on Human Rights." *Yearbook of European Law*, 2003: 483–97.

Huntley, Wade. 1996. "Kant's Third Image: Systemic Sources of the Liberal Peace." *International Studies Quarterly*, 40: 45–76.

Husa, Jaakko. 2000. "Guarding the Constitutionality of Laws in the Nordic Countries: A Comparative Perspective." *American Journal of Comparative Law*, 48: 345–81.

Ignatieff, Michael. 2001. *Human Rights as Politics and Idolatry*. Princeton: Princeton University Press.

Ingram, James. 2013. *Radical Cosmopolitcs: The Ethics and Politics of Democratic Universalism*. New York: Columbia University Press.

Itzcovich, Giulio. 2013. "One, None and One Hundred Thousand Margins of Appreciations: The *Lautsi* Case." *Human Rights Law Review*, 13(2): 287–308.

Jackson, Miles. 2016. "Freeing *Soering*: The ECtHR, State Complicity in Torture and Jurisdiction." *European Journal of International Law*, 27: 817–30.

Jacoby, Wade. 2004. *The Enlargement of the European Union and NATO: Ordering from the Menu in Central Europe*. Cambridge: Cambridge University Press.

Jarvis Thomson, Judith. 1985. "The Trolley Problem." *Yale Law Journal*, 94: 1395–415.

Jiang, Na. 2014. *China and International Human Rights*. Berlin: Springer-Verlag.

Joseph, Sarah. 2011. *Blame it on the WTO? A Human Rights Critique*. Oxford: Oxford University Press.

Kant, Immanuel. 2006 (P. Kleingeld, ed.) [1795]. "Toward Perpetual Peace: A Philosophical Sketch." In, *Toward Perpetual Peace and Other Writings on Politics, Peace, and History*. New Haven and London: Yale University Press.

Kant, Immanuel. 1996 (M. Gregor, ed.) [1797]. *The Metaphysics of Morals*. Cambridge: Cambridge University Press.

Kant, Immanuel. 1994 (H. Reiss, ed.) [1784]. "An Answer to the Question: What is Enlightenment?" *Kant's Political Writings*. Cambridge: Cambridge University Press.

Kant, Immanuel. 1991 (H. Reiss, ed.) [1792]. "On the Common Saying: 'This may be true in theory, but does not apply in practice.'" *Kant's Political Writings*. Cambridge: Cambridge University Press.

Kant, Immanuel. 1970 (H. Reiss, ed.) [1784]. "Idea for a Universal History with a Cosmopolitan Purpose." *Kant's Political Writings*. Cambridge: Cambridge University Press.

Kant, Immanuel. 1900. *Critique of Pure Reason*. New York: Colonial Press.

Kelemen, R. Daniel. 2017. "The Assualt on Poland's Judiciary." *Foreign Affairs*, available online at: https://www.foreignaffairs.com/articles/poland/2017-07-26/assault-polands-judiciary.

Kelemen, R. Daniel. 2010. *Eurolegalism: The Transformation of Law and Regulation in the European Union*. Cambridge, MA: Harvard University Press.

Keller, Helen and Alec Stone Sweet, eds. 2008. *A Europe of Rights: The Impact of the ECHR on National Legal Systems*. Oxford: Oxford University Press.

Klabbers, Jan, Anne Peters, and Geir Ulfstein. 2009. *The Constitutionalization of International Law*. Oxford: Oxford University Press.

Kleingeld, Pauline. 2011. *Kant and Cosmopolitanism: The Philosophical Ideal of World Citizenship*. Cambridge: Cambridge University Press.

Kleingeld, Pauline. 2004. "Approaching Perpetual Peace: Kant's Defence of a League of States and his Ideal of a World Federation." *European Journal of Philosophy*, 12: 304–25.

Kleingeld, Pauline. 1999. "Kant, History, and Moral Development." *History of Philosophy Quarterly*, 16: 59–80.

Korsgaard, Christine. 2009. *Self-Constitution: Agency, Identity, Integrity*. Oxford: Oxford University Press.

Koskenneimi, Martti. 2006. "Constitutionalism as Mindset: Reflections on Kantian Themes About International Law and Globalization." *Theoretical Inquiries in Law*, 8: 9–36.

Krasner, Stephen, ed. 1983. *International Regimes*. Ithaca: Cornell University Press.

Krisch, Nico. 2010. *Beyond Constitutionalism: The Pluralist Structure of Postnational Law*. Oxford: Oxford University Press.

Kuijer, Martin. 2013. "The Right to a Fair Trial and the Council of Europe's Efforts to Ensure Effective Remedies on a Domestic Level for Excessively Lengthy Proceedings." *Human Rights Law Review*, 13(4): 777–94.

Kumm, Mattias. 2010. "The Idea of Socratic Contestation and the Right to Justification: The Point of Rights-Based Proportionality Review." *Law & Ethics of Human Rights*, 4: 141–77.

Kumm, Mattias. 2009. "The Cosmopolitan Turn in Constitutionalism: On the Relationship between Constitutionalism in and beyond the State." In

J. Dunhoff and J. Trachtman, eds., *Ruling the World? Constitutionalism, International Law and Global Governance*. Cambridge: Cambridge University Press: 258–325.

Kumm, Mattias. 2005. "The Jurisprudence of Constitutional Conflict: Constitutional Supremacy in Europe before and after the Constitutional Treaty." *European Law Journal*, 11(3): 262–307.

Kumm, Mattias. 2004. "Constitutional Rights as Principles: On the Structure and Domain of Constitutional Justice." *International Journal of Constitutional Law*, 2: 574–96.

Lambert Abdelgawad, Elisabeth and Anne Weber. 2008. "The Reception Process in France and Germany." In H. Keller and A. Stone Sweet, eds., *A Europe of Rights: The Impact of the ECHR on National Legal Systems*. Oxford: Oxford University Press: 107–64.

Lasser, Mitchel. 2009. *Judicial Transformations: The Rights Revolution in the Courts of Europe*. Oxford: Oxford University Press.

Laursen, John Christian. 1986. "The Subversive Kant: The Vocabulary of 'Public' and 'Publicity.'" *Political Theory*, 14: 584–603.

Law, David and Mila Versteeg. 2013. "Sham Constitutions." *California Law Review*, 101: 863–950.

Layne, Christopher. 1994. "Kant or Cant: The Myth of the Democratic Peace." *International Security*, 19(2): 5–49.

Leach, Philip, Helen Hardman, and Svetlana Stephenson. 2010. "Can the European Court's Pilot Judgment Procedure Help Resolve Systemic Human Rights Violations? *Burdov* and the Failure to Implement Domestic Court Decisions in Russia." *Human Rights Law Review* 10: 346–59.

Legg, Andrew. 2012. *The Margin of Appreciation in International Human Rights Law*. Oxford: Oxford University Press.

Leib, Ethan, David Ponet, and Michael Serota. 2013. "A Fiduciary Theory of Judging." *California Law Review*, 101: 699–753.

Letsas, George. 2013. "The ECHR as a Living Instrument: its Meaning and Legitimacy." In A. Føllesdol, B. Peters, and G. Ulfstein, eds., *Constituting Europe: The European Court of Human Rights in a National, European, and Global Context*. Cambridge: Cambridge University Press: 106–41.

De Londras, Fiona and Kanstantsin Dzehtsiarou. 2015. "Managing Judicial Innovation in the European Court of Human Rights." *Human Rights Law Review*, 15: 523–47.

Macdonald, Ronald. 1999. "The Charter of the United Nations in Constitutional Perspective." *Australian Year Book of International Law*, 40: 205–32.

Maduro, Miguel. 2009. "Courts and Pluralism: Essay on a Theory of Judicial Adjudication in the Context of Legal and Constitutional Pluralism." In J. Dunhoff and J. Trachtman, eds., *Ruling the World? Constitutionalism, International Law and Global Governance*. Cambridge: Cambridge University Press: 356–80.

Mathews, Jud and Alec Stone Sweet. 2011. "All Things in Proportion? American Rights Review and the Problem of Balancing." *Emory Law Journal*, 60: 798–875.

Miller, Sarah. 2010. "Revisiting Extraterritorial Jurisdiction: A Territorial Justification for Extraterritorial Jurisdiction under the European Convention." *European Journal of International Law*, 20: 1223–46.

Moravcsik, Andrew. 1997. "Taking Preferences Seriously: A Liberal Theory of International Politics." *International Organization*, 51(4): 513–53.

Moreno-Lax, Violeta. 2012. "*Hirsi Jamaa and Others v Italy* or the Strasbourg Court versus Extraterritorial Migration Control?" *Human Rights Law Review*, 12: 574–98.

Morgan, Patrick. 1993. "Multilateralism and Security: Prospects in Europe." In J. Ruggie, ed., *Multilateralism Matters*. New York: Columbia University Press: 327–64.

Motoc, Iulia and Ineta Ziemele, eds. 2016. *The Impact of the ECHR on Democratic Change in Central and Eastern Europe*. Cambridge: Cambridge University Press.

Mowbray, Alistair. 2015. "Subsidiarity and the European Convention on Human Rights." *Human Rights Law Review*, 15: 313–41.

Nichol, Danny. 2005. " Original Intent and the European Convention on Human Rights." *Public Law*, 2005: 152–72.

Nickel, John. 2006. *Making Sense of Human Rights*. Oxford: Blackwell.

O'Neal, John and Bruce Russett. 1999. "The Kantian Peace: The Pacific Benefits of Democracy, Interdependence, and International Organizations, 1885–1992." *World Politics*, 52: 1–37.

Parish, Randall and Mark Peceny. 2002. "Kantian Liberalism and the Collective Defense of Democracy in Latin America." *Journal of Peace Research*, 39: 229–50.

Peers, Steve. 2015. "The EU's Accession to the ECHR: The Dream Becomes a Nightmare." *German Law Review*, 16: 213–22.

Petersmann, Ernst-Ulrich. 2009. "Constitutional Theories of International Economic Adjudication and Investor-State Arbitration." In P.-M. Dupuy, F. Francioni, and E-U. Petersmann, eds., *Human Rights in International Investment Law and Arbitration*. Oxford: Oxford University Press: ch. 8.

Pogge, Thomas. 2000. "The International Significance of Human Rights." *Journal of Ethics*, 4: 45–69.

Pogge, Thomas. 1988. "Kant's Theory of Justice." *Kant-Studien*, 79(1–4): 407–33.

Pollicino, Oreste. 2018. *Protection of Fundamental Rights in Internet and Judicial Interaction. A Constitutional Comparative Perspective*. Oxford: Hart.

Priest, George and Benjamin Klein. 1984. "The Selection of Disputes for Litigation." *Journal of Legal Studies*, 13: 1–55.

Quint, Peter. 1989. "Free Speech and Private Law in German Constitutional Theory." *Maryland Law Review*, 48: 247–347.

Rainey, Bernadette, Elizabeth Wicks, and Clare Ovey. 2014. *The European Convention of Human Rights* (6th ed.). Oxford: Oxford University Press.

Raponi, Sandra. 2014. "What is Required to Institutionalize Kant's Cosmopolitan Ideal?" *Journal of International Political Theory*, 10(3): 302–24.

Rawls, John. 1999. *The Law of Peoples*. Cambridge, MA: Harvard University Press.

Ripstein, Arthur. 2009. *Force and Freedom*. Cambridge, MA: Harvard University Press.

Rosecrance, Richard. 1986. *The Rise of the Trading State*. New York: Basic Books.

Sabel, Charles and Oliver Gerstenberg. 2010. "Constitutionalising an Overlapping Consensus: The ECJ and the Emergence of a Coordinate Constitutional Order." *European Law Journal*, 16: 511–50.

Sadurski, Wojciech. 2016. "European Court of Human Rights in Pursuit of Public Reason? A Study of Lost Opportunities." *Workshop on Courts and Public Reason in Global Public Law*. Berlin, July 11–12, 2016. Unpublished, on file with the authors. 14 pp.

Sadurski, Wojciech. 2009. "Partnering with Strasbourg: Constitutionalization of the European Court of Human Rights, the Accession of Central and East European States to the Council of Europe, and the Idea of Pilot Judgments." *Human Rights Law Review*, 9: 397–453.

Sadurski, Wojciech. 2008. "Solange, chapter 3: Constitutional Courts in Central Europe—Democracy—European Union." *European Law Journal*, 17: 1–35.

Sadurski, Wojciech, Adam Czarnota, and Martin Krygier, eds. 2006. *Spreading Democracy and the Rule of Law? The Impact of EU Enlargement on the Rule of Law, Democracy and Constitutionalism in Post-Communist Legal Orders*. Dordrecht: Springer.

Sainati, Tatiana. 2015. "Human Rights Class Actions: Rethinking the Pilot-Judgment Procedure at the European Court of Human Rights." *Harvard International Law Journal*, 56: 147–205.

Sajó, András ed. 2004. *Human Rights with Modesty: The Problem of Universalism*. Leiden: Martinus Nijhoff.

Scheinen, Martin. 2011. "Lecture of the Ombudsperson." National Autonomous University of Mexico, June 24, 2011, available online at: http://www.un.org/en/sc/ombudsperson/pdfs/Mexico%20Presentation%20-%2024%20June%202011%20%28English%29.pdf.

Scheinen, Martin. 2009. "Is the ECJ Ruling in Kadi Incompatible with International Law?" *Yearbook of European Law*, 28: 637–53.

De Schutter, Olivier. 2006. "Globalization and Jurisdiction: Lessons from the European Convention on Human Rights." *Baltic Yearbook of International Law*, 6: 183–245.

Seymour, James and Patrick Yuk-tong Wong. 2015. "China and the International Human Rights Covenants." *Critical Asian Studies*, 47(4): 514–36.

Shapiro, Martin and Alec Stone Sweet. 2002. *On Law, Politics, and Judicialization*. Oxford: Oxford University Press.

Shapiro, Martin and Alec Stone Sweet, eds. 1994. *The New Constitutional Politics of Europe*. Special Issue of *Comparative Political Studies*, 26(4).

Shelton, Dinah. 2016. "Significantly Disadvantaged? Shrinking Access to the European Court of Human Rights." *Human Rights Law Review*, 16: 303–22.

Shelton, Dinah. 2003. "The Boundaries of Human Rights Jurisdiction in Europe." *Duke Journal of Comparative and International Law*, 13: 95–153.

Skaar, Elin, Jemima García-Godos, and Cath Collins, eds. 2016. *Transitional Justice in Latin America: The Uneven Road from Impunity towards Accountability*. London and New York: Routledge.

Slaughter, Anne-Marie, Alec Stone Sweet, and Joseph Weiler, eds. 1998. *The European Court and the National Courts—Doctrine and Jurisprudence: Legal Change in its Social Context*. Oxford: Hart.

Smith, Matthew. 2008. "Rethinking Sovereignty, Rethinking Revolution." *Philosophy and Public Affairs*, 36(4): 405–40.

Stein, Eric. 1981. "Lawyers, Judges, and the Making of a Transnational Constitution." *American Journal of International Law*, 75: 1–27.

Stone, Martin. 2011. "Legal Positivism as an Idea about Morality." *University of Toronto Law Journal*, 61(Spring): 313–41.

Stone, Alec. 1994. "What is a Supranational Constitution?: An Essay in International Relations Theory." *Review of Politics*, 55: 441–74.

Stone, Alec. 1992. *The Birth of Judicial Politics in France*. Oxford: Oxford University Press.

Stone Sweet, Alec. 2017 (4th ed.). "Constitutions, Rights, and Judicial Power." In D. Caramani, ed., *Comparative Politics*. Oxford: Oxford University Press: ch. 9.

Stone Sweet, Alec. 2013. "The Structure of Constitutional Pluralism." *International Journal of Constitutional Law*, 11(2): 491–500.

Stone Sweet, Alec. 2012a. "Constitutional Courts." In *Handbook of Comparative Constitutional Law*. Oxford: Oxford University Press: ch. 38.

Stone Sweet, Alec. 2012b. "A Cosmopolitan Legal Order: Constitutional Pluralism and Rights Adjudication in Europe." *Journal of Global Constitutionalism*, 1: 53–90.

Stone Sweet, Alec. 2010. "The European Court of Justice and the Judicialization of EU Governance." *Living Reviews in EU Governance*, available online at http://europeangovernance.livingreviews.org/Articles/lreg-2010-2/.

Stone Sweet, Alec. 2009a. "Constitutionalism, Legal Pluralism, and International Regimes." *Indiana Journal of Global Legal Studies*, 16: 621–45.

Stone Sweet, Alec. 2009b. "Sur la constitutionnalisation de la Convention européenne des droits de l'homme: cinquante ans après son installation, la Cour européenne des droits de l'homme conçue comme une Cour constitutionnelle." Special Issue Commemorating the 50th Anniversary of the European Court of Human Rights. *Revue Trimestrielle des Droits de l'Homme*, 80: 923–44.

Stone Sweet, Alec. 2004. *The Judicial Construction of Europe*. Oxford: Oxford University Press.

Stone Sweet, Alec. 2002. "Constitutional Courts and Parliamentary Democracy." *West European Politics*, 25: 77–100.

Stone Sweet, Alec. 2000. *Governing with Judges: Constitutional Politics in Europe*. Oxford: Oxford University Press.

Stone Sweet, Alec. 1999. "Judicialization and the Construction of Governance." *Comparative Political Studies*, 32: 147–84.

Stone Sweet, Alec. 1995. "Constitutional Dialogues in the European Community." *Robert Schuman Workingpaper No. 95/38*. European University Institute, Florence.

Stone Sweet, Alec and Thomas Brunell. 2013. "Trustee Courts and the Judicialization of International Regimes: The Politics of Majoritarian

Activism in the ECHR, the EU, and the WTO." *Journal of Law and Courts*, 1: 61–88.

Stone Sweet, Alec and Florian Grisel. 2017. *The Evolution of International Arbitration: Judicialization, Governance, Legitimacy*. Oxford: Oxford University Press.

Stone Sweet, Alec and Jud Mathews. 2017. "Proportionality and Rights Protection in Asia: Hong Kong, Malaysia, South Korea, Taiwan—*whither Singapore*." *Singapore Academy of Law Journal*, 29: 774–99.

Stone Sweet, Alec and Jud Mathews. 2008. "Proportionality and Global Constitutionalism." *Columbia Journal of Transnational Law*, 47: 73–165.

Stone Sweet, Alec and Eric Palmer. 2017. "A Kantian System of Constitutional Justice: Rights, Balancing, Trusteeship." *Journal of Global Constitutionalism*, 6(3): 377–411.

Stone Sweet, Alec and Kathleen Stranz. 2012. "Rights Adjudication and Constitutional Pluralism in Germany and Europe." *Journal of European Public Policy*, 19(1): 92–108.

Taylor, Robert. 2006. "Democratic Transitions and the Progress of Absolutism in Kant's Political Thought." *The Journal of Politics*, 68(3): 556–70.

Teubner, Gunther. 2004. "Societal Constitutionalism: Alternatives to State Centered Constitutional Theory." In C. Joerges et al. eds., *Transnational Governance and Constitutionalism*. Oxford: Hart: ch. 1.

Thatcher, Mark and Alec Stone Sweet. 2002. "Theory and Practice of Delegation to Non-Majoritarian Institutions." *West European Politics*, 25: 1–22.

Vachudova, Milada. 2005. *Europe Undivided: Democracy, Leverage, and Integration After Communism*. Oxford: Oxford University Press.

Voeten, Erik. 2014. "Domestic Implementation of European Court of Human Rights Judgments: Legal Infrastructure and Government Effectiveness Matter: A Reply to Dia Anagnostou and Alina Mungiu-Pippidi." *European Journal of International Law*, 25(1): 229–38

Von Bogdandy, Armin and Ingo Venzka, eds. 2012. *International Judicial Lawmaking: On Public Authority and Democratic Legitimation in Global Governance*. Berlin: Springer.

Waldron, Jeremy. 2006. "The Core of the Case against Judicial Review." *Yale Law Journal*, 115: 1346–406.

Waldron, Jeremy. 2004. "Some Models of Dialogues Between Judges and Legislators." *Supreme Court Law Review*, 23: 7–46.

Walker, Neil. 2015a. *Intimations of Global Law*. Cambridge, UK: Cambridge University Press.

Walker, Neil. 2015b. "Subsidiarity and the Deracination of Political Community: The EU and Beyond." *Europa Working Paper*, 2015/04.

Walker, Neil. 2008a. "Taking Constitutionalism beyond the State." *Political Studies*, 56: 519–43.

Walker, Neil. 2008b. "Beyond Boundary Disputes and Basic Grids: Mapping the Global Disorder of Normative Orders." *International Journal of Constitutional Law*, 6(3): 373–96.

Walker, Neil. 2002. "The Idea of Constitutional Pluralism." *Modern Law Review*, 65: 317–59.

Waltz, Kenneth. 1979. *Theory of International Politics*. New York: McGraw Hill.

Walzer, Michael. 1994. *Thick and Thin: Moral Argument at Home and Abroad*. Notre Dame: University of Notre Dame Press.

de Weck, Fanny. 2016. *Non-Refoulement under the European Convention on Human Rights and the UN Convention against Torture*. Leiden: Brill.

Weiler, Joseph. 1991. "The Transformation of Europe." *Yale Law Journal*, 100: 2403–83.

Weinrib, Jacob. 2016. *Dimensions of Dignity: The Theory and Practice of Modern Constitutional Law*. Cambridge: Cambridge University Press.

Weinrib, Jacob. 2014. "The Modern Constitutional State: A Defence." *Queen's Law Journal*, 40: 165–211.

de Wet, Erica. 2008. "The Reception Process in Belgium and the Netherlands." In H. Keller and A. Stone Sweet, eds., *A Europe of Rights: The Impact of the ECHR on National Legal Systems*. Oxford: Oxford University Press: 229–309.

de Wet, Erica. 2006. "The International Constitutional Order." *International and Comparative Law Quarterly*, 55: 51–76.

Wiklund, Ola. 2008. "Norway and Sweden." In H. Keller and A. Stone Sweet, eds., *A Europe of Rights: The Impact of the ECHR on National Legal Systems*. Oxford: Oxford University Press: 165–228.

Williams, Howard. 2015. "Kantian Underpinnings for a Theory of Multirights." In A. Føllesdal and R. Maliks, eds., *Kantian Theory and Human Rights*. New York and Oxford: Routledge: ch. 2.

Wright, Thomas. 2014. *Impunity, Human Rights, and Democracy: Chile and Argentina 1990-2005*. Austin: University of Texas Press.

Yap, Po Jen. 2017. *Courts and Democracies in Asia*. Cambridge: Cambridge University Press.

Yildiz, Ezgi. 2015. "Judicial Creativity in the Making: The Pilot Judgment Procedure a Decade after its Inception." *Interdisciplinary Journal of Human Rights Law*, 8: 81–102.

Zylberman, Ariel. 2016. "The Public Form of Law: Kant on the Second-Personal Constitution of Freedom." *Kantian Review*, 21: 101–26.

Zylberman, Ariel. 2014. "Kant's Juridical Idea of Human Rights." In A. Føllesdal and R. Maliks, eds., *Kantian Theory and Human Rights*. New York and Oxford: Routledge: 27–51.

Index